Work without Salvation

By the Same Author

Designing the Industrial State:
The Intellectual Pursuit of Collectivism in America

Writers and Partisans:
A History of Literary Radicalism in America

JAMES B. GILBERT

Work without Salvation

America's Intellectuals and
Industrial Alienation, 1880–1910

The Johns Hopkins University Press
Baltimore and London

To William R. Taylor, a fine teacher and friend

Manufactured in the United States of America

The Johns Hopkins University Press, Baltimore, Maryland 21218
The Johns Hopkins Press, Ltd., London

Library of Congress Catalog Card Number 77-2249
ISBN 0-8018-1954-7

Contents

Introduction

America is and always has been a nation defined by devotion to work. Although the ethic of work and individual effort has been interpreted and stated in various ways, it has always been a principal metaphor indicating the relationship of the individual to society. The ideologies of self-explanation and national self-justification, whether these are derived from the "puritan ethic," the manifest destiny of an unfilled continent and its promise of endless mobility and success, or the almost continuous dominance of society by middle-class ideals, have all related to hard work and its rewards.

In the twentieth century, this has been an uncomfortable ideal. As Studs Terkel in his recent survey *(Working)* found, the bitter reality of modern work does not fit the ideal. The reality is "ulcers as well as accidents," "shouting matches as well as fist fights," and, above all, "daily humiliations." Contemporary commentators like Terkel have rediscovered what was well known by their predecessors—that the human spirit is often repressed and distorted by the regime of industrialism.[1]

It has been apparent since the conspicuous development of capitalism in the nineteenth century that the reality of industrial labor does not match the work ideal. But the sense of social crisis and change that typified the late part of the century up to the First World War was accompanied by an intensified feeling that work, the sacred myth of mobility and individualism, was undergoing a rapid and crucial degeneration; by the turn of the century the apparent had become the unavoidable. This book attempts to explain the relationship of the myth of work and that *fin de siècle* feeling of crisis. It explores the development and the implications of new attitudes toward the relationship of individuals and labor.

The reexamination of work coincided with several important changes in intellectual life. In the 1880s American philosophers and psychologists began to examine several problems that led them to develop a pragmatic and functional view of intelligence. They wondered if ideas had any decisive effect upon the exterior, real world or upon the interior, psychological world, if individuals made a difference in society, and if conscious will and effort or intentional activity changed behavior. Such deliberations became necessary and inevitable because modern science and psychological experimentation made it increasingly unattractive to speak of human reason as if it were something apart or even distinct from the flow of body juices and electric currents. Because they could define the human mind as the stirring of organs and sinews, philosophers were hard pressed to discover any independent function for individualism, reason, and will. The result was a vigorous debate and the development of a distinct, new view of human personality and destiny that stressed, not the intent of action, but actual behavior and the determining factors of heredity and environment. In opposition were those who continued to support the claims of reason and the special nature of human intelligence.

These developments in psychology and philosophy impinged upon another turn-of-the-century debate among social commentators. American society appeared to be changing rapidly and deeply—with distressing side effects. Observers saw these effects in a variety of problems. Some pointed to moral degeneration. Others were irate over the growth of labor violence and radicalism. Others feared the decline of the family, the growth of vagabondage, the influx of foreigners, and the rapid, delirious mobility of the captains of industry. Many of these thinkers felt that the aggregate of such problems suggested the possibility of a transformation in the work ethic.

By 1900 the definition of "work ethic" had become synonymous with the idea of social order. The work ethic represented a complex, ethical statement of the interrelationship between the individual, what he or she produced, and society. It represented an ideal situation in which individuals received, not just payment, but ethical and aesthetic enrichment for their work as well. It was, in effect, a utopian description based upon an idealized American past.

Part of the importance of the term "work ethic" derived from this utopian quality. No doubt the enormous attention to work and striving embodied in the success literature that deluged the country in the early twentieth century was partly a reflex of the discovery that the work ethic was only an ideal. This tide of literature that promised individual regeneration through work contained, therefore, as much of an implied critique of society as it did straightforward advice.

The term "work ethic" as it is used in this book refers to the idealized relationship between individuals and their labor. This relationship was considered to be reciprocal—one in which each person derived a full range of benefits from labor. It is a term deeply imbedded in the traditional American description of human labor derived from the Bible and embodied in the puritan notion of the "calling." This calling (the labor to which God summons each individual) was at first apprehended as a conservative notion of social order. Labor, success, and mobility distorted this early concept, and success emerged as an imperative. Earthly reward, class mobility, and the fulfillment of any ambition were all elements that lent credence to the notion that America was an economic democracy. The nation, it was hoped, could become a paradise where talent and perseverence were inevitably rewarded. This was the dream promised to boatloads of immigrants who touched shore in the late part of the nineteenth century. But, simultaneously, this idea of the calling flowered into a new variation. Work had become a means of self-discovery and the basis for individualism. Quite literally (as Ralph Waldo Emerson had written), a man was what he made of himself.

In the 1890s the aesthetic and ethical overtones of the work ethic seemed especially relevant to those who felt the brunt of social change. Joy and a sense of accomplishment from the creation of beauty and order, some commentators argued, came from older forms of labor: handicraft and manual effort. They felt that the success of the traditional work ethic depended upon the type of environment that existed in a small town or village, where each citizen could learn the values of community through the contribution of his labor.

Inevitably, the idea (or ideas) of work in this period developed in contradictory directions, with one emphasis upon financial success and class mobility, and another on the potential for moral development. This confusion over meanings did not, however, diminish the importance of the work ethic as a focus through which to view the crisis of a society in rapid transformation.

A sense of crisis was not universal in American culture, nor can it be compared in intensity to the feeling of *Weltschmerz* that struck some of the advanced industrial nations of Europe at this time. Nonetheless, among an important group of academics and social commentators, there was a strong feeling that society was falling apart under the strain of corporate consolidation and centralization in government. Intellectuals perceived such changes on several levels. A prevailing sentiment was, however, that work had drastically changed. To many serious social and economic observers, this reorganization appeared at every level in the giant new corporations that suddenly appeared in this era.

Industrial transformation was accompanied by well-publicized labor violence and even revolutionary activity. The fact that the assembly line manufacture that was revolutionizing the shop had overflowed into the offices was less widely noted. The result was the trivialization of white-collar functions and the creation of a large class of workers— secretaries and office functionaries—whose labor was manipulated and organized according to the new principles of scientific management.

Most of the movements and individuals in this study were associated with New England. There are a number of reasons why this section of the country gave special attention to the relationship of the work ethic and the sense of social crisis in the late nineteenth century. There was a relative decline in the industrial and intellectual predominance of New England (and of Boston in particular) during this period. New England (and, again, especially Boston) was an area that had witnessed and worried over the growth of industry for a long time. New England was the parent of both the "puritan ethic" and the transcendental movement of the 1830s, which, through the works of Emerson and Thoreau, had brilliantly transformed Calvinism into a philosophy of individualism. The growing inappropriateness of the work ethic as a description of American ethics was strikingly evident to intellectuals raised in the traditions of this region.

The rapid changes that were taking place in America's larger cities before and during the Gilded Age riveted the attention of social observers, statistics-takers, and reformers to the workplace itself. As Carroll Wright, chief officer of the 1890 census (and perhaps the most influential social statistician of his day) noted, the extensive project of gathering labor statistics in Massachusetts (the first state to do so) began in response to an incipient labor crisis in 1869, but blossomed into a national movement. The precedent of the Massachusetts State Bureau of Labor Statistics was quickly copied by other states with large industrial populations; New York, Maryland, Pennsylvania, Ohio, Connecticut, Illinois, and New Jersey were among twenty-eight states to have their own bureaus by 1892. In 1884 there was sufficient national pressure to establish the post of commissioner of labor in the Department of the Interior. Carroll Wright was the first to fill the post; his initial report in 1886 concerned the causes of industrial depressions.[2]

The preliminary facts that social statisticians discovered (despite their often crude and incomplete inquiries) demonstrated their assumption that modern work had been greatly altered. Even in gathering facts about industrial life they were biased by the belief that the nature of the industrial worker was different, and that this and other alterations in modern labor boded ill for society. For Wright, the great effort to put information about work at the disposal of government was nothing less than putting "Christian Religion into social science."[3]

One of the early problems that faced social statisticians who were looking at the workplace was that of making sense of the figures they gathered. Because of short funds and a lack of expertise, many bureaus of labor statistics initially relied upon owners and workers to fill out circulars and voluntary information sheets. Even when this inadequate method brought responses, there were fundamental problems. Returns were incomplete because of oversight and because of the hostility of some corporations, unions, and workers to answering any personal questions about working conditions. Furthermore, there was the dilemma of comparing results in one state—or even in one industry—with those in another. If returns were partial and incomplete and categories varied from survey to survey, how could statisticians compare what they had learned?

In 1872 the Massachusetts Bureau of Labor Statistics examined these problems and faulted the 1870 census specifically for its confusing and inappropriate use of job categories such as blacksmith and carpenter. In the industrial workplace these terms, which referred to older craft functions, could be misleading as to the work actually performed. The problem was still acute in 1886, when the commissioner of labor made his first report. In charts depicting numbers of employees in similar manufacturing industries in various states, job descriptions varied widely for the same function; in some states workers were listed according to older craft terms, and in others, those apparently doing the same work were given different titles.[4] This problem suggests that, until an appropriate language was invented, modern work could not even be defined.

Another difficulty encountered by those who were trying to gather and compare figures as a way of confirming changes in work was the lack of reliable estimates about past conditions. At the seventh annual convention of the Commissioners of Bureaus of Labor Statistics in Connecticut in 1889, for example, Carroll Wright disagreed with reformer Frances Kelly's contention that cases of child labor were increasing in the United States. The real argument between the two, however, was diverted to a debate over whether or not existing statistics could prove anything about child labor.[5]

Nevertheless, whatever the precision of facts and figures, many observers would have agreed with the Lowell, Massachusetts, correspondent who, in 1873, wrote of the cotton mills in that pioneer industrial city, "We are gradually creating—what the founders of Lowell never looked for—a permanent body of factory employees, composed in part of American stock, but more largely of Irish and

French Canadian elements, with English, Scotch, and German blood commingled."[6]

In pointing to the existence of a permanent industrial working class, this observer might well have also cited the very rapid growth of industrialized manufacture in New England towns like Lowell and in the cities of Boston, New York, and Chicago in the late nineteenth century. There was ample confirmation of such larger, momentous changes in industrial life. The rapid increase of capitalization in the shoe industry (which was one of New England's primary industries) between 1865 and 1885 is illustrative of the change in the character of the workplace. While capitalization increased by about five and a half times over these decades, the number of employees increased only slightly, by about 25 percent, indicating both larger establishments and increased use of machinery.[7]

The 1890 census documented the obvious shift in work that had taken place during the century. In Massachusetts, 47 percent of gainfully employed males and 52 percent of women were employed in manufacturing and mechanical industries. The figures were higher in Rhode Island, where they were recorded as 48 percent and 63 percent respectively, and lower—33 percent and 38 percent—in New York State.

Another indication that the character of work was altered was the slight but significant rise, between 1880 and 1890, of the percentage of persons gainfully employed. This trend was most marked in the North Atlantic and North Central areas of the United States, and was strongest for women. Another figure suggests that, while the amount of work—at least in mining and manufacturing—increased, it was very unstable work. Of the five million workers employed in these industries in 1890, as many as 560,000 experienced unemployment for one or two months and 112,000 for between seven and twelve months. This contrasts with white-collar unemployment among bookkeepers and clerks, which was approximately 14,000 and 4,000 for the same periods per one million workers.[8]

There was a surprising increase between 1870 and 1890 in the number of persons engaged in white-collar jobs. The number of journalists, teachers, doctors, artists, and architects—as well as clerks, bookkeepers, and salesmen—tripled in three decades, while those in manufacturing increased at a rapid but less striking rate. The employment of more and more women in industrial and white-collar positions led many commentators to suggest that divorce and prostitution would automatically be increasing. In two studies of divorce statistics and prostitution in 1886 and 1888, Carroll Wright agreed that divorce rates seemed to increase with urbanization, but he did not find that prostitution—contrary to what many assumed—was automatically incited by exposure to industrial work. He noted, instead, that the highest percentage of prostitutes were either servants, hotel workers, seamstresses, or women who had no previous occupation at all.[9]

A different nineteenth-century prejudice about industrial work and its effects was, however, confirmed by census statistics and reports of state industrial commissions. This was the idea that industrial work was dominated by immigrant, urban labor. The growth of urban areas in late-nineteenth-century America far outstripped population increases in other sectors. While the populations of American cities had increased rather gradually and steadily until 1880, the 1890 census reported a rapid acceleration of this trend from 1880 to 1890, "thus illustrating in a forcible manner the accelerated tendency of our population toward urban life." The population growth was even more obvious in selected urban areas. Between 1880 and 1890, the urban element of the population of the North Atlantic region increased by 44 percent, while the whole area grew only about 20 percent. The same characteristics were present in other states, including Maryland and Illinois, which were located at the extremes of the manufacturing belt stretching down and across the eastern United States. This differential pattern was also found even within rapidly growing cities; Boston, St. Louis, Baltimore, Philadelphia, and New York City all experienced unbalanced growth by wards, with some filled to overcrowding and others increasing at a more leisurely rate.[10]

The greatest factor in this urban-industrial phenomenon was foreign immigration. The flow of immigration had been relatively stable—at around 2,500,000 entries into the United States per decade—between 1851 and 1880. In the 1880s it more than doubled, reaching about 5,250,000 entries that decade. This new population appeared disproportionately in larger urban areas and in manufacturing industries. The population that was foreign-born or of foreign-born parentage increased in Massachusetts between 1870 and 1890 from 43 percent to 56 percent of the total population. In New York, the change was from 51 percent to 57 percent, and in Illinois it was from 39 percent to 49 percent. In manufacturing and mechanical occupations in 1890, 41 percent of white employees were native-born with native-born parents, but about 55 percent of such jobs were held by foreign-born workers or those with one (or both) foreign-born parent. In the whole working force, 51 percent were native-born whites with native-born parents, while 38 percent were foreign-born or had at least one foreign-born parent. This latter group also had a significantly higher number of gainfully employed members than did similar age groups for native-born whites.[11]

These statistics indicate only a small portion of the material that was available to social commentators and reformers by the end of the nineteenth century. While the statistics suggested many things to such observers, one conclusion was inescapable. The great force of industrialism had brought a sudden and obvious concentration of population to large cities, and it had gorged these cities and their factories with immigrants. Industries most associated with the great transformation of American society and work were being infiltrated by an army of foreigners. It could be said, with partial truth, that the modern American industrial worker was a stranger in the land.

The rapid urbanization of large commercial centers such as New York, Chicago, and other midwestern cities quite literally transformed the visage of the nation; the small village communities that had nurtured the work ethic and hand labor were pushed out of sight. Large-scale immigration peopled American cities with foreigners who seemed capable of hard work and even of success, but who did not fit into the preconceived notion of the perfect, Protestant commonwealth. Nor did the rise of great industrial leaders follow the prescriptions of the work ethic. When William James asked during a lecture how one could speak in the same sentence of Andrew Carnegie and Napoleon as great men, he was referring to an unexpected by-product of the drive for success. The American class system, he hinted, was producing a new aristocracy, an aristocracy that had little merit.

All of these transformations in American society can be and were seen as a growing discontinuity between the ideal and reality. Work, as a specific activity and as the expression of larger philosophic attitudes, seemed to be the key to a condition of alienation between individuals and their creative efforts. The problem of the work ethic touched the practical activity of laboring conditions, social ideals, and, finally, even the most profound problems in modern philosophy.

There are three divisions in my examination of the idea of work and its relationship to the social crisis at the end of the century. The first recounts the discovery of the crisis and the exploration of its causes and effects. The argument then proceeds to a discussion of individuals and movements that proposed to put the old order back together again and sought to reestablish the hegemony of the work ethic. A final section examines movements in psychology and philosophy that attempted to restate the relationship of mankind to work in a new, behaviorist form. This restatement shuffled the philosophic premises of individualism and led to a critique, initiated by William James, that pointed to the futility of the older justifications of individualism as well as to the dangers of modern behaviorist and scientific dogmas. As James discovered, the discontinuity between individuals, their work, and society implied that modern mankind was hopelessly and perhaps permanently alienated* from the philosophic, psychological, and industrial world that had suddenly appeared.

*In the interest of coherence and uniformity, I have employed the term "alienation" in summarizing various late-nineteenth-century descriptions of the effects of modern work. Although the figures discussed in this book almost never used the term, the substance of their complaints about industrial labor coincides closely with the word "alienation" as it is used later.

I

Defining the Problem

Stenographic department, Montgomery Ward and Co., Kansas City, Missouri, November 8, 1913.

1

Work and the
Crisis of Self-Control

From the beginning of the American industrial revolution until the end of the nineteenth century, the concept of work regulated the definition of human personality and its relation to society. The American guiding principle of the work ethic, with its strong religious overtones demanded, among many things, the existence of a distinct and autonomous character. An individual was seen as a conglomeration of faculties and potentialities that required exercise and practice for fulfillment. Strenuous in its demands and rigorous in the responsibilities it implied, this concept suggested two primary and opposite states of being—motion and rest, action and inaction, work and contemplation. From movement flowed the enrichments and ethical benefits that nourished citizen and nation. From sloth, lassitude, and weakness flowed unhappiness and crime.

The work ethic was a convincing explanation of the nineteenth-century social order because it was apt as both a sociological and idealogical interpretation of the origins of social hierarchy. It pointed to the origins of the complex relationship of duties and responsibilities between citizens and the state. As a corollary, it contained the notion that expended effort would be rewarded. It implied, above all, that the individual was the master of his own fate.

This concept of work was formulated in the secularization of Protestant theology at the beginning of the industrial revolution in the United States; it contained an exhortation to work hard and find fulfillment in labor. During the nineteenth century, however, the craft and agricultural society that it had been designed to fit was rapidly changing. Manual labor—the basis of the work ethic—was being replaced by machine manufacture and the intensive division of labor. The work ethic was, therefore, a definition of human labor and participation in society that, even at the height of its popularity, was becoming abstract, detached, and ideal. It was a myth that quickly overgrew its original function.[1]

Ralph Waldo Emerson's thoughts on self-reliance already had a faintly nostalgic ring when he recorded them. "A man is relieved and gay," he said, "when he has put his heart into his work and done his best; but what he has said or done otherwise, shall give him no peace." This was a simple program for gaining the Kingdom of Heaven on earth, but of course Emerson held to no such simplicities. "Society everywhere is in conspiracy against the manhood of every one of its members," he wrote. Emerson expressed here the age-old paradox that mankind essays and society conspires. The result was stalemate and compromise. But effort had its rewards because the expenditure of force in honest pursuits marked the human personality and changed society itself. Emerson proposed to judge character by the indelible imprint work made upon it: "But do your thing, and I shall know you. Do your work, and you shall reinforce yourself." Work was not mere toil or unending drudgery, but salvation. Creative labor was rich in ethical and social overtones. This remarkable and persistent tradition that Emerson summarized held the promise of great rewards—it was the very cornerstone of individualism.[2]

Like his fellow transcendentalist, Henry David Thoreau was impelled by the promise that a man was what he made of himself. But, unlike Emerson, Thoreau took his dictum literally and retired to Walden Pond outside Concord, Massachusetts, where he constructed his society of one. The record of this sojourn—Thoreau's literary masterpiece—provided the outline for a moral and economic utopia in much the same way that Daniel Defoe's *Robinson Crusoe* had. But, as Thoreau noted often in his manuscript, his world was one in which working and becoming were synonymous: "All men want, not something to *do with*, but something to *do*, or rather something to *be*." Instead of transforming natural objects into commercial objects as Defoe had Crusoe do, Thoreau realized the function or utility of nature itself. In this self-sufficient empire of the individual soul, Thoreau exposed the romantic ideal of work for what it really was; a theory and justification of individualism.

After the Civil War another New Englander, Louisa May Alcott, wrote *Little Women,* one of the most important nineteenth-century American novels concerning work and child nurture. Her message was similar to Emerson's. Although her characters sometimes chafe at the narrow limits of their world, they ultimately find success and fulfillment in the labor to which they are called. The mother tells her four daughters that "work is wholesome, and there is plenty for everyone, it keeps us from ennui and mischief, is good for health and spirits, and gives us a sense of power and independence better than money or fashion." As each of the sisters is led through her particular "Pilgrim's Progress"—through temptation and back to the acceptance of limitation and sacrifice—the author seeks to convince the reader that she deeply believes that work can be defined as the labor God (or society) calls each person to perform, and that success in a given métier will bring ethical enrichment and happiness.[3]

Emerson, Alcott, and scores of writers, religious men, business leaders, and teachers accepted the work ethic as the American ideal and human labor as the source of personality and citizenship. But what did this ethic mean to men and women who grew up in an age of consolidated, corporate industrialism? By 1900 the work ethic seemed to describe another era, a time of more perfect harmony between man, society, ethics, and religion. When doubt came, it was intense and overwhelming. Clearly, self-activated individualism was an inappropriate social philosophy for the new age. Isolated assertion, hard work, and ethical behavior scarcely affected the fate of the new industrial laborers who were regulated by the demands of machinery and maximum profit. When work became a continuous process and the laborer became an appendage of the machine, such attitudes rarely mattered. Was there not the risk that the work ethic would dissolve under the pressures of modern capitalism into something entirely different—a compulsion to work?

The progress of industrial civilization challenged the ethic of work and gave rise to a number of specific fears about the direction of social evolution. New, statistical descriptions of behavior suggested a different interpretation of personality formation. The pioneers of a scientific description of human character and development insisted upon explaining moral phenomena in terms of facts and figures. In their theories, impersonal causation replaced moral responsibility as an explanation for social behavior. They admitted that the advance of civilization had had unfortunate side effects. Social disorder might indicate declining individual morality, they said, but this new situation ought to be described in terms of a physical or mental pathology with tangible causes that could be distinguished and treated. In this interpretation, the place of traditional individuality was precarious at best. The discovery of "self" came neither through introspection nor through the expression of one's creative potential in the calling. The self was created by the blind forces of nature and social environment.

This approach was impossible to square with the traditional work ethic, which had derived much of its persuasive power and sanction from religion. American Calvinism had elevated work from the penalty imposed upon man by original sin to the mode of demonstrating the existence of grace; this laid a strong foundation for associating human labor and achievement with salvation; thus the relationship between craft labor and work was firmly cemented. But in the late nineteenth century, this amalgam seemed to be disintegrating. In Europe this led to the development of theories that social commentator Lewis Mumford has aptly called the "religion of utility." In America the separation of work from its ethical bases led to a reorientation in social theory.[4]

The degradation of work in all of its facets was a popular and important subject of social commentary at the turn of the century. Besides the central question of surviving industrial accidents, unemployment, and low wages, specialization, ennui, and the division of work tasks became serious problems for sociologists and economists. First of all, the division of labor seemed destined to separate the nation into classes whose antagonisms would spill over into revolution. The emptiness of modern physical labor and the lack of intellectual stimulation on the assembly line threatened the work ethic itself, which by definition had promised a reciprocal relationship between effort and psychological reward.

The middle classes also appeared to be victims of changes in work. As essayist Randoph Bourne said, the mind of the ordinary worker reflected the vacuous but intense labor of the shop, the "regimen of mechanical labor and a minute division of labor, and so devitalizing and distorienting the normal satisfactions for great masses of men." The attempt to bend the worker to the needs of the machine reproduced in each worker's psyche a "gigantic silent struggle that is in progress, a struggle far more momentous than the open dramatic features of the class struggle." Citing the warnings of the English critics of industrialism, Bourne concluded that what they had observed to be true of workingmen in the early nineteenth century in England was now true of white-collar workers in America. The modern clerk, Bourne noted, looked upon his working hours "as an empty waste in his life." Everywhere in modern society labor was losing its social and cohesive force, and, Bourne concluded, there were some movements, such as scientific management, that were consciously attempting to remove any intellectual or moral content that remained in labor.[5]

All of this suggested a crisis in social order; it was not difficult in the 1890s to discover indications that American society was losing cohesiveness as it entered the age of rapid industrialization. The nation seemed to be flying asunder at the same time that it was expanding economically. Did this mean that traditional ideas of social order were inadequate? In the face of mounting evidence of increased suicide, crime, and divorce, the simple exhortation to work hard and receive the just deserts of ethical life was no longer useful.

In 1899, sociologist Charles Cooley expressed the vague but common uneasiness of his era: "A large class of persons, including many of the wisest and finest minds of the day, dislike and denounce the time, and pray that it may soon be over."[6] Cooley's statement reflected the feeling that social change was occurring too rapidly and that social and moral discipline was declining. This perception of rapid, uncontrolled change haunted a number of American thinkers who, like Cooley, felt that society was becoming unmanageable.

Others experienced this change as a religious crisis; there was a tide of suspicion that the traditional ethical and theological adjustments of American Protestantism were inappropriate for modern times. Doubt engulfed Protestant orthodoxy. In 1871 the publication of Darwin's *Descent of Man* exposed a part of Darwin's thought that every close reader—and every skeptic—knew to be there. Darwin contended that man's evolution (as well as that of the animals) was guided by the laws of natural selection. For some, this demonstrated tie to the animal kingdom threatened to sever man's ties to divinity.

Still others were troubled by a feeling that the social efficacy of religion was declining. The power of individual morality was ineffective against the temptations and tribulations of modern society. While there were frequent religious revivals and theological stirrings at the end of the nineteenth century, they were imbued with the feeling that religious sanctions over American institutions were becoming weak. This sentiment was particularly strong in New England, the geographic heartland of the traditional Protestant conscience in the United States.

Whether the crisis was felt to be moral, religious, social, or even geographic in character, it was affected by several profound and fundamental intellectual reorientations. The first of these was the acceptance of statistical and aggregate descriptions of human behavior. There was a shift of focus from individual responsibility to social, graphic, or comparative explanation for individual behavior. Another reorientation, based upon the first, included a widespread belief that aberrant behavior in the form of suicide, crime, vagabondage, and mental disorder was rapidly increasing—or at least becoming more obvious. There was also a mounting reluctance on the part of intellectuals to accept a moral or religious interpretation of such behavior. They looked elsewhere for explanations, utilizing a whole range of new deterministic theories that made it impossible to believe that crime was always malicious behavior, that suicide was immoral, that vagabondage implied laziness, or that divorce resulted from a loosening of morals. Certainly these changes in thinking had deep roots in earlier nineteenth-century intellectual and social thought; they no more appeared full-blown than the older secular Protestant description of personality and behavior evaporated in an instant. There had been moments when such new interpretations were suggested. For example, the 1881 trial of President Garfield's assassin, Guiteau, brought to public attention a dispute in American psychology and medicine about the meaning of insanity and criminal responsibility.[7]

The 1890s saw the arrival of new methodologies and resources for gathering the facts that were required to examine questions of social decline and moral laxness. Statistical interpretations of America's moral character focused on the 1890 census because it was the first national survey to incorporate extensive sections and comparative figures on crime and other deviant behavior. The Congressional Act of 1879 had instructed the census to broaden its inquiry to consider specifically those statistics that might gauge a rising or falling social cohesion. As a confidential plan of inquiry suggested, "The statistics of crime and of misfortune, which are great social evils, are an index to the social condition of a state and reveal the degree of its civilization as well as the character and effect of its laws."[8]

Several of the very groups most worried about a decline in public morality had been responsible for pushing the government in this direction. One such organization was the National Divorce Reform League (later the National League for the Protection of the Family). The League cooperated with Labor Commissioner Wright to persuade Congress to commission a survey of statistics on the laws governing marriage and divorce in the United States. Reverend Samuel W. Dike, secretary of the organization, also claimed some part in convincing the State Department to prepare a statistical report on immigration in 1885. Wright and others who labored over the census and other surveys had great faith that such studies would incite reforms. The mission of these early scientific surveys was, therefore, synonymous with reform and amelioration.

Organizations (such as the Divorce League) that were predisposed to discover an increase in family dissolution and a decline of public morality helped push the government to gather the sort of information that they confidently felt would prove their jeremiads about the decline of modern morals. The conclusions drawn from the 1890 census figures by Dike demonstrated this point. Using aggregate figures and speaking about social problems and long-range trends, he argued that social critics should stop using the individual as the basic unit for study. He felt that something larger—such as the family—should be considered the primary unit of society.[9]

Perhaps the most hotly debated figures of the 1890 census related to suicide rates. Suicide statistics had been recorded in many New England states since the 1850s, but the returns from other areas were sketchy. One result of this incomplete information was a popularization of the belief that suicide and insanity had a greater incidence in industrialized areas. In a long article published in *Arena* magazine in 1893, Frederick Hoffman speculated on the trend in New England suicide rates. His conclusion that suicide and industrial progress were inexorably linked was not uncommon or surprising. Because his method of argument is representative of other commentators, it is worth discussing in some detail.

Hoffman began by noting that, since 1868, the number of suicide cases in New England had been steadily increasing in both absolute and relative terms. This deplorable trend, he continued, was obviously related to the growth of large cities, since increases were greatest there. This was an unfortunate illustration of the validity of the Belgian statistician Quetelet's law of felo-de-se, which stated that an inevitable percentage of citizens in a given population would take their own lives. The cause of suicide, Hoffman argued, was the growing tension that derived from the stress of modern civilization. The result was a plague of social disorder in which the incidence of madness, crime, and suicide was increasing.

Hoffman suggested that progress and social change accounted for this dangerous situation. But he also used strong words against the perversion of the work ethic: "It is a diseased notion of modern life— almost equal to being a religious conviction—that material advancement and prosperity are the end, the aim and general purpose of human life; that religion and morality, art and science, education and recreation, are all subordinate to one all-absorbing aim, the struggle for wealth."[10] The pursuit of materialism by itself was nothing new, but its separation from the ethical context of work had profound significance. A new ethic, Hoffman argued, was pushing modern mankind into ruthless competition and class warfare. Thus suicide (or the complete denial of individual significance) was symptomatic of the worst effects of new character traits in American social morality.

Other explanations for increasing suicide rates enlivened the debate over the figures published by the 1890 census. The first was most notably presented in Emile Durkheim's work on suicide, which became available in the United States after 1898. Durkheim's thesis proposed to remove the moral stigma from self-destruction and to explain suicide in terms of the social life of a nation. This clinical consideration betrayed no lack of humanism—quite the contrary—but it did signal a shift in emphasis away from the individual and toward larger aggregates of the population. A far more controversial form of Durkheim's argument had been made slightly earlier by Felix Adler of the Ethical

Culture Society in a speech to the Plymouth School of Ethics in 1891. Adler's comments, reported in *Open Court* magazine (which was devoted to the reconciliation of science and religion), suggested that suicide might be justified in some cases, and that under no circumstances should it be described as a criminal act. Like Durkheim's, Adler's argument lessened the degree of personal responsibility in this ultimate act of self-destruction. The individual pieces in the puzzle of suicide could not be placed until the general laws of social behavior were deduced.[11]

Census figures from 1890 also appeared to indicate a serious increase in the crime rate of the United States—again, with particular severity in the cities of the industrial Northeast. Reverend Frederick Wines, special agent responsible for gathering statistics on crime, suicide, literacy, and benevolence, reported in 1890 that available figures demonstrated a rapid increase in the number of criminals incarcerated. This was not conclusive evidence of a rise in criminality, he admitted, but such a trend was strongly suggested. Other writers were not so hesitant. David A. Wells, Henry M. Boies, and the Italian criminologist Cesare Lombroso all interpreted the 1890 census results as indicative of the growing degeneracy of American society. In his book *Prisoners and Paupers*, Boies tied crime to increasing prosperity and moral laxity. The city was particularly to blame, he wrote, because it tolerated the existence of intemperance and other forms of debauchery. Boies bolstered his argument with figures from other sources. The study of the Jukes family, published in 1876, the social surveys of the English Salvation Army leader General Booth, and the works of the English psychologist Havelock Ellis on criminality, all suggested spreading social degeneracy and a rapid increase in crime, he wrote.[12]

Not every interpreter agreed. Roland Falkner, editor of the *Annals* of the American Academy of Political and Social Science, thought he found a serious error in the argument that crime was increasing. Statistics, he wrote, were inevitably subject to contradictory interpretations, and at most, the census only indicated a modest rise in the crime rate. In any case, such phenomena should be considered from a social and scientific, and not from a moral, point of view. The ferver and judgmental attitude of some commentators, Falkner continued, confused the issue. Bois and Reverend Wines had used figures from the census to issue warnings about the state of modern morality; Falkner summarized this sort of argument by saying, "in the race for wealth our people have been losing that wholesome respect for law and righteousness which formerly prevailed."[13] While Falkner may have felt that he had disarmed such commentators by citing their moralism, it is more likely that he had simply pointed out why their arguments were so attractive. Such notions were grounded in the widespread feeling that society was undergoing rapid change and moral crisis.

What the census suggested, other sources confirmed. Additional statistical evidence made the same disquieting point about increasing social degeneracy. Studies made of the incidence of mental disease among American soldiers during the Spanish-American War suggested that there were severe problems among some troops. As a result, a number of experiments were performed in army camps near the Mexican border using varied forms of work and recreation to eliminate the source of malaise. In another, widely noted study, the British Inspector General reported in 1902 that the English working classes were deteriorating physically. As proof, he offered the fact that 60 percent of those who volunteered for active army duty during the Boer War were found to be unfit for service. American observers in the 1890s suddenly discovered another group of misfits in the large number of tramps who were roaming the slums, countryside, and railroads. George McNeill of the Knights of Labor argued that these victims of the new industrial system were a "standing threat against the stability of our institutions."[14]

For those who wished to find it, there was a casual relationship between industrial progress and the physical and moral degeneration of the American population. This proposition was an enormously controversial one, for it invoked a number of dubious assumptions in sociology, psychology, and medicine. But whatever specific cause was blamed—sexual excitement, use of alcohol and drugs, or degenerate racial or ethnic heredity—many observers were sure that they could prove that there was a linkage between the general loss of native intelligence and morality and advancing civilization and urbanization. As W. I. Thomas of the University of Chicago argued in 1909, "The rapid increase in idiocy and insanity shown by statistics indicates that the brain is deteriorating slightly, *on the average,* as compared with earlier times." How Thomas or any psychologist or sociologist could provide even a crude estimate of intelligence or morality in "earlier times" is an enigma. But next to the need to prove that modern times and contemporary social order were plagued by an increase in degeneracy, such problems mattered little.[15]

An examination of the literature devoted to explaining the increase in social misfits reveals that interpretations were as diverse as commentators were numerous. The multitude of explanations suggests that, although there was no clear understanding or agreement about the causes, there was a strong (and perhaps hasty) desire to do something about the consequences. Spicy foods, alcohol, overwork, public education, easy divorce, decline of religion, and contact with foreigners were all given as explanations for the decline of public morality that had, presumably, been revealed by the census of 1890 and other statistical studies of behavior at the end of the century.

There was, however, one general conclusion that enormously worried moralists, and intrigued social theorists. It appeared to almost every observer that individual responsibility and self-control were declining. The president of Harvard University, Charles W. Eliot, succinctly stated this observation in a 1914 article for the new American Social Hygiene Association. The association, he argued, should work hard to prevent venereal disease from attacking the white race. "The Association," he continued, "ought to advocate actively the common use of the recognized safeguards against sexual perversions—such as bodily exercises, moderation in eating, abstinence in youth from alcohol, tobacco, hot spices, and all other drugs which impair self-control, even momentarily."[16]

The crisis of self-control (made apparent to Eliot through figures relating to venereal disease) seemed to lie behind almost all other frightening statistics that showed a decline in public and private morality. The suggestion that society had lost its self-control was impetus for a broad inquiry by American thinkers into the nature of individual development and social order at the turn of the century. Something of the mechanics of this inquiry is revealed in the table of contents for the March 1898 issue of the *American Journal of Sociology*. The problem of control is the focus of each article. Among the articles included were a description of character-building at Elmira prison, a statistical study of the causes of poverty, and a report on the means of relief and care of social dependents, part of sociologist E. A. Ross's series *Social Control*, and a portion of sociologist George Simmel's work "Persistence of Social Groups."[17]

To some observers the lack of self-control in society indicated the presence of a new disease. As self-help adviser Annie Payson Call postulated, the crisis in social order revealed the existence of a pathology to which all Americans were susceptible. "The advertisements of nerve medicines alone," she wrote in her book *Power through Repose*, "speak loudly to one who studies in the least degree the physical tendencies of the nation." When the Germans looked at American civilization, she continued, they were right to give the name *Americanitis* to the endemic nervous fatigue that resulted from overwork and the unending American pursuit of materialism.[18]

Thus the decline of self-control was used as a way of linking the two apparently uncontestable trends of material progress and moral and physical degeneracy. In part this idea derived from the persistence of traditional Calvinist hostility to overt materialism, but it was, surely, also a response to the change in the physiognomy of American society. The contradictions between progress and poverty and between pursuit of success and pursuit of calling could not be resolved. Observers who issued stern warnings about the moral fate of the nation were not prepared to reject industrialism or significantly alter the relationship between capital and labor. One could, it seemed, be disquieted and optimistic at the same time. This is precisely the tone of E. A. Ross's work *Social Control*. He argued that "individualism, voluntarism, melioristic reforms," were no longer effective, but that the new subject matter and the new scientific tools of sociology gave some promise that social problems could be solved.[19] It might be regrettable that society was no longer a collection of autonomous individuals, but the study of social phenomena must advance—it could not remain forever trapped by nostalgia.

2

Genius:
The Problem of Deviant Intelligence

For those who defined human behavior in terms of science and statistics, normality often meant conformity to the dictates of the industrial environment. Exceptional personality types of all sorts were lumped together; the average—not outstanding or the heroic —became the norm in discussions of social and intellectual behavior. The dominant force in the creation of character seemed to be what determined the personality and not what the individual determined. This implied a fundamental attack upon traditional American social ethics, for it shifted responsibility for moral actions and intellectual achievements from the individual to the environment. Some observers felt that in the measurement of the cranium, of the whorls of finger-prints, of the sensitivity to pain, or of the intelligence quotient lay an infallible indication of character.

While searching for a new definition of normality and abnormality, many thinkers spent considerable time discussing the nature of genius. Around the definition of genius there swarmed a controversy that produced a remarkable amount of interest and that accumulated a wide sampling of theories about human behavior. The debate over genius uncovered an important and widespread disagreement about the meaning and origins of personality. The extent of this discussion is a gauge for measuring the declining faith in individual self-reliance, and the growing suspicion that the dominant characteristic of modern man was internal division and contradiction.

There were enormous implications in the shift in emphasis from individualism to normality in defining intelligence and capability. The question was, as Jack London wrote in his preface to Osias L. Schwarz's *General Types of Superior Men*, one of the nature of human originality and its uses. As William Hirsch quite accurately noted, the whole discussion was animated by the fear that modern man was

14

degenerating physically and mentally under the pressure of industrial life. Psychologist Lewis Terman put it in more American terminology when he wrote in 1911: "The *problem of vitality* underlies almost every social and political situation confronting us."[1]

Debate over the nature of genius was not unique to the late nineteenth century, nor were all of the theories advanced necessarily new. But many observers argued that modern science and statistical methods would enable them to settle age-old questions in a new way. One such observer was Frederick Woods of the Massachusetts Institute of Technology, who, in the course of several articles on genius, called for the creation of a new science, *historiometry*, which would be devoted entirely to an analysis of history and genius.

Sifting through the voluminous arguments about the nature and origins of special intelligence and talent, several preoccupations of the age emerge. Was genius creative or destructive? Was its incidence decreasing? What caused its appearance? Was it a form of behavior that, as philosopher James Mark Baldwin asked, society ought to consider part of the general category of insanity, idiocy, and criminality? A good deal was at stake in the answers to such questions—nothing less, indeed, than the role, meaning, and worth of the individual intelligence in modern society.[2]

One of the most interesting documents in this discussion was produced by fifteen French specialists who conducted an intense psychological and physical examination of the writer Emile Zola. The results were published in 1896 by Eduard Toulouse, in his study of the relationship between neurosis and genius. Enthusiastically cited by Arthur MacDonald, an American criminologist and government expert attached to the United States Bureau of Education from 1892 until 1902, the report conceded that Zola was not insane or physically degenerate, but that he nonetheless possessed a number of nervous disorders. These were revealed through anthropometric studies (physical measurements) that included descriptions of his fingerprints and measurements of his sensitivity to pain. MacDonald as well as the French scientists hoped to answer one question: Was the neuropathic condition they discovered "an excitation that has given rise to the intellectual ability of Zola?"[3] Was genius neurosis? The evidence suggested that it was.

Identification of genius with madness or insanity (or neurosis, to employ the modern term) is a very old tradition in Western thinking. But in an era when science was increasingly bent to the study of specific mental characteristics, this belief took on new vitality and form. By analyzing genius, experts were also (by implication) questioning the validity of self-expression and individuality itself. As sociologist

Charles Cooley wrote in his article, "Genius, Fame, and the Comparison of Races," the problem of genius was inevitably linked to a larger question: "the very root problem of sociology, of history, perhaps of psychology, the question of how man makes society and society makes mankind."[4]

The first widely recognized figures to give the analysis of genius in its modern form were Francis Galton and Thomas Carlyle in England, J. J. Moreau in France, and Cesare Lombroso in Italy. Galton, half-cousin to Charles Darwin, was instrumental in developing the premise that physical traits revealed mental characteristics. Applying statistical methods to corrolate the facts he gathered, Galton studied the coincidence of eye color, right- and left-handedness, and physical height in relation to accepted rank in society or intellectual renown. In the resulting studies, marked by a crude and naïve scientism, he saw causal relationships between factors where probably only fortuitous ones existed. But these ideas nonetheless constituted compelling evidence for an age that desired scientific certainty in such matters. His words were clear and revolutionary: "I propose to show," he wrote in *Hereditary Genius*, "that a man's natural abilities are derived by inheritance, under exactly the same limitations as are the form and physical features of the whole organic world." The program of eugenics or selective human breeding that he proposed was based upon an unexamined premise buried in his viewpoint. Genius developed, he assumed, from the superior breeding of the upper class. Thus fame, ability, and social position coincided. Likewise, the poor and the mentally deficient were inevitable products of the inferior stock of the lower classes. Not every partisan of hereditary causation of genius could be friendly to the eugenic implications that Galton drew from his research. Nonetheless, his arguments and the apparent factual basis of his conclusions were seconded by such English philosophers as Herbert Spencer and the American sociologist and philosopher John Fiske.[5]

Also in the ranks of Galton's followers was the psychologist Havelock Ellis, who was well known to American psychologists and criminologists in the early part of the twentieth century. In an analysis of the British *Dictionary of National Biography*, Ellis reached what would strike the modern observer as a foregone conclusion: acknowledged British political and artistic genius stemmed from the Anglo-Norman upper classes. (Ellis's book was reprinted in the American journal *Popular Science Monthly* in 1900–1901, touching off a good deal of discussion and criticism.) Quoting from a broad selection of English and American literature on genius and its characteristics, Ellis concluded that neither education nor improvement of the environment could do much to alter the fact that the proletariat was incapable of producing men of genius.[6]

Another important European definition of genius came partly from the French psychologist Moreau and partly (and more noticeably) from Lombroso of Italy. Lombroso's pioneering work *Insanity and Genius*, published in 1864, together with subsequent articles and commentaries, influenced the direction of the American discussion of genius. Of course countless writers had associated exceptional intelligence or ability with madness before Lombroso. But in his version of this ancient theme, Lombroso's discussion was nearly always clinical, not cultural. Thus he side-stepped the theory of divine madness, clairvoyance, or mysticism that was sometimes associated with the poet or the musician. He was interested not in the Roman *furor poeticus*, but in demonstrable physical and mental characteristics.

Lombroso's "discovery" of ties between physical and mental characteristics was grounded, as Galton's work was, upon the assumption that mental traits made observable marks upon the individual. But his purposes were different from Galton's. His writings tended to discredit genius. As he suggested in his article "Genius, a Degenerative Epileptoid Psychosis," madness and genius were inextricably tied together. "If the lives and works of the historically great morbid minds be examined," he wrote, "it is found that they, as well as the men who have passed through the glorious parabola of genius without demonstrable mental taint, are distinguishable by many traits from ordinary." Thus, creative inspiration was, to Lombroso, the equivalent of an epileptic psychic phenomenon, and this, in turn, was one of the symptoms of criminality.[7]

Another widely discussed European book on genius was Max Nordau's *Degeneration*, translated from the German and published in the United States in 1895. This work was dedicated to Lombroso, and developed and extended many of the Italian psychologist's ideas. Lombroso had argued that criminals and certain politicians were physical degenerates. He had discovered what he thought was a psychic similarity between madness and genius. Nordau extended this analysis and found that artists and writers were also quite often physically degenerate. He was specific about whom he meant and why he chose them. When he denounced the culture of the *fin de siècle*, Nordau singled out for particular scrutiny Richard Wagner, Oscar Wilde, Frederick Nietzsche, and Emile Zola. Their art, he argued, constituted the record of an outstanding increase in hysteria and mental disorder that was becoming the most noticeable characteristic of modern society.[8] With Nordau's book, the myth of divine madness ceded to psychological analysis. Inspiration, mystical states, and genius were presumed to be forms of mental aberration.

It is, perhaps, surprising that the rigid and often class-conscious views of Galton, Ellis, Lombroso, and Nordau found a favorable reception in America, for they contradicted the native notion that genius was an endowment of special individuals in all social groups. Lombroso, Galton, Nordau, and Ellis all had their American followers *and* critics, however. Perhaps the most interesting of these was Arthur MacDonald. Something of a maverick in a department dominated by the Hegelian William Torrey Harris, MacDonald spent many years, beginning in the late 1890s, attempting to pursuade Congress to fund an extensive anthropological study of genius, insanity, and criminality in the United States (thereby giving him an independent position of operation). MacDonald accepted Lomborso's anthropometric method of identifying mental and physical degeneracy. He was somewhat cautious about certain aspects of the Italian's "criminal typology," but was obviously convinced about the utility of a physical analysis of genius. In his article "Genius and Insanity," written in 1892, he suggested that, if genius and insanity were not precisely the same, they were similar: "Thus the frequency of delerium, the numerous signs of degeneracy, the commonness of epilepsy, precocity, and melancholia, the tendency to suicide, and the special character of inspiration favour the idea that genius is a mental and degenerative disease."[9]

Even for those American writers (and there were many) who rejected the conclusions of Galton, Lombroso, and Nordau, the manner in which European thinkers posed the question of genius, and their subsequent search for an explanatory coincidence in physical characteristics or heredity, helped determine the nature of the argument. Thus in his article on genius, Charles Cooley spent considerable time unraveling Galton's arguments, pointing out, for example, that the Englishman has assumed that fame was an automatic indication of genius.

Although it may have been easy to poke holes in Galton's hereditarian assumptions, the more sophisticated physical determinism of Lombroso and Nordau was another matter. James Kiernan, a leading American psychologist, attempted to refute both. Attacking Nordau specifically, Kiernan first conceded the popular impact of *Degeneration* in the United States. Nonetheless, he contended, there was no reason to believe that genius and insanity were causally linked. To suppose so was to commit a gross scientific error: "In the art, as well as the literature of the insane," Kiernan concluded, "evidence is found that insanity mars, but does not make genius."[10]

The writings of Kiernan and others like him certainly did not settle the argument or convince the scientific and psychological community that Nordau was wrong. As late as 1912, Nordau's hypothesis still smouldered in the discussion of genius. In that year, *Popular Science Monthly* published a series of articles written by Charles Kassel and devoted to the examination, one by one, of the sorts of characteristics that Nordau had identified as the physical evidence for examining links between genius and mental disorder.

The exploration of genius and its origins troubled many social commentators and scientists during this period, but it was perhaps the philosopher William James who best understood what was intellectually at stake in the argument, because he tied it directly to the problem of individuality. James considered exceptional intelligence or ability in the light of nonpathological sorts of departures from ordinary behavior. Thus they were aspects of the general problem of individualism and character. James entered into a spirited dispute with two disciples of Herbert Spencer's who, he felt, defined genius, and hence personality itself, in an unacceptable, mechanical, and deterministic fashion. The first thrust in this intellectual duel was an article published in 1878 in *Gentleman's Magazine* by Grant Allen, an American student of Herbert Spencer. *Atlantic Monthly* printed a reply by James in 1880, followed by a rejoinder from Allen and a commentary by the philosopher John Fiske. James submitted a further reply that the *Atlantic* refused to publish but that, finally, appeared in *Open Court* in 1890 under the title "The Importance of Individuals." Somewhat later James wrote a review of several of the major European books on genius in which he touched upon the principal ideas of Nordau, Hirsch, and Lombroso.

Grant Allen's original ideas on genius were simply and rigidly stated, and they went straight to the traditional foundations of individualist theories of self-creativity and control. Great men were "wholly created by the external circumstances," he wrote. Rejecting Galton's suggestion that genius might be only a slight variation from the normal, Allen argued that exceptional talent was inexplicable except in terms of general laws of human development. Those forces which created the normal or average, he said, also created the exceptional. "What we have really to explain," he summarized, "is the force which produces the average man of each race; and the extraordinary men must come in their turn."[11] Therefore the normal—the collectivity —defined what was considered exceptional.

This argument, as James pointed out in his rejoinder "Great Men, Great Thoughts, and the Environment," was an extraordinary turn of the tables. Allen's argument, with its heavy emphasis upon environmental determinism, could account for everything in general and nothing in particular. Yet the particular and the exceptional were the only significant issues at stake. The environmental explanations of genius had to be rejected, he explained, because the forces that produced great individuals "lay in a sphere wholly inaccessible to the social philosopher." A genius or a great man was a person who by definition altered existing social relations; he was an individual who broke the rules of conduct. Therefore his activities could scarcely be accounted for by those rules. He was creator, not created.[12]

With these words James developed an argument that lay within an earlier, romantic tradition enunciated by Carlyle in his theory of great men and by Ralph Waldo Emerson in his notion of the representative man. As Grant Allen and John Fiske were quick to realize, however, James's real purpose in this article was to attack the whole idea of mechanical determinism as a metaphysical proposition.

John Fiske, in his retort to James published in early 1881, granted the young psychologist several inessential points. But he stood firmly against James's central proposition that humans consciously created history. The genesis of genius might be difficult to explain in social or general terms, he conceded, but human history—the story of human development and the impact of genius and innovation—was far more complicated than James or Carlyle pictured it. "Since the middle of the nineteenth century," Fiske generalized, "the revolution which has taken place in the study of history is as great and as thorough as the similar revolution which, under Mr. Darwin's guidance, has been effected in the study of biology." This revolution altered the aim of study from individuals to institutions.[13]

Better than Allen's, Fiske's argument placed the dispute where it belonged; he understood that he was challenging the validity of traditional concepts of individuality. Fiske paid lip service to the historical importance of individuality and human distinction, but he carefully argued that differences derived from the operation of the large, impersonal laws of social behavior. The general thus flowed into and determined the particular. When James finally published his rejoinder in 1890, he focused upon the functional meaning of individual distinctions. The problem of genius was part of the larger debate over individuality, he wrote. James's ultimate opinion on the matter rested upon faith and common sense. The only differences between humans worth discussing, he noted, were those which affected behavior. Yet precisely on this point, knowledge was weakest and least secure: "There is thus a zone of insecurity in human affairs in which all dramatic interest lies," he wrote. "The rest belongs to the dead machinery of the stage."[14] Thus human creativity was an unmeasurable but vital force.

In 1917 Boris Sidis, a former student and colleague of James's published a work, *Philistine and Genius,* in which he embellished and extended James's arguments in a manner that was more extreme and, perhaps, more pessimistic than his mentor would have allowed. But Sidis did capture the drift of James's thoughts, even if he could not write with his teacher's grace and generosity. Sidis feared for the future of genius in a society that he characterized as repressive, mediocre, and unoriginal. "Instead of growing into a people of great independent thinkers, the nation is in danger of fast becoming a crowd of well-drilled, well-disciplined, common-place individuals, with strong philistine habits and notions of hopeless mediocrity." Sidis concluded (and James would have concurred) that individuality and the free exercise of intelligence made the difference between civilization and barbarism.[15]

Thus James and, after him, Sidis, recognized the key philosophic dilemma posed by the late-nineteenth century attack on the definition of genius as originality and self-motivated individualism. To isolate, categorize, and explain talent and special intelligence in terms of abnormal behavior (or even normal behavior), they realized, was, in effect, to attack all individual distinctions; it was a sign of the modern drift toward self-doubt. James, moreover, recognized an equal if not greater danger in the less offensive attempt to explain genius as the operation of laws in the natural or social environment. He perceived this debate for what it was, an indication of growing suspicion among philosophers, psychologists, and sociologists that traditional explanations of human personality and individualism were inadequate: genius was an unwelcome risk for any society that defined itself in terms of the collective mediocrity of the average.

The primary approaches raised in this discussion of genius reveal the basic polarity around which were formulated arguments about the meaning and origins of personality in modern society. One side in this discussion may be characterized as the modern scientific attitude, which, in effect, meant that several positions were loosely associated by an emphasis upon facts, statistics, and generalized scientific laws. Scientific analysis of personality could mean, as Fiske had argued, for example, an explanation of the particular in terms of general laws of behavior. It could also mean the refusal to admit any discussion of ethics, judgments, or aesthetics into considerations of personality. Scientific theory could also mean the classification of facts into significant categories, tendencies, or laws. In the late nineteenth century, science applied to the mysteries of the individual could result, as Lombroso and Galton believed, in the detection of signal physical traits for mental abilities. Finally, science used as the measure of personality could mean, simply, the substitution of mechanical language and metaphors for traditional moral or ethical terms. The distinction between individuals was thereby reduced to questions of operating efficiency attained by the human mechanism. The other pole in this argument was tradition itself, with all the compromises, confusions, and faiths that went with it. That tradition specifically centered around the concept of the individual as creative and self-made, enriched and proven by labor, and defined by effort.

The debate over which side would prevail became more intense because of the feeling on both sides, sometimes bolstered by an impressive array of figures, charts, and graphs, that the traditional moral order of the United States was crumbling. Thus whatever its value, traditional morality, even to its defenders, appeared to hold less sway over the loyalties of modern man. However rich in ethical potential, work did not automatically incite faith and good behavior. Worst of all, perhaps the other side was right to proclaim that the most admired and powerful intelligences in history were nothing more than neurotics or physical degenerates.

3

Vagabondage: The Symbol of Industrial Malaise

In the 1890s the man who would not or could not work was a symbol of maladjustment to industrial America. He also represented, in growing numbers, an actual and highly visible form of discontent in modern society. Curiously, much of the discussion of vagabondage assumed that this age-old phenomenon was something new. Indeed, "tramping" may have appeared to be a new element of industrial life at this time because scores of unemployed men and boys adopted rail travel and thus became more mobile. But whatever the causes of their new visibility, tramps were often regarded as the sign of declining public morality. Vagabondage was thus the social malady of modern industrialism. It represented the failure of traditional institutions to form and sustain individuals with a robust and persistent will to achieve success. It represented a failure of the work ethic and a condemnation of the "American dream."

To many American sociologists and social critics, the tramp was also a victim of industrialization. The philosopher James Mark Baldwin, in his book *Social and Ethical Interpretations in Mental Development,* posed a hypothetical moral dilemma. Should an individual help a tramp or not? Should he grant charity to this outcast from modern society, even though he risked perpetuating the vagabond's slothful, antisocial behavior? The answer to this question, Baldwin contended, was immensely complicated and depended, ultimately, upon the predominant moral sentiment in the situation, one's charitable instincts or social consciousness, and, vis-à-vis the tramp, the possibilities of reinforcing antisocial behavior or depriving him of necessary food and shelter in hopes that he would be forced to seek work. But, whatever one's view of the dilemma, the tramp was a perfect symbol of the problems in modern social ethics.[1]

The Civil War marked the beginning of the period in which the problem of vagabondage became apparent and serious to American legal and charity officials. Although the roots of this problem lay in early American history, Henry Shaw, writing in 1900 in a report to the Massachusetts Association of Relief Officers, argued that there had been almost no tramps in America before 1850. The vagabond was, therefore, "one of the very latest fruits of civilization."[2]

In what sense did vagabondage stem from the exigencies of progress and the advance of civilization? This question appeared repeatedly in contemporary literature on vagabondage, although few observers offered much hard evidence that progress and tramping were associated. Often, commentators, even public charity officials, gave little proof for the hypotheses they advanced. Thus Shaw offered two explanations for vagabondage: Civil War pensions, which rewarded men who did not work, and immigration, which brought a new sort of population to America—one that was unaccustomed to the rigors of industrial labor. Simply put, Shaw was arguing that the function of the traditional work ethic had been disrupted because many Americans had either been taught not to obey its dictates or came from cultures where it did not exist.

The public discussion of tramping centered in several leading journals of popular sociology and political commentary during the 1890s. Charles Ely Adams, in *Forum* magazine, summed up the results in 1902. The hobo had become a symbol for a variety of theories. To the sociologist he was a problem, to the clergyman or philanthropist, an example, "to the criminologist a scapegoat," and to others, he was an object of charity or "quarry for the law." He was alternately "discussed in books, fed at free soup houses, mauled by police, [and] 'rescued' by the Salvation Army."[3]

Behind this outpouring of theories and attachment of symbols to them lay a feeling of emergency. Vagabondage became an important political controversy when the severe depression of the 1890s brought this part of the population to the public's attention in a new guise. To some observers the march of "Coxey's army" of unemployed workers from Ohio to Washington, D.C., in 1894 raised the threat of revolution. Although the "army" consisted of only about five hundred men, some commentators denounced it as a wild mob of hobos who threatened the very existence of the nation. As Henry Rood wrote in the *Forum* in 1898, Coxey's army was a magnet for the criminal elements in America. The overemotional men who initiated the march had fallen prey to demagogic leaders. As the army crossed the country, it was joined by "scores of tramps and other vagabonds as well as by hundreds of ill-balanced laboring-men, who actually quit work to further the 'demonstration against capital.'"

In a sharp rejoinder to Rood, E. Lamar Bailey disagreed with the belief that tramps were either criminals or revolutionaries. But even he agreed that they represented a serious threat to social stability. They could not, as some suggested, be suppressed by forced labor. Hobos, he concluded, were "products of industrial conditions and of the attitude of society toward unfortunate able-bodied men." Their vast numbers (Baily estimated that there were 100,000 tramps in 1898) presented a grave social dilemma. Coxey's army simply highlighted the potential political threat of such men.[4]

Refusal to work in a society where every dream was based upon the rewards of labor was an intriguing but disturbing phenomenon. The degenerated or incapacitated industrial laborer and social outcast—the tramp—symbolized a problem that demanded solutions from sociologists, political writers, criminal experts, and even moral philosophers.

Three general explanations of tramping appeared in the literature of this era. Tramps were designated as physical or moral degenerates whose weaknesses were inherited and whose treatment should be limited to incarceration and isolation from the rest of society. A second explanation blamed tramping upon institutions that disrupted the stern discipline of the traditional work ethic and thus encouraged the lazy and morally lax to throw themselves upon the mercy of society for care. Charity itself was the instigator of tramping. A final explanation cited a profound alteration in the nature of industrial work, which had destroyed the moral and aesthetic rewards of labor. Thus the tramp could be seen as something of a hero, or at least as a misfit whose lifestyle highlighted the problems of the entire industrial system.

The hereditarian explanation of tramping was a strong and attractive theory to an age that was intrigued (if not absolutely convinced) by Lombroso's theories of physical degeneracy, and that practiced an active racism in a large part of its popular and professional sociology. Modern criminal anthropology, in part based upon the theories of Lombroso, seriously considered racial degeneration as a cause for the appearance of the large and growing class of persons that was unable to adjust to modern society. Charles Henderson, sociology professor at the University of Chicago, in his 1901 work *Introduction to the Study of Dependent, Defective, and Delinquent Classes*, argued that there were broad anthropological laws governing the development of all advanced countries. These acknowledged the inevitable appearance of a large group of criminals and outcasts who were easily identifiable because of their family histories, and, in some cases, because of certain suggestive physical features. Syndromes of physical and mental traits thus linked crime, moral degeneracy, and dependency. The modern delinquent came, generally, from a family that had evidenced some prior serious difficulty; the members, of these families, he argued, would most likely drift into asylums for the incurable. Whereas the normal home was the "garden of virtues," the wandering, shiftless life-style of the tramp encouraged laziness and shiftlessness.

When Henderson linked immorality and physical degeneracy he echoed the popular wisdom of all ages concerning the nature of crime and social outcasts. But, like many sociologists and criminologists of the day, he was convinced that crime and immorality were psychic and social stigmata of physical degeneracy. Science, by examining criminals and noting significant statistical trends, could isolate those physical features—left-handedness coupled with a particular cranial slant, for example—which indicated the presence of criminal potential. It could isolate that crime-prone element which lay submerged in society. To facilitate such a study, Henderson suggested that sociologists accept the French system of classifying social misfits by the shapes and sworls of fingerprints. He argued that this system, developed by Bertillon, would help bring about the "social control of members of the criminal class."[5]

In spite of his emphasis upon heredity in explaining crime and vagabondage, Henderson, like most other Americans who wrote on the subject, hoped, paradoxically, to cure some individuals. The treatment he suggested had remarkable similarities to contemporary cures for hysteria. No doubt the sociologist was thinking in the same, basic nineteenth-century medical tradition that convinced doctors to attempt restoration of individual will power through physical therapy, herbal baths, massage, and electric treatments. To this primarily physical regimen Henderson proposed other activities, including manual training and vocational education. Thus he hoped to treat both the physical condition of the criminal and vagabond and his moral attitude toward the work situation.

The similarity between such an analysis of vagabondage and the analyses that had been made of criminality and mental diseases did not escape contemporary observers. Some of them hoped to discover a single treatment for all of the varieties of contemporary lapses of will, melancholy, and laziness. For such writers, it seemed possible that tramps suffered neurotic disorders similar to the disease neurasthenia. Thus the refusal to work might be considered a social symptom of a profound psychological disorder.

Implicit in all of these physical or hereditarian views of vagabondage was an abiding pessimism. If, as many analysts insisted, tramping developed because of some inherent degeneracy of the racial stock, then little could be done, except through selective breeding of populations to end it. In a 1916 new publication, the *Journal of Delinquency,* J. Harold Williams published an article entitled "Hereditary Nomadism and Delinquency," in which he agreed with Charles Davenport, America's leading advocate of eugenics, that vagabondage was an inherited trait. It occurred, he argued, in families already marked by hysteria, epilepsy, and depression. Nomadism was a sign of feeble-mindedness. Little could be done to help cases of it.[6]

Although a good deal more sympathetic to tramps, writer Jack London nonetheless subscribed to a version of the degeneracy argument to explain modern vagabondage. As a young man, London spent much of his time among hobos. He joined General Kelly's corps of Coxy's army in 1894. After this experience, he recognized that the widespread fear of tramping was largely based upon the political potential of this group, and he agreed that they represented such a threat.

London's most interesting work on tramping was his report on England, *The People of the Abyss,* published in 1903. To undertake this study of poverty and urban nomadism, the author lived, temporarily, the life of a city tramp. Before he went underground and took on the disguise of his surroundings, the novelist presented himself at the London offices of Cooks Tours to secure advance verification of his identity and plans as a precaution against the chance that he be arrested or incarcerated and require help. The company refused to book this odd tour, but London eventually secured the aid of an American friend. Nonetheless, the incident is revealing, for it shows that the author, like many of his contemporaries, considered slums as unknown, dangerous, and the remotest part of the world. His reportage was, inevitably, the study of a "foreign" country populated by unknown, exotic peoples. When he emerged, he stated his conclusion that this underworld was crushed by exploitation, poverty, disease, and government bureaucracy. The result was a new race of degenerates who occupied urban slums and who could not and would not work. Even in this account, which was certainly sympathetic—written as it was by an author who was widely known for riding the rails and living a life of tramping—vagabondage and racial degeneracy were linked. The early twentieth century found this conclusion hard to escape.[7]

A second group of writers blamed the sudden appearance of tramping upon a national decline in morality and the creation of institutions, in the name of charity, that often, inadvertantly, promoted vagabondage. Thus the railroad encouraged young men to abandon their homes because it did not adequately prevent hobos from hitching rides. By a little effort and ingenuity, anyone could find free transportation to almost any place in the United States. Indiscriminate charity, free housing, or even free temporary lodging in police stations all made tramping easy and even pleasant. Mrs. Charles Russell Lowell, who was active in urban reform in New York, specifically cited cheap hotels and lodging houses as a major cause of vagabondage. Fellow reformer Edward T. Devine disagreed, but only in part. He argued that at least a few organizations, such as the Salvation Army, considered part of their legitimate work to be providing housing for tramps.[8]

Behind the reappraisal of charity institutions lay the question that the philosopher Baldwin had used to illustrate his discussion of modern ethical problems. The dimension of urgency that filled such books as Robert Hunter's *Poverty* and Jacob Riis's *How the Other Half Lives* indicates how much the fear of tramps and the urban poor was part of a larger doubt. The traditional moral attitudes toward charity and the work ethic appeared to be disintegrating. The deserving poor (that is, those who worked and remained poor) had once been the favorite objects of almsgiving. But at the turn of the century, there was no longer any easy guide for giving. By traditional standards, there existed a large number of social outcasts who did not deserve any help. Many among these were defined as the products of mental instability, environmental conditions, or racial and ethnic inheritance. Traditional charity was designed to reinforce the work ethic, but how could it affect this population?

Charity organizations themselves were well on their way to rejecting any rigid, moral interpretation of vagabondage by the turn of the century. Alice Solenberger, head of the Chicago Bureau of Charities, in her study *One Thousand Homeless Men* for the Russell Sage Foundation, argued in 1911 that industry had most contributed to the growth of tramping. She presumed that vagabondage was a new phenomenon in America. As proof, she noted that the word "tramp," had not appeared in American lawbooks before 1865. The larger trends that had caused vagabondage were outgrowths of industrial change. For one thing, the American family had been disrupted. Even more serious was a revolutionary change in the conditions of industrial work. Modern labor required two major alterations in habits. Workers had to accustom themselves to high speed and repetitive output, and they had to adjust themselves to seasonal work, which demanded geographic mobility. Both of these changes encouraged tramping. As Charles Ely Adams conceded, the hobo was very possibly a necessary part of modern industrial conditions.[9]

Solenberger and Adams were both wrong in their analyses. Vagabondage was certainly not new, nor was labor different in precisely the way they imagined it. But their description of the tie between industrial progress and social disarray was of symbolic importance, for it illustrated the way in which modern commentators conceived the crisis of work.

Josiah Willard who, like Jack London, traveled with tramps, suggested a third interpretation of vagabondage. In articles for *Atlantic* and *Harpers*, he suggested that tramps were neither degenerate nor immoral, but that their most important characteristic was the result of a new social attitude. Vagabonds refused to accept the traditional work ethic because they could not subscribe to the notion that success came through perseverance and hard work. As Lamar Bailey put it, in some work "there is something lacking; it may be variety, it may be hope, it may be freedom. . . ." In a life of tramping, men could exchange "hope for unconcern, and they are free."[10]

Avant-garde writers and literary critics of Greenwich Village after 1911 took this argument one step further. The bum and the tramp came to represent the proletarian hero, the man who refused to be crushed or shaped into a cog in the industrial mechanism. The natural genius "on the bum"—the urban and industrial noble savage—was pictured in the pages of the *Masses* and the novels of Floyd Dell as the last free man in modern society. The tramp was transformed into a literary vagabond.[11]

Few observers chose to follow the romantic logic of this argument. To a majority of writers, the tramp remained both a victim of industrialization and a threat to society. He represented a challenge to the American dream and case study in the breakdown of the work ethic.

Reinstilling the traditional work ethic in the midst of industrialism and urbanization was a perplexing dilemma. It demanded a reexamination of the sequence of social events and a study of institutions that formed personality. Institutions such as the family or apprenticeship training, which once had operated naturally and effectively in a rural or craft society, were clearly ineffective in modern circumstances and, in some cases, they had ceased to operate at all.

In his 1897 article "Shiftless Population," Edward Devine suggested that responsibility for part of mankind's inability to adjust to modern work be laid upon the institutions that formed character. The nature of labor had changed, and its psychological rewards were often scanty. The family structure as a producing unit no longer existed. Therefore, a conscious, special effort was required to create a strong, work-oriented personality. To accomplish this end, Devine argued that the burden of personality formation in modern America ought to be shifted from private to public institutions. He advised additional kindergartens, manual training schools, care for homeless children, social work for families in distress, and, above all, the study and research of modern social problems. Only in social reformation, he concluded, would society ever find the means for eliminating "our shiftless and floating population." Socialist Robert Hunter agreed, although he seemed a good deal more sensitive to the problems of this population.

Tramps were, he claimed, an exploited, unemployed population, untrained and unfit for modern life. It was not their fault; they were not immoral. But something had to be done, for lack of work had made them degenerate. They openly bore the physical marks of their low position in society.[12]

The various suggestions for the cure and prevention of tramping indicate something of the range and intensity of feelings involved in seeing this population as a threat to social stability. In undertaking the cure of these misfits—the most glaring failures of American capitalism—social critics and government officials proposed a range of solutions that, taken together, indicate the impetus behind thinking about the modern crisis of work. Solutions to vagrancy problems and tramping ranged from the Rahway, New Jersey, plan, under which hobos were arrested, placed into chains, and put to hard labor, to medical treatments conducted in modern, sanitary institutions. Some commentators suggested posting signs promising vagrants nothing but hard labor and meager food. Others, more sociologically oriented, argued for a national system of classification and study of tramps.[13]

Whatever the viewpoint, whether tramping was linked to racial inheritance, drink, laziness, or environment, and whether the treatment advised was brutal incarceration or medical therapy, most observers agreed on one thing: something had to be done to reinstill traditional attitudes toward work and achievement in a population that was increasingly urban and immigrant and that seemed decreasingly susceptible to exhortations to follow well-worn paths to social achievement. New means were required to revise the attitudes of modern Americans to their work or, better, to recreate the conditions that had once created strong, persistent, and uncomplaining workers.

4

Neurasthenia:
The Mental Illness of Industrialism

In the debates over genius and vagabondage there was an implicit assumption that traditional concepts of individualism and work were ineffective in explaining the problems of modern society. "Neurasthenia" was the name given by psychologists to the breakdown of the structure of a personality when it proved incapable of adjusting to the regime of modern industrialism. Well before the flowering of behaviorism and psychoanalysis prior to the First World War, there were signs that psychologists and physicians questioned the efficacy of traditional methods of forming personality structures. The isolation of a specific category of symptoms called neurasthenia and the development of several important forms of treatment suggest that some observers were deeply distressed by the threat industrial progress posed to human personality. Neurasthenia was the disease of progress, brought on by the disruption of the traditional work ethic. It was a specific name given to a category of symptoms that an increasing number of doctors and alienists believed to lie behind the bloated figures of suicide, crime, divorce, and psychosis, which were especially high in America's urban areas. Neurasthenia was the disease of the traditional personality divided against itself.

Whatever the particular refinements or definitions of the disease, it was identified as a paralysis of will caused by insufferable conditions of modern life. Neurasthenia was the name given to a divided and weakened sense of identity. It was an explanation for the nervous and discontented appearance that unmistakably marked the American physiognomy. Foreign visitors were apt to remark upon this worried aspect of American countenances and upon the American obsession for work and excitement. As Charles K. Mills of the Philadelphia Polyclinic and College for Graduates in Medicine wrote, such characteristics could even be regarded as typical of "American civilization."

The problem of a divided psyche or some form of mental schism, or even the mind-body problem, had been the cause of longstanding and feverish debates in European and American philosophy and psychology. The study of the pathology of the divided or unbalanced self was a traditional part of European medicine. During the nineteenth century two major psychological theories, phrenology and faculty psychology, elaborated upon the divisions of the mind. Both argued that the human spirit was divided into separate functional parts that had specific ties to the material world. In the early part of that century medical writers and food faddists had accepted and elaborated several complex theories about the nature of the interlocking, but antagonistic, parts of the self. In part, neurasthenia belongs to this tradition of analysis, but it also represents a specific refinement based upon modern social conditions. It was the disease of the impotent will.[1]

Isolation of the symptoms of neurasthenia coincided with the beginning of a serious discussion in the United States about the psychological and ethical meaning of work, human efficiency, and social order. Described as a disease of social crisis, it was, according to its discoverers, the result of the intense and contradictory demands made upon the personality by modern industrial civilization. It was a medical metaphor for moral paralysis and unexplainable lapses in the effectiveness of personality and individual effort. Pathological indecision was its most frequent symptom. It appeared because excessive energy was committed to the pursuit of work and success.

George Beard, medical lecturer at City University in New York, isolated and defined the symptoms of neurasthenia in the 1880s. This disease, like hysteria, he wrote, manifested itself in the total collapse of personality. It was most likely to strike citizens of the United States, because of a variety of factors that made this civilization unique. The malady had two sorts of origins. One was biological, manifesting itself in the physiological symptoms of exhaustion and nervousness. The body, he wrote, possessed only a limited supply of nervous energy, and this was electrical in nature. If this energy were dissipated by evil habits, excesses, drugs, or worry, then physical damage might result. But disruption of the electrical circuits did not by itself explain the origin of the disease. Behind the physical mechanism that triggered neurasthenia were social and cultural problems. American civilization, he concluded, created serious nervous tensions that induced the disease.[2]

Beard was not the first to remark upon the speed of change and personal agitation of Americans in their pursuit of fortune and success, but he was one of the first to call this a primary cause of mental disorder. This observation, together with his description of the body as a dynamo, gave his theory some semblance of modern experimental medicine. Beard was in part, however, serving up an older theory of medicine, one that linked disease to vice and dietary excitement. In his modernization of this tradition, however, he added social pathology to neurotic symptoms.

The environmental causes of American nervousness, Beard argued, included climate, diet, and specific, indigenous institutions. Of the secondary factors, climate was of great importance. The degree of moisture (or, rather, the lack of moisture) in the air was a major cause of nervousness. At this point Beard was echoing a much older body of accepted medical wisdom, which defined illness as an imbalance among the basic elements or humors of the body. Climate had another destructive effect, for it helped to create beautiful women who, in turn, incited excess nervous excitement.

The exhausting American climate was a major contributor to neurasthenia, but the burden of Beard's analysis was concerned with the mental and psychological factors that led to the condition. The chief among these, Beard wrote, was modern civilization itself, which he defined as "steampower, the periodical press, the telegraph, the sciences, and the mental activity of women." Behind this phenomenology of industrialism lay one more profound and principal cause—the modern division of labor and the devolution of work into specific, repetitive tasks. Specialization in work touched off an "increase of insanity and other diseases of the nervous system" among the working and poor populations. The effects were even worse for those whose labor was mental. Excessive intellectual strain, he warned, was ravaging the American middle classes and, together with other excitements, was inciting nervous dissipation and mental disease. Progress, regulation of life by clocks, specialization, and the noneconomically determined function of women (as objects of beauty, not utility) dislodged the healthy structures of personality and led first to physical degeneration and, finally, to collapse.[3]

As might be expected, Beard compromised himself in defining neurasthenia as a disease of overspecialization of labor, for he employed a contradictory standard in analyzing the social causes of the disease. Sympathetic as he was to its sufferers, Beard ultimately stated that the increase in mental disease was a necessary by-product of progress. It was simply a price paid for the advance of civilization and the elaboration of social hierarchy. Without this progress and material and scientific expansion, America would descend into barbarism. Moreover, if the middle classes were particularly susceptible to neurasthenia, they, at least, were compensated by a longer, richer life than that of manual laborers.

The crisis of will that Beard called a neurological disorder had become more severe, he wrote, because of inappropriate traditional attitudes toward work and career that invested every individual effort in the pursuit of success. Rest, relaxation, and moderation had been and still were associated with sin and weakness. The obsession for work thus made man the victim of changes in the marketplace. Divided labor inevitably split the personality or absorbed the individual entirely in one narrow activity. "The gospel of work," he wrote, "must make way for the gospel of rest. The children of the past generation were forced, driven, stimulated to work, and in forms most repulsive. . . ." In Beard's view, education and upbringing had to prepare new generations for a different form of civilization with new attitudes toward labor.[4]

In treating the neurasthenic patient, the doctor acted much like a sociologist or psychologist. Cure depended upon the ability of the patient to understand and bear modern civilization and its stresses. Thus Beard suggested changes in the patient's life: dietary alterations, rest, and electrical therapy. Most important, however, was a reversal of attitudes toward work. In this way, Beard updated and put into modern usage the ancient medical wisdom that defined health as a perfect balance of bodily forces and mental effort. Output must be matched by input; physical labor should be balanced by mental output; specialization by generalization.

Several important members of the American medical and psychology professions accepted the outlines of Beard's analysis of neurasthenia although, of course, they modified some of his ideas. Perhaps the most important American to second his work was the physician and novelist S. Weir Mitchell. Mitchell's forced-rest cure became one of the most widely practiced treatments for the disease, especially among female patients. Like Beard, Mitchell diagnosed physical and social causes of the disease and, if anything, he was more explicit in his denunciation of the destructive effects of divided labor and intensified work among the middle classes. In the first edition of his book *Wear and Tear*, written in 1875, and throughout the nine subsequent editions that appeared before the end of the century, Mitchell blamed the intensity of "brain work" for the growing tide of neurasthenia.

Mitchell discovered the highest incidence of mental disturbance to be in crowded, urban areas of America. Although he neglected to cite precise figures to support his contention, he noted that "maladies of the nervous system" were rapidly spreading in American cities. This wave of mental disease struck the population unequally, affecting some classes far more than others. It did not infect physical laborers as severely as others, for they were being "better and better paid and less and less hardly tasked." But those who lived "by the lower form of brain work" were increasingly prone to the disease. The intensification of labor among the lower-middle classes constituted, for Mitchell, the principal cause of neurasthenia.

To illustrate his point about work, Mitchell arranged a list of professions in descending order according to their susceptibility to mental strain: "Manufactures and certain classes of railway officials are the most liable to suffer from neural exhaustion. Next to these come merchants in general, brokers, etc.; then less frequently clergymen; still less often lawyers; and more rarely doctors; while distressing cases are apt to occur among the overschooled young of both sexes."[5] This classification, Mitchell felt, would also help to explain the rising statistical rate of suicide and mental illness. Industrialism and the increasing tempo of work brought on serious paralysis of the will.

Following Mitchell and Beard the literature on neurasthenia branched into two directions. The first included technical examinations of patients to determine what, if any, organic and cellular changes occurred as a result of the disease. Researchers also sought to differentiate the specific symptoms of hysteria and melancholy from neurasthenia. Another group of researchers continued to examine the social causes of the disease. For example, Edward Cowles, professor of mental diseases at Dartmouth Medical School in 1891, defined the essential early symptom of the disease as the inability to support a "prolonged effort at attention." Additional indications of infection might be mental depression, loss of mental control, excessive introspection, or physical irritability. In cases of two patients analyzed by Cowles, overwork was the catalyst for breakdown. Both the businessman who worried too much about his financial affairs and the harried female clerk succumbed to the disease. Most physicians would agree, Cowles concluded, that, whatever the trigger for the mechanism, neurasthenic patients generally evidenced a high level of toxic substance in their blood systems. Unable to eliminate this because of a generalized dissipation of energy, patients were, in effect, poisoning themselves. Thus worry, fatigue and overwork touched off physical and organic changes.[6]

In his book *Nerve Waste: Practical Information Concerning Nervous Impairment in Modern Life,* written in 1889, H. C. Sawyer argued that neurasthenia resulted from overstrenuous activity, tension, and monotony. The physical ravages of nerve waste were likely to remain for a long time. "An incessant mental and nervous over-activity," he wrote, "seems to be inseparable for many vocations." This tendency appeared to be spreading in American society. The author even found a new symptom to add to the list that Beard and Mitchell had compiled.

Writers' cramp, he suggested, was also a major indication of the disease. With this addition neurasthenia, more than ever, was defined as the disease of the sensitive soul, the intellectual confronted by an insurmountable obstacle in his life and calling.[7]

From 1900 to the end of the first decade of the twentieth century, literature on neurasthenia proliferated. As the English physician Thomas D. Savill noted, the disease was more and more becoming a symbol for the infection of the intelligence by lassitude and inaction. It was possible to compare it with hysteria, except that the latter disease was much more likely to strike women in the form of emotional paralysis. Closer medical attention to neurasthenia had given rise to a debate among medical experts. Was neurasthenia, they questioned, exclusively the disease of the upper classes and intellectuals, or could it strike anywhere in society? Thomas Savill felt that the preponderant medical opinion of his day was still that anyone could fall prey to the disease.[8]

Although Savill's work suggests some departure from the original Mitchell-Beard diagnosis of neurasthenia as the disease of middle-class alienation, there remained a strong tendency to define it as the result of a malfunctioning work ethic. An anonymous author, in the article "The Autobiography of a Neurasthenic," published in *American Magazine* in 1910, wrote that his problem stemmed from his inability to adjust to urban life and competition. "Never again," he concluded, "will I listen to the promptings of the miserable fever of emulation that drives so many American men to sickness, despair, and madness."[9]

Treatments advised for neurasthenics suggest that physicians and patients were deeply worried about the pace of American life and the intensity of work; the cure was, most often, enforced rest. The best known cure was prescribed by Weir Mitchell in his popular book *Fat and Blood: An Essay on the Treatment of Certain Forms of Neurasthenia and Hysteria*. Mitchell's cure developed out of his experimentation with nervous female patients. Most of them, he noted, suffered a serious loss of weight, indicating a lack of blood and, more particularly, an absence of fat cells. To reverse this condition, he attacked the moral and physical causes of the infection. He demanded absolute rest and immobility of the patient, excessive (forced if necessary) feeding, and artificial stimulation of the muscles through electric therapy. For some patients (generally male neurasthenics) he prescribed a "testicular elixir" developed by Brown-Sequard. But he also recognized that his work had a psychological side. The doctor, by imposing his will and strict control of the patient, forced a pattern of physical behavior that would, ultimately, have moral effects.[10]

The noted Boston physician Morton Prince pointed to a dilemma in

Mitchell's advice. The rest cure and excessive feeding might have beneficial effects, but it was more likely that cure occurred because of the role of the doctor in asserting his will over the patient. In this process of substitution of the doctor's will for the patient's, Prince continued, great care should be exercised. Every element of routine, every reaction of the patient should be anticipated. Of course, medical suppression of symptoms should be continued through whatever means; electric therapy, suggestion, improved nutrition, rest, and isolation from a destructive environment. But treatment should also include a frank discussion of the disease with the afflicted person and the development of new rules of conduct and occupation. As Prince argued, the doctor should become more open and explicit about the physical and mental retraining and reformation that he was promoting.[11]

Electric therapy, advised by Prince, Mitchell, and Beard, was justified by the psychological and physiological theories then popular, which described the body as a closed energy system. Expended energy required refurbishing. In a work written primarily for other doctors and entitled *Electro-Therapeutics of Neurasthenia*, W. F. Robinson described two principal sorts of electric treatment and their different purposes. One was *faradism*, a mild current designed to stimulate the muscles of a particular area. Weir Mitchell in particular advised this treatment to preserve the muscle tone of his patients who were forced to remain immobile in the course of their rest cure. Another form of electric therapy was the static electric shock, again, of a relatively mild sort. Robinson preferred this latter treatment because he felt that it might shatter the syndrome of laziness, nervousness, and lassitude characteristic of most neurasthenics.[12]

If physicians advised both a physical and moral approach to the disease, it was primarily because they saw, as Beard did, a parallel between the physical energy system of the body and a moral and ethical energy system of the intellect and will. This parallelism implied a general, orderly mechanical universe that obeyed similar physical and moral laws. The health of the whole man depended upon, as Arthur Carey put it in 1904 in his book on nervous prostration, "obedience to spiritual law on the part of the soul and obedience to natural law on the part of the body." Mental disease, following this definition, came from the reckless excitement and overexpenditure of physical and mental energy. The body could infect the mind, but also, the mind could destroy physical health. Cure represented a return to a proper balance and harmony of physical and mental functions.

Among all doctors of neurasthenia, the activity most advocated to restore the mental and physical self-regulation of the patient, considered to be the proper antidote to neurasthenia, was work. There was no paradox in this prescription, even though many doctors argued that modern forms of labor caused the disease. Most of them clung to the traditional view that human labor was the source of physical and moral satisfaction and ethical growth. As Richard Cabot, professor of medicine at Harvard, wrote in 1915, finding suitable work meant finding "one's place in the world." Disease, by implication, was the pathology of dislocation, caused because a subject did not know where he belonged and because he committed his energies in the wrong place. The lack of creative work, the increase in specialization, and the wrong attitude toward labor (emphasizing merely the financial rewards of work) perverted the human personality. To innoculate society against neurasthenia and similar diseases of mental and physical breakdown, Cabot proposed a new and more creative work ethic and a reintegration of the personality through physical activity. Social workers should preside over this program and, together with the physician, help to redirect and train the will of neurasthenic personalities.[13]

Writing somewhat later, Boris Sidis extended and developed several ideas that he (and William James) shared with Beard and Mitchell about the relationship of industrial culture to mental illness. Sidis and James both resented what they called the growing mediocrity of American civilization, by which they meant its growing conformity to routine. Sidis, in his book *Nervous Ills,* made this commentary the cornerstone of his analysis. Habit, work, and monotony, he wrote, were creating a servile spirit in America and a class of unconscious automatons who suffered from prolonged depression and fear. Neurosis and psychotic symptoms emerged from extremes of routine. Cure might be effected (and here he credited James with an important psychological discovery) by liberating the pent-up reserve energy in each human personality.[14]

As evident in the work of Sidis, the diagnosis of neurasthenia coincided, during the late nineteenth century, with a very active philosophic and psychological interest in the problem of the divided will. In 1884 the Humbolt Library of Popular Science Literature published a translation of *Diseases of the Will* by the French psychologist Theodule Ribot. Ribot explicitly linked the philosophic problem of free will to the incidence of neurasthenia. Drawing heavily upon the works of the French philosopher Charles Renouvier and the American philosopher William James, Ribot noted parallels between medical theory and philosophic inquiry. It could be enormously fruitful, he contended, if a single definition of the will were developed to serve in both areas of study. Such a definition might be the following: the will is a force that balances and creates coherence in the body and mind. Diseases of the will are, therefore, indicated by incoherence and incomplete attention. A crisis of will would bring about extreme symptoms of ennui and ineffectuality. Psychologically, it would distort the personality. Philosophically it would cast doubt upon the meaning of freedom and individuality.[15]

As Prince, Ribot, and Sidis described it, neurasthenia can be considered part of the development of modern psychological theories. The majority of doctors who concerned themselves with the disease, however, subscribed to a more traditional version of personality. They assumed a parallelism of mind and body where the human spirit coincided with, but remained distinct from, the physical elements of existence. In their stress upon the will, individual regeneration, and (even) conversion, they were responding to deeply ingrained secular protestantism. The doctors who linked mental disease to modern industrialism were making a moral critique of society as much as they were exploring nervous disorders. They were asking if the traditional personality, as they understood it, formed with specific aspirations, expecting visible satisfactions and ethical enrichment from work, could survive in a much-changed, complicated, industrial society.

In a different form the phenomenon of neurasthenia worried nonmedical circles. A school of self-help and mind cure writers appeared toward the end of the nineteenth century that also blamed modern society for a paralysis of will and suggested a variety of homeopathic treatments that would reestablish the power of the will. More frankly conservative, their goal was to spread the gospel that intense effort and single-mindedness could bring financial and social rewards to any believer. The tone of this literature was irrepressibly enthusiastic and confident. But behind the optimism there lay strong doubts. Many writers seemed to suspect that success had become too elusive a goal. Citizens therefore needed special instruction in how to achieve it. Other writers argued that the moral quality of work was changing because of developments in modern industry and bureaucracy; therefore, new attitudes were necessary.

The appearance of success literature, like the discussion of neurasthenia, strengthens the sense that there was a deep ambiguity about individualism and the work ethic by the turn of the century. Versions of the success ethic in parables, novels, and political and religious tracts inundated American society at all levels. But this rush of propaganda, despite its enthusiasm, suggests rising doubts about self-help and individualism—the very message preached. Self-help literature crested and then broke upon the very issue it was designed to overcome: the insufficiency of the older, private definition of the self.

Advice literature of this era propagated an ideal that was rapidly declining as an appropriate or useful mode of behavior. In the eyes of contemporary sociology and psychology, self-help, mental regeneration, and recrudescence of the will were all viewed as insufficient means to overcome the problems of modern social adjustment. Thus the self-help movements of this period indicate a pervasive feeling that the traditional description of effort and reward was indeed in crisis. Unsuccessful confrontation with modern working conditions led to futility and failure; self-help was a way of reentering the contest. Doubtful as it may have been, the advocates of self-help invoked traditional wisdom. They proposed that each individual achieve success and fulfillment through personal effort and will power. Paralysis of the will in the economic sphere could be overcome by an act of will itself.

There was, however, a measure of difference. The modern restatement of this formula distorted the work ethic by stressing the financial rewards of effort. Work brought reward but not dignity. Economic activity ought to be conducted according to ethical standards, not because these were of themselves right or because they were the basis of human community devoted to exchange, but because they brought bigger rewards.

Of course the inculcation of the success elements of the work ethic had been widespread throughout the nineteenth century in such important books as the *McGuffy Reader* as well as in the stories and novels of popular culture. Historians of American culture have extensively explored the reinforcement of the success motif at the end of the nineteenth century and, although there are different emphases among them, several points are clear. In the late nineteenth century the meaning of success underwent changes in emphasis. The modern success ethic was distorted to stress techniques of getting ahead financially. This focus indicated a concern and, often, an obsession for hard work, proper manners, perseverance, and a yen for cutthroat competition. Reward was increasingly defined as social mobility. Success came through objects of consumption, not the intangible elements of ethical satisfaction.[16] Obviously, such ideas had appeared in American culture before the 1890s, but there was a difference. In the works of Emerson (often invoked as the patron saint of self-help advisers) personal effort was a primary value. But the reward, while it might include financial success, was, primarily, the achievement of self-reliance and self-fulfillment.

Another characteristic of this vast new success literature was its revision or elimination of the religious and democratic elements that had once been the principal sanctions of wealth. Nineteenth-century textbooks such as the *McGuffy's Reader* defended success in religious terms, as the symbol of reward for virtuous action. Typically, moral virtue could be discovered in every parable of work well done. Mind cure movements also related religious sanction and success, but differently. The most popular modern tracts, such as Elbert Hubbard's "A Message to Garcia," William Makepiece Thayer's "Turning Points in Successful Careers," and Ralph Waldo Trine's "In Tune with the Infinite," were imbued with religious justifications and religious allusions. But the purpose of their advice was to prepare the personality, not for grace or service, but for seizing the moment.[17]

Modern success literature discovered what George Beard and Weir Mitchell assumed: the conditions of labor and brainwork were rapidly changing and, therefore, the individual stood in a new relationship to work. Advocates of success, unlike neurasthenic specialists, however, called for a reintensification of effort and competition. What was disease to some became cure to others.

In some cases the paradox of success advice was openly admitted. The *Retail Clerks International Advocate*, one of the few white-collar union papers of the age, contained the sort of advice that reflected the contradictions of modern work. "Clerkology," a series of articles by George Putnam appearing in 1908, captured this paradox of a changed world. Success, wrote the author, resulted from unremitting commitment to hard work. But modern laboring conditions had changed: "Monotonous? Certainly! But in some respects blessed by monotony. We know how to do what is expected of us and we are therefore more or less satisfactory to our employers and we feel that we are worth the amount which comes in our envelope every Saturday night." As another writer put it in the same journal, the successful merchant almost always rose by force of honesty and truthfulness from the position of sales clerk. Thus a clerk must "prove his real worth by applying energy at all times." Work, in this scheme, was not rewarding because human labor was dignified. It led to financial success. High ethical standards were simply the wisest policy.[18]

The history of the *Advocate* itself illustrates the problems in defining work and success for a growing body of white-collar workers. From 1903 until about 1910 the paper repeated much of the then-standard success advice: hard work, good manners, and extra effort bring financial reward. After 1909 its writers became more interested in news of strikes and labor-organizing activity. After 1911 its emphasis shifted to the problems of organizing working women who, it recognized, now constituted a large element in the clerking vocation.

There was also a deprecation of talent and creativity and a singular emphasis upon perseverence implicit in the advice literature of the early twentieth century. As Ernest Johnson wrote in 1914 in his advice book *Working and Winning*, "Now and then it is said of some successful insurance man that 'he is a genius'; but a genius has been defined as a man with an unlimited capacity for hard work." The hard worker shared with the specialist and the highly trained brain worker a constant vision on the small steps that he might take toward success. The road to financial heaven was thus paved with effort and sacrifice.[19]

The heroes of modern popular individualist fiction and advice literature also changed from the natural heroes of the early nineteenth century—military, intellectual, or ministerial giants—to those individuals who successfully took advantage of the economic system. This apparent democratizing of success was accompanied by other changes in tone. Modern heroes generally received some sort of social or financial reward rather than glory or esteem. So, too, the successful person did not contribute to society through charity, but by perfectly performing his function. As reformer Ernest Poole stated this idea, "And self-help, in spite of all its mistakes, is to-day the main force in blotting out what is worst in a sweatshop."[20]

Several American writers recognized a serious problem in the character-building advice literature of this modern period. In the novels of the era there is a persistent questioning of the facile ethic of self-improvement. In the works of Mark Twain and William Dean Howells, the doubt was clear and profound. Other writers, such as Theodore Dreiser, who once worked for *Success* magazine (a leading "new thought" journal), returned again and again to explore this theme about which he was deeply ambiguous.

Personality advice, like Weir Mitchell's rest cure, represented an extension and transformation of traditional assumptions about the character and its relationship to work. Both recognized that modern society often failed to provide the personality with the defenses which would enable it to survive in an environment of intensified competition and labor.[21]

The Emmanuel movement recognized this similarity between neurasthenic diagnosis and mind cure. Begun in Boston in the first decade of the twentieth century, it was led by the Reverend Elwood Worcester of Emmanuel Church. Worcester held classes in his church beginning in 1906 that were designed to treat the increasing number of mentally ill who came to his attention. During these sessions he informed his parishioners of the dangers of neurasthenia and suggested ways to rejuvenate the will. A self-styled follower of William James, Worcester devoted himself to the cause of the "nervously and morally diseased." His analysis of neurasthenia echoed Beard's words. "Unless," he wrote, "we find some better means than we possess at present to calm and simplify our lives, the end of our civilization is in sight, for we cannot continue to use up our forces faster than those forces are generated." Unlike Beard or Mitchell, Worcester advised mind control through auto-stimulation and self-induced will power. He treated only the mental and spiritual symptoms of neurasthenia, in much the same way that mind cure approached the problem of the feeling of failure, even though he reiterated the energy theory of Mitchell and Beard.[22]

Although the Emmanuel movement was limited in influence and was controversial (Sigmund Freud attacked it, for example), it bridged the gap between serious medical research and popular sentiment, demonstrating that both were based upon the feeling that American society was undergoing a revolution in morals and a weakening of traditions. Neurasthenia, mind cure, and the Emmanuel movement all stressed the need for moral regeneration through the invigoration of the individual will. Each movement explicitly recognized that the cause of modern psychological malaise was the increasing tempo and specialization of industrial activity.

There were, according to doctors and mind curists, only a few ways to overcome the destructive effects of modern work. Only by restoring the will through faith or resignation could the personality return to the competitive world. The picture of the modern businessman drawn by Annie Payson Call in her tract, *Power Through Repose,* perfectly captured this reluctant acceptance of the hostile world of modern economic life.[23] In the face of the difficult and enervating new world, Call advised repose and a private restoration of the self's resources. Salvation was, by implication, a kind of retreat from modern life. Like other mind curists and even neurasthenic experts, her advice was contradictory. Given the destructive nature of modern economic competition and specialization, rest and rejuvenation cures—even absolute faith in will power—would only enable a person to return and survive the debilitating conditions that had led to retreat, collapse, and failure in the first place.

5

Alienation in Industry:
The Division of Labor

Industrial alienation or the divorce of mankind from satisfying labor has become one of the major themes in modern
social thinking. At the turn of the century discussion of the
specific ways in which work had become degraded was already well
under way. Industrial accidents, unemployment, low wages, and
sweated labor were important results of industrialism, but the psychological and moral problems brought on by specialization, ennui, and
the division of work tasks were just as significant. The proliferation of
terms describing work and the argument over which should fit each
category of activity marked the writings of sociologists and industrial
commentators, indicating a confusion over terms and meanings. As
working conditions altered rapidly and extensively, verbal distinctions
developed in the usage of words such as "career," "profession," "calling," and "vocation."

The symptoms of dissatisfaction, mental disorder, and boredom that
Americans discussed at the end of the century and the questions that
they asked about the formation of personality were intimately related
to and based upon the discovery of industrial alienation. Observers in
this period hoped that they could discover the economic factors in
society that had provoked this feeling of crisis. And, inevitably, they
focused upon the rapidly changing conditions of industrial labor.
These conditions appeared to challenge traditional wisdom about work
and its effects in a particularly distressing manner. That traditional
wisdom had been no mere simplistic morality. It was a profound and
important explanation for the way citizens constructed their lives and
gained membership in society through their activities in the workplace. Any disruption of this process was, therefore, a serious problem
for a society that based itself upon the rightful relation of individuals to work.

Although few Americans would have used the term "alienation" or employed such words as "lumpen proletariat" to describe the large under class that would not or could not adjust to modern work, they did, nonetheless, broach precisely the sorts of problems that had interested Karl Marx fifty years before. Marxism might have been overlooked in this discussion, but there is no doubt that what preoccupied Marx about modern capitalist development also worried many Americans during this period. But the debate over problems such as the division of labor and industrial alienation (to name two) led the United States in a different direction. Reacting to the same kinds of problems, perceiving some of the enormous difficulties inherent in modern industrialism, and just as sympathetic to the human damage wrought by such changes, Americans worked out a new industrial sociology in terms of two positions that Marx had given up. One was the necessity to preserve society much as it was and to leave economic and social relationships fundamentally untouched. The other was to work out the destiny of the nation within a Protestant, Christian context. Because of these commitments few American thinkers were prepared to admit Marx to the discussion. He was too abrasive and too much interested in the class struggle to have much impact. Even those (like Thorstein Veblen) who agreed with the core of Marx's critique of capitalism rarely invoked the German revolutionary's name or referred directly to his work.

Since the major assumptions of Americans who worried about industrial alienation were inherently conservative, the actual and the imagined history of industrial development in the United States was of great importance to them. To preserve an older set of economic and social relationships, it was necessary to know what those relationships had been. Therefore the passing of the traditional work ethic, especially as it was associated with the apprenticeship system, was something most critics lamented. This idyllic system of labor became, in fact, the ideal against which modern industrialism was judged.

The appearance of industrial alienation depended upon the division of labor that marked advanced industrialism. Social critics, moral philosophers, and economists were seriously worried by what most of them deemed to be destructive effects of specialization. This division, they argued, separated work into small compartments and meaningless activities. It altered the nature of labor and removed economic activity from its traditional moral and social context. Work had once been the end as well as the means of achieving a fulfilled life; it had provided social cohesion; it had educated; it had provided aesthetic training. Piecemeal tasks required by the assembly line and intensified, middle-class office work (generally referred to as the "intensification of competition") separated effort from any of these rewards. Work, rather than being an enriching experience, had become alienating. The enormous effort and total commitment invested in it brought only monetary wages as a return.

Much of the discussion of modern work was tied to economic questions, but beneath each suggestion and most of the reforms advocated there lay one predominant question: what was the nature of human personality and how was it related to labor? The answers to this question allowed a profound assumption to surface. Work and the preparation for work, in spite of the new industrial reality, constituted the quintessential human experience. Economics was foremost a moral science.

Otto Spengler, in his *The Decline of the West,* argued that this moral definition of work was invented by the eighteenth century. "*Work* becomes the great word of ethical thinking," he wrote. "The machine works," he continued, "and forces the man to cooperate." Spengler's interest in the modern revolution of attitudes toward human labor and its ties to the beginning of the industrial revolution was heightened by his belief that the creative force of the machine and the ideology of work had crested, and were in decline. Self-willed creativity and the control of mechanical invention had evolved into self-enslavement to mechanical forces.[1] The German author's sweeping pessimism was uncharacteristic of American thought. Yet his insights might have helped to explain the paradox of the work ethic itself. He understood that what had been progressive and revolutionary in one age had grown to be destructive in another because the circumstances had dramatically altered.

Thorstein Veblen characterized industrialism in another fashion. The life of modern man, he wrote, was regulated by the clock: "as a factor in shaping the habits of thought of the modern peoples, it is itself moreover, a fact of the first importance." In modern times there was, he continued, a strain "against the drift of the machine's teaching" that erupted particularly among the middle classes and the well-to-do who sought refuge in fantastic and archaic cults, all bent upon restoring the mystical powers of the individual personality. Reaction to alienation among such groups produced fantasy, not analysis, mysticism, not rebellion. Although few could match the wit or incisiveness of Veblen's analysis, it was obvious to many Americans that the traditional ethics and culture of work were missing from the assembly line. When asked to compile a book of work songs, contemporary sociologist Nels Anderson discovered that there were cowboy songs, logger songs, hobo songs, and labor union songs, but that none could be found that were "associated with modern industrial work."[2] This failure to celebrate the joy or even the tragedy of the modern work-place was itself an indication of a profound change in the meaning of labor.

Many thinkers discussed what they defined as a revolution in the social and cultural meaning of work during this period, but, of course, not everyone agreed. The expectations of the traditional work ethic did not die, nor did praise of individualism diminish. Popular writers in particular continued to extol the virtues of work, even in a modern factory, and claimed that it could be as enriching as any other exper-ience. As Waldo Warren wrote in his book *Thoughts on Business*, cen-turies of experience had accumulated evidence that "the Golden Rule stands preeminent as the world's greatest business maxim." William Armstrong Fairburn made the point more concretely in his book on work and genius. "There is often more poetry in the daily product of a factory," he concluded, "teeming with the spirit of universal brother-hood, than in a whole book of rhythmic verse."[3]

With this important qualification—that the question of industrial alienation was raised in the midst of a culture that still strongly ad-hered to the traditional work ethic—in mind, it is apparent why the issue of work and its relationship to human nature was so important and controversial. A culture that could not give up the compulsion to work hard could scarcely be unconcerned as the rewards for that com-pulsion appeared to be diminishing.

The history of the work ethic in its broadest sense is certainly the history of industrialization. Andriano Tilgher, in his book *Homo Faber*, underscores this point by arguing that work was the seminal concept of the nineteenth century, "so closely related to modern conceptions of liberty and of progress—of practically every activity—that to give anything like a complete account of it would be to write the history of economics, ethics, sociology, pedagogy, applied science—in fact of every branch of modern culture."[4] By 1900, when commentators began to recognize serious changes in the terms of work, the relationship between industrialism and work had become a paradoxical, even a contradictory, one. Up to then the history of industrialism and work had been reciprocal, but by the turn of the century changes in the nature of industrial labor threatened to alter this history. The creative manual labor that had sustained the work ethic at the beginning of the industrial period was fast disappearing.

Some of the most incisive critiques of modern industrialism came, particularly in England, from those who idealized the apprenticeship and manual labor systems. This nostalgic view of a craft society where apprenticeship, stability, and close social relations prevailed had been a major sentiment behind the romantic movement that flourished in

England at the beginning of the 1800s. Resistance to the divisions and exigencies of a mechanical civilization, fought in the name of a smaller, more intimate craft society, became a major premise in the works of Thomas Carlyle, John Ruskin, and William Morris. Ruskin captured the essence of the matter in his discussion of the nature of the gothic: "We have much studied and much perfected of late, the civilized invention of the division of labour; only we have given it a false name. It is not, truly speaking, the labour that is divided; but the men. . . ."[5]

Ruskin understood that the discussion of work and alienation in Europe and, later, in America, was a debate over the future of societies devoted to individual creativity. Looking back on this era, Peter Drucker argued in his *The New Society* that the major documents of social and religious thoughts in the nineteenth century all related to the effects of separating the worker from the control and understanding of what he produced. "Industrialism therefore," he wrote, "destroys the social prestige of traditional occupations and skills, and with it the satisfaction of the individual in his traditional work."[6]

This separation of work from its anticipated Christian rewards did not, however, release labor from its Christian sanctions. When intellectuals lamented the decline of craft society and the growing alienation of modern labor, they did not suggest giving up the moral exhortation to work. Escape from labor itself was never seriously proposed as a meaningful alternative in this discussion.

Because there already existed in England, France, and Germany a fully developed literature on the subject from which to draw ideas, European theories influenced the American discussion of alienation during the 1890s. Quite early, European thinkers recognized that work and ethics were becoming separated and that labor no longer brought its expected social and psychological rewards. The most radical elements to write in this tradition, including the English romantics and Pre-Raphaelites, the French utopians, and the German Marxists, stressed the need to restore harmony between man's work and his psychological and social instincts. In a great many writings the workshop was pictured as a place where individuals might achieve happiness and fulfillment. Indeed, the standard for judging any economy was, as often as not, the degree to which the fruits of labor, including moral and psychological rewards, were returned to the worker. Despite the disclaimers of even the most secular thinkers, this labor theory of value remained tied to the historical relationship between religious sanctions and the work ethic.

In France discussion of the work ethic achieved important dimensions in *Emile*, written by Jean Jacques Rousseau in 1762. But it was

Charles Fourier who wrote what was, in some ways, the most profound and strange tract on human labor in an industrial setting. Like a great many thinkers of the second and third decades of the nineteeth century, Fourier was greatly concerned with social changes that accompanied the early industrial revolution. He was particularly interested in the social effects of divided industrial tasks and factory work. In the utopian phalanstery that he imagined, the problems of the new industrial system could be resolved. In this harmonious, industrial village, the proper relationship between human instincts and work could be reestablished. Fourier divided the tasks of his utopian society minutely, according to his own sense of the division of labor. But, at the same time, he proposed to fulfill the sexual and psychological desires of every one of its citizens through an elaborate form of pageantry and ritual. As he wrote, "Love, which is so useless today, will become one of the most brilliant mainsprings of the social mechanism."[7]

Fourier's picture of a harmonious industrial world had many characteristics that reappeared in the writings of Americans seventy years later. He criticized the effects of the division of labor just as Edward Bellamy did in his utopian novel *Looking Backward,* published in 1888. He devised, just as Bellamy later did, a system whose purpose was to provide the psychic and sociological rewards of work without sacrificing industrial and agricultural progress.

Another influencial critic of the division of labor was the Frenchman Pierre-Joseph Proudhon. Like Fourier, Marx, and many of the major English economists of the day, he based his thought upon the labor theory of value. Unlike Fourier, however, Proudhon was unwilling to employ organizational novelties to overcome the alienating features of modern industrialism. Denouncing inequality and coercion, he suggested that men and women live together in mutual relationships based upon the exchange of goods. To this French political thinker the specialization, separation, centralization, and repression that existed in factories was particularly dangerous for the soul of modern man. The division of labor symbolized this problem. The just society, he continued, should overcome the inequalities of human beings by providing equal guarantees to life, work, and education.

Such anarchists as the Russian Leo Tolstoy extended Proudhon's attack upon modern industrialism and its class system. Tolstoy advised a return to rural virtues and economic activities as he stressed the need to refashion a creative and varied agricultural system. The Russian writer thus turned the utopian and anarchist critique of modern industrialism into a plea for a return to a more primitive social organization.[8]

Marx, in his early writings, attempted to mediate between nostalgic humanism and faith in progress. The inherent division of man from the product of his labor, which Hegel had posed as a central dilemma for modern society, was exactly the problem Marx tackled. His description of alienated labor in *The 1844 Economic and Philosophic Manuscripts* began with the origins of psychic division and exploitation. The industrial division of labor, he wrote, resulted in the production of objective commodities embodying labor time. But this product, under modern capitalism, did not belong to the worker. "Work," he wrote, "is external to the worker, that it is not part of his nature; and that, consequently, he does not fulfill himself in his work but denies himself, has a feeling of misery rather than well being, does not develop freely his mental and physical energies but is physically exhausted and mentally debased."[9]

Marx's elaboration of this argument included a further reproach against the division of labor. Not only did it divide men from what they produced, it also divided the personality into useful talents, exploiting some while eliminating others. This state of alienation was perpetuated by social institutions. Human will and effort were transformed into money with which the bourgeoisie, at any rate, attempted to repurchase those elements of humanity and happiness lost in the very process of gaining a living.

Other than proposing an abrupt, thorough change in the course of history, it is difficult to imagine how Marx might have escaped a very pessimistic conclusion to his discussion of alienation. Only by recapturing the self, objectified in created objects, did he see an end to alienation. This could be accomplished by the revolutionary act of destroying capitalism. But there remained the problem of industrialism itself, which Marx did not deal with, but which most intrigued American commentators. Was not the division of labor required by modern technology, they might have retorted, was it not an alienating force in itself, however it might be used?

Marx's demand for a change in the ideological and sociological context of work paralleled the more nostalgic arguments of Fourier and Tolstoy, who also sought to replace the sterile surroundings of labor. One assumption reappeared in each argument, whether it was a call for returning to a time and mode of production favorable to creative work, whether it was an outline of a utopia of pleasure or a festival of human labor, or whether it was a call for millennial change. All of these arguments were firmly grounded in the tradition of nineteenth-century thought that rejected any state of alienation as the natural end of human history.

But another position, developed in Europe, took a very different sort of perspective on this question. In the works of Emile Durkheim, published toward the close of the nineteenth century, modern industrial alienation and the division of labor are treated dispassionately, as natural effects of progress. The French sociologist suggested—and many American sociologists and psychologists agreed with him—that the division of labor was a positive force because it enhanced progress. The good effects of modern civilization far outweighed whatever individual damages might occur. Durkheim argued persuasively that the division of labor, far from separating individuals, created a higher level of interdependence. The reliance of each upon the other created law, order, and harmony.

Durkheim was not insensitive to the psychological disturbances induced by modern industry. He chose a special word, "anomie," to indicate just such a situation. But cases of maladjustment were the exception and, he continued, they developed because the individual failed to realize his place in society or perceive the growing social solidarity that accompanied industrialization. The division of labor, he admitted, might loosen traditional family ties that had once mediated between individual and society, but this situation simply indicated that cohesion was taking place at another level, in the social institutions erected by the state. Durkheim rejected the nostalgic medievalism contained in the works of contemporary Pre-Raphaelite thinkers such as William Morris. The division of labor and industrialism were natural stages in human evolution; to deal with the problems they created merely demanded a revision of social ethics.[10]

The German sociologist Max Weber recognized, as Durkheim did, that modern work had destructive features. He too proposed a way out of the dilemma of progress that would preserve the fundamental elements of work as then organized. The fundamental problem, he argued, was not work, but administration. He proposed new forms of bureaucracy that he hoped would eliminate the traditional class system and replace it with a mass democracy that would liberate the modern spirit and commit it to building a more just society.[11]

Durkheim and Weber, together with the bulk of early American sociologists they influenced, hoped to end alienation through the creation of compensatory institutions. Both accepted and welcomed progress with its faults and virtues. While the workplace might not create solidarity and social cohesion, they felt other institutions might do so. The opposing tendency in this debate, the socialists, utopians, anarchists, and Pre-Raphaelites, argued that nothing short of a revolution or a fundamental change in the mode of production could terminate this severe social and ethical crisis.

The contradiction between these two approaches to modern work was also apparent in the United States. President Charles Eliot of Harvard, writing in 1904, raised the dilemma unequivocably: "The winning of satisfaction and content in daily work is the most fundamental of all objects for an industrial democracy. Unless this satisfaction and content can be habitually won on an immense scale, the hopes and ideals of democracy cannot be realized." Most labor, even extremely dangerous or exhausting work, he argued, was rewarding. It could be as adventurous and exciting as sports. Since Eliot realized that the very nature of human personality was at stake in his discussion of contemporary industrial ethics, he could not admit the obvious —that in many cases work was menial, unrewarding, and destructive.[12]

Even socialist William D. P. Bliss contradicted himself when he discussed the term "Division of Labor" in his *The Encyclopaedia of Social Reform*, published in 1897. Like Eliot, he spoke about the problem of alienation but then dismissed it. The moral and aesthetic elements of modern work were destructive, he argued, although the division of labor that created them was also responsible for progress, production, and civilization. Bliss's solution was rather simple: he thought the importance of work should be reduced. Shorten the hourly burden of work, he suggested, and let men develop "in other ways," to recoup the elements of social and ethical satisfaction that their labor did not contain.[13]

For some commentators, such as the Reverend Heber Newton, an active New York reformer, the problem of alienation existed, but the solution was simple. A mere psychological change was necessary. Many men, he noted, did mechanical labor that brought them no satisfaction, "whereas they might find in those labors a bubbling-up of the waters which make life beautiful in the commonist surroundings." To find this respite from monotony, the worker should seek education to understand the whole process of manufacture of which his labor was such a small ingredient.[14]

Single tax reformer Henry George examined the problem more profoundly but, unfortunately, many of his insights were obscured by the political movement he launched. George's notions of modern social reform were explicitly and firmly based upon a labor theory of value and upon his vision of an agricultural America where he felt the proper relation of work, society, and reward had prevailed. George believed in a harmony of nature and society, a rapport that industrialism and capitalism had disrupted. In this natural state the fruits of man's labor were returned, undiminished, to him. In modern society rents, interest, and taxes had disrupted the free flow of this exchange. Society had become deeply divided. As George put it, "The rewards which nature yields to labor no longer go to the laborers in proportion to industry and skill; but a privileged class are enabled to live without labor by compelling a disinherited class to give up some part of their earnings for permission to live and work." Like the American socialists with whom George made an uneasy alliance, the advocate of the single tax believed that the alienation of human labor could be ended through some form of institutionally imposed equality.[15]

A different but equally important approach to the question of alienation focused upon the problem of the "work instinct." Frank Taussig, in his 1915 discussion *Inventors and Money-Makers*, noted that the modern division of labor had substituted monotonous assembly-line work for the random but complete experience of manual labor. Taussig examined the biographies of a number of contemporary inventors, trying to understand the source of their creativity. Invention, he concluded, came from the release of an inner urge, a will to expression that, unfortunately, modern society threatened to suppress by the imposition of repetitive and divisive work. Inventiveness, workmanship, and play were all related, and they were the normal human instincts that the regime of modern industrialism was destroying.[16]

Thorstein Veblen made the most interesting and profound use of the instinct theory. His description of the leisure class, together with his work on the instinct of workmanship, constitute the most comprehensive theory of industrial alienation developed in America during this period. To the maverick sociologist, the social and psychological superstructure of society had quite literally reversed the order of values. This process he described in 1898: "According to the common-sense ideal, the economic beatitude lies in an unrestrained consumption of goods, without work. . . ." Influenced by this prevailing attitude all occupations, he continued, that were not based upon a "capacity for predatory exploit" were considered dishonorable. With nonwork and even exploitation as the social ideal, the true instincts of mankind for creative work remained unexpressed and distorted. The predatory ethic overwhelmed the instinct for workmanship. The values held highest by society were, therefore, competition and conspicuous waste.

Veblen's discovery of an instinct of workmanship enabled him to imagine an ideal man. This ideal personality structure was, he felt, repressed by the practical and profitable arrangements of modern industry. The result was an inevitable and growing social tension. In *The Instinct of Workmanship*, written in 1914, Veblen remarked at length on the efforts of some Americans to undo the psychological damage that was created because of the repression of the work instinct. His remarks indicate the extent to which he used the concept of alienation as a social critique.

The work instinct could be distorted into strange behavior if it was unconscious or repressed. This frustration erupted into the strong contemporary tendency toward animism and the belief that objective, physical objects had spiritual characteristics. Escape from the real, industrial world, he continued, often expressed itself in worship of the primitive, in sport and brutality, and in the definition of mankind as a predatory animal. But this evasion, like the pursuit of monetary values, also had destructive side effects, and, in particular, it threatened to squeeze off the flow of technological inventiveness. Sport and violence merely reinforced the structural inequalities of society that had led to alienation in the first place.

Veblen's description of the "sports and primitive craze" at the end of the century underscored its relationship to work. The social and cultural activities of the leisured classes were not, as they seemed, merely diversions from the alienating life of industrial society. They also reinforced those features. Thus Veblen did not blame technology for the adverse effects of the division of labor; social and cultural institutions were at fault for distorting the impact of inventiveness on society.

Veblen's remarks upon what he deemed another evasion of alienation were also to the point. In the reappearance of occultism, neurasthenic cures, and homeopathic movements, he wrote, men and women hoped to avoid facing the dilemmas of modern industrial society. The "manner of life imposed by the machine process and its logic," he wrote, bore heavily upon them. Fantastic cults and beliefs were spreading. Middle-class people constructed make-believe worlds that could offer relief from the melancholy industrial universe. Veblen continued with a satiric reference clearly directed at William James. Laymen, he wrote, fall back upon "the will to believe things of which the senses transmit no evidence." "So there comes," he concluded, "an irrepressible—in a sense, congenital—recrudescence of magic, occult science, telepathy, spiritualism, vitalism, pragmatism."[17] As Veblen understood it, the large and variegated movement (or movements) that sought to reintegrate the human personality through one or another form of appeal to exercise of the will were fruitless efforts to overcome individual symptoms of industrial alienation without ever attacking the root causes. Veblen's own answer to alienation depended upon his concept of the natural economic man. Unlike those observers who turned their backs upon progress, he believed that human instinct for craft, work, and creativity could conquer the petty tyrannies of industrialism. But this could only be accomplished if modern society rid itself of its archaic elements—only if it eliminated the social and political causes of alienation. This argument, similar to one made early by Marx, assumed that progress, industrialism, and work could be united into a creative system of values only if the surrounding political and social system were changed.

Veblen's analysis of industrial alienation and his understanding of the self-cure movements have a coherence and sharpness unmatched by other American commentaries on the problem of work. But he stood outside the main thrust of the discussion, not because he misunderstood it (the contrary is true), but because his sardonic manner, his wit, and his penchant for integration and theory did not meet the needs of a debate that was dispersed, hesitant, and consistently aimed at practical results. Veblen's interpretation amounted to a brilliant and devastating appraisal of the culture of modern industrialism, a satire of those who misunderstood or rejected it, and an attack on the archaic social network that surrounded labor.

Many critics took a different tack. In their thinking the problem lay with technology itself, which seemed invariably antagonistic to the elements that had created the work ethic. The problem was not a cultural lag, as Veblen suggested, but the inevitable decline and fall from the golden age of handicraft and agriculture. This nostalgic and pessimistic attitude toward the effects of modern industrialism was a persuasive and widespread position that occupied the forefront in the discussion of work from the 1890s to the First World War.

These critics suggested that the context of labor had abruptly changed. They cited as evidence the separation of labor from ethical and moral relationships, the division of society into classes, and the increasing problems of leisure. All of these mutations challenged the old, carefully structured concept of the calling. With the rewards of labor increasingly limited to financial gain, it became very difficult, if not impossible, to believe that work could be the basic and fundamental activity of social integration. Indeed, modern work appeared to have precisely the opposite effect—it disintegrated home and community.

The religious crisis that this development suggested was a central concern of George Herron, itinerant minister and socialist intellectual. The tragedy of modern times, he wrote, was apparent in the chasm between civilization and conscience. "The facts and forces which now organize industry and so-called justice violate the best instincts of mankind," he wrote. The contemporary relationship between "master and men" subverted freedom and workmanship to the point where the words "Christian business life" had become a disguise for evil-doing.

Herron's bitter denunciation of modern work and exploitation was mollified by his faith in changing such practices through "social redemption." He appealed for economic justice and equality of opportunity and for the return of the fruits of labor to the producer. Although it was placed in a socialist framework, this suggestion had a strong conservative ingredient. Herron had in mind a return to the Populist paradise of the early nineteenth century that he and so many of his contemporaries imagined had existed. "The vast majority of human beings," he wrote, "must live their lives in the machinery of civilization; we can only save the people from being ground to profit by capturing the 'machine.' "[18]

Herron's proposal to throw a net of Christian restraints around the machinery of modern industrialism was a persistent tendency in an era that exhibited a complex and often contradictory religious critique of industrialism. If, as he felt, mechanical society was now separated from moral society, the dilemma of industrial progress was critical. Francis Peabody, professor of Christian ethics at Harvard, suggested in 1900 that such was the case. Modern laboring conditions seriously disrupted the operation of the work ethic. Undoubtedly it was still a moral virtue to commit oneself to work and toil, but in so doing one could become a slave to economic activity. The virtues that once accompanied work now existed only away from the marketplace. Thrift, for example, was no longer necessary to the economic system, so the moral value of it could not be acquired through experience in labor. Peabody sympathized with those who rejected modern society and found "signs of social bankruptcy and approaching chaos" in the growing chasm between ethical ideas and practice. Peabody's suggestion, like that of Herron, envisioned an ethical revolution, a reinvigoration, and a reapplication of Christian principles to industrial life. In this way he hoped to use the concept of Christian brotherhood to fill the interstices left by the disappearance of the comraderie of craft and the joy of creativity from labor.[19]

Jane Addams pointed to the same moral emptiness of work in her book on democracy and social ethics. Modern workers "desire both a clearer definition of the code of morality adopted to present day demands and a part in its fulfillment, both a creed and a practice of social morality." Unfortunately Addams detected a "dreary round of uninteresting work" and a sense of "declining consciousness of brain power." To reverse this decline, she hoped to bring ethical coherence into the workplace. Her own contribution to this goal involved plunging into a career of social effort and reform. The whole society, she concluded, must come together also, in order to eliminate industrial and class divisions.[20]

Such moralistic or religious attitudes toward industrial alienation were quite natural in America during this period because of the long-standing and intense identification of the calling and secular Christianity in the traditional definition of the work ethic. Quoting John Ruskin on the Christian nature of manual labor, Charles Roads, in his work *Christ Enthroned in the Industrial World*, insisted that a proper mental attitude brought to labor by the worker could make any effort —even garbage collecting—a rich and rewarding experience: "none can be more useful; and in those and other lowly work there is room for skill and mind and conscience to grow in fullest exercise."[21] As Roads in his optimism and Peabody, Herron, and Addams in their more critical attitude agreed, every effort to overcome modern alienation should be judged for its efficacy in enabling the worker to achieve self-mastery and then control over the machine. The principle question left to debate was which ingredients should be added to work to help the laborer achieve the enrichment, growth, and happiness that were rightfully his.

The moral-mechanical division that Addams, Herron, and a host of social critics detected in modern industrialism was given a less religious formulation by Albert Shaw in his advice book to young men in search of a career. The modern work world, he admitted, had altered greatly since earlier times, and young men hoping to make a success could expect to experience "considerable anxiety by reason of the disappearance of traditional landmarks." Shaw dismissed the religious lament over this situation and condemned the "timorous and painful arguments pro and con that one finds running through the columns of the press, particularly of the religious weeklies." Nonetheless, his own argument that work, especially middle-class work, should have some social service function amounted to a restatement of the same sense of crisis that existed in the calling. With less competition and shorter working hours, Shaw hoped that the intense drive for personal success might be deflected. But his suggestions, constituted nothing more than a proposal to return to the "traditional landmarks" of self-appraisal and moral reward for work well done.[22]

Class divisions, which deeply distressed many social observers, also sprang from modern laboring conditions. Some commentators argued that this separation damaged exploiters as much as it did the exploited. The enormous gap between worker and owner extended to questions of culture. While the wealthy had access to universities and education, they suffered from what Jane Addams described as the "snare of preparation." Thomas Davidson, philsopher and social theorist and founder of Breadwinners College of adult education in New York City, put it this way: "The rich and the learned are poorer and meaner because they cannot enter into brotherly and sisterly relations with the toilers; and these suffer equally because they are sundered from those."[23]

One sign of the recognition of divisions between classes and between types of work was the proliferation of words describing modern laboring situations. Work, as William Fairburn wrote, was directed physical and mental exercise. Labor, on the other hand, was mere expenditure of energy. Declining opportunities for individual expression through labor bolstered a social class system. "If his inner self," Fairburn wrote, "battles to overcome the world, he becomes a worker." But if his "inner self is overcome by discouragement, slumbers through indifference, or is hypnotized by avaricious materialism, the man degenerates to the status of a toiler or drudge." Fairburn's understanding that attitude toward work helped determine feelings of class is characteristic of his day. The danger of a wrong attitude on the part of the worker, he concluded, might induce him to join a labor union or, worse, a revolutionary socialist movement.[24]

Increased use of words like "profession" reflected the changing evaluation of activities such as architecture, engineering, and business. These varieties of work clamored to be deemed as morally remunerative as the older professions of law, medicine, and the ministry. Louis Brandeis's commencement address to Brown University in 1912 caught the spirit of this movement. Brandeis argued that business ought to be called a profession because it required all of the social attributes and training of the highest of careers. "Real success in business is to be found in achievements comparable rather with those of the artist or the scientist, or the inventor or the statesman," he noted.[25]

Brandeis's attempt to raise the verbal status of business to match its financial position indicates the swelling gap between what was meant by ordinary work and what was called a profession. The former, he told the Civic Federation of New England in 1906, was not rewarding. Leisure time was therefore required to compensate workers for lost elements of educational, recreational, and ethical development. Professions, on the other hand, still provided both spiritual and financial advancement.

The language describing work could be refined into more precise categories than two, but most writers used "profession" and a newer term, "vocation." By 1910 the term "vocation" had achieved wide usage, particularly in describing industrial work that did not require professional membership or licensing. The Library of Congress definition of this word for use in cataloging indicates the sense in which it was often employed: "Here are entered works dealing with the occupation of an individual in the sense of employment to which he is destined by nature, or called, as it were, by some higher power." Whether that higher power was God, the state, or a local vocational association, the use of this word, as well as the appearance of a new profession composed of advisers, testers, and social scientists called "vocational experts," signified a distinction in the sorts of work available to citizens according to the expectations of effort and reward in each.

A further troubling division, one that was even more puzzling for those who attempted to redefine work, was the separation of labor from pleasure. While the average hours of labor in 1900 surely entitled no one to worry that the American public had too much unfilled time, leisure was nonetheless a much-discussed problem. It became so because observers felt that work was no longer the moral and social center of civic relationships. Consequently leisure time offered possibilities for instilling values. This was not a wished-for development, wrote George Cutten, president of Colgate College, in his history of leisure, but the machine had forced leisure upon Americans. Whatever its origin, increased free time, said socialist Algie Simons, could be and should be used to fill the life of each worker with the moral and ethical enrichments that the mechanical workshop did not offer. Although Simons did not see it, his suggestions undermined the whole ethic of work.[26]

A less revolutionary substitute for moral and social satisfaction formerly associated with work was advocated by educationists who proposed that young people received special training in sport, exercise, or some "moral equivalent" of violence. Such suggestions underscored the proposition that work was being transformed into mechanical labor divorced from its traditional and Christian ethical values.

From the perspective of traditional work, the separation of mental and moral qualities from physical endeavor could be defined as the root cause of modern alienation. Put another way, explanations for the transformation of work converged upon one key phenomenon—proletarianization. Although this term was rarely, if ever, used to explain the emptiness of work, it was what lay behind the concrete and piecemeal observations that American commentators made in their efforts to explain the degradation of modern labor.

Insights into the nature of modern work depends upon the answers to two historical questions. What was the nature of work in the early nineteenth century? How had labor evolved from being the keystone of social unity into a force that threatened to explode the social order? By 1900 it was obvious that training for work and the manner of selecting one's vocation had radically changed since the first years of the industrial revolution. The selection of jobs had become much freer but, to some critics, this freedom was illusory, for it was accompanied by a decline in demand for special skills. Therefore, fitting the right person to the right job was more a psychological problem than it was a practical one. A number of writers agreed that apprenticeship training was the missing element in modern work that accounted for the vocational crisis of modern industrialism. As a viable system of labor training, of course, apprenticeship had long been on the decline. But the idea of apprenticeship training was enormously appealing to many commentators, and its disappearance was deeply regretted. Unfortunately, in modern factories positions were filled haphazardly; as long as the employee could turn the proper screw and keep up with the cadence of production, he was deemed a success. The extended family relationship that had once characterized apprenticeship evaporated into the anonymity of mass employment. Monotonous, industrial manufacturing had conquered the process of American work.[27]

To find out how far this revolution had progressed, the U.S. Congress instructed the Commissioner of Labor in August 1894 to report on the use, cost, and effectiveness of hand labor and machine labor in the United States. One surprising discovery that Commissioner Carroll Wright, author of the resulting study, noted was the amount of hand work that remained in industries where one might expect greater mechanization. In a similar sort of study done for the United States Bureau of Education in 1908, Wright noted the widespread and persistent use of apprenticeship training in industry. But Wright added a caveat; this persistence of hand work and apprenticeship, these older customs, existed in the context of modern technical training. Therefore, they did not have the same social and ethical results. Apprenticeship in the twentieth century had a much narrower base and purpose and it did not offer moral or academic training.

Wright estimated that the older system had changed after 1860 because of state regulation of job training. A more important cause, suggested by economic historian Paul Douglas, was the rapid growth of industrialism after the War of 1812.[28] However apprenticeship had died, it was no longer a viable system of job training.

While some spoke nostalgically of training systems that prevailed in the early nineteenth century, not every observer had the same feelings. As Charles Eliot of Harvard noted, the fashion of studying medicine by caring for the doctor's horse and buggy or the study of law by copying deeds was, happily, gone forever. There were "better ways of studying medicine or law, namely, by going to professional school, where progressive, systematic instruction rapidly developed is to be had."[29]

Carroll Wright also warned against any effort to turn back the clock and restore cottage industry. Technical knowledge, he suggested, imparted two immense benefits. It enabled a person to find a position in life. Furthermore, if he worked successfully, the laborer would develop "ethical relations." But this was not so simple, warned Walter Lippmann: "When you think of the misfits among your acquaintances—the lawyers who should be mechanics, the doctors who should be business men, the teachers who should have been clerks, and the executives who should be doing research in a laboratory—when you think of the talent that would be released by proper use, the imagination takes wing at the possibilities."[30]

Lippmann suggested, quite rightly, that vocational education in modern schools represented an attempt to fill the gap left by the disappearance of older formal institutions of job training. H. J. Hapgood asked if men drifted into work or were assisted by some larger, natural force. "The man who investigates this question, whether for practical or sociological reasons, finds unmistakable traces of a law which puts the right man in the right place—sometimes." But, he concluded, because this law worked imperfectly, society needed the services of a new professional, the employment expert.[31] Through conscious and explicit education the moral qualities of a good worker could be developed as each job required. As the *Business Journal* noted in 1916, these generally included clean habits, willingness to work, untiring energy and loyalty, "initiative . . . originality, the ability to use good judgment, painstaking thoroughness and enthusiasm."[32]

If these were the desirable mental attitudes of the modern worker, they had little to do with the habits of mind that the industrial tasks in modern society inculcated. Industrial work was increasingly and more obviously a monotonous activity divorced from serious intellectual input. Frederick Taylor's application of scientific management to the process of continuous production and planning was merely an explicit recognition of this situation. It was an effort to speed up and complete the separation between idea and execution for the purposes of increased production. Under the ideal regime of clocks and graphs, he felt industrial work could be subdivided and scheduled so that it was impossible for the worker either to exert any personal initiative or to understand the contribution of his own repetitive motion to the rhythm of the whole process.

This sort of modern work, Paul Douglas noted, contradicted the first assumptions of the work ethic: "Emerson himself would not have put much faith in the quality of self-reliance caused by carrying parcels, tending a cotton loom, stitching button holes, canning oysters, rolling cigarettes, and opening doors." Somewhat later Stuart Chase summarized this feeling when he wrote that Americans were the most mechanized people on earth, but that progress had rendered them nervous, restless, and at odds with their world. "This is the more tragic," he continued, "in that the specialization and frequent monotony of our daily work, however skilled, clamour for psychic equilibrium." Helen Marot made much the same point in 1918 in her discussion of industry for the New York Bureau of Educational Experiments. The degeneration of the work environment under modern industrialism was unmistakable: "the modern factory organization destroys creative desire and individual initiative as it excludes the workers from participation in creative experience."[33]

Human effort and the overcoming of obstacles—the release of creative energy—had once defined the function of the will and the effect of honest work. The assertion of control over human nature and the ethical mastery of the passions had thus once been the most important psychic by-products of human labor. Essayist Edwin Bjorkman noted the decline of such uses of the will in the workplace. Speaking of the citizens of Pittsburgh, he noted, "Elsewhere, people may work to exist; here, if anywhere, they exist to work. And this applies with equal force to rich and poor, to high and low to native and foreigner." Man the toolmaker had become an appendage of the machine.[34]

The transformation of white-collar labor no doubt forced American intellectuals to consider the psychological effects of work in terms of their own lives. This transformation was not as extensive as the *Nation* suggested in 1913 when it noted that the typewriter had transformed literary creation into a matter of business ledgers and balance sheets. Nonetheless, the division of labor had also changed middle-class work. Even elite institutions of learning were threatened by this encroachment. Efficiency advocate Morris L. Cooke quite seriously suggested in 1910 that American universities judge their performance by standards of "formal organization" and special sorts of "machinery of administration." In a chapter entitled "The College Teacher as Producer" he argued that the professor would someday measure what he produced by the prevailing standards in other occupations. In his proposals for standard room sizes, buildings, blackboards, and evaluations of performance, Cooke proposed to submit the university to a system that already reigned in industry—the separation of intellectual from practical activity.[35]

If such advice was seriously intended, then the independence of middle-class institutions and their function as refuges from the routinized life of industrialism was at stake. How threatening and bizarre such threats had become is demonstrated by an article written in 1903 by David Graham Phillips. Phillips enthusiastically commented on the transformation of St. George's Church of Stuyvesant Square, New York City, into a model business organization. In an article for *Harpers* magazine he noted that the church was run as if it were a railroad. Every member was given some task in caring for the building plant. Even the physical layout reminded him of a factory: "There is the the church proper, steepleless and with two massive towers, whose clocks seem to be keeping time upon its toilers, warning them that a moment is approaching when a great whistle shall blow the close of the day's work."[36]

Certainly not all American institutions were similarly assaulted and transformed into models of industrial efficiency. But the effects of this general transformation of work were strongly felt in office work. The revolution of clerical and white-collar labor at the end of the nineteenth century and during the following two decades derived from the mechanization of bureaucratic functions. The tools of white-collar labor were perfected and applied in this period with amazing rapidity. Jobs were routinized with the introduction of shorthand methods of note-taking and the use of office machines and record-keeping devices and systems. The social character of this work changed as increasing numbers of women were hired as secretaries, clerks, and assistants.

One indication of the intensity of this transformation can be seen in the appearance of over 200 systems of copyrighted shorthand methods during the 1890 to 1920 period. Methods of penmanship were perfected—that is, standardized—with the publication of A. N. Palmer's *Guide to Business Writing*. After 1890 the use of typewriters and numerical filing systems became widespread. Production of office machines and supplies, in percentage terms, grew rapidly between 1900 and 1919, as did the number of employees occupied with such tools.

Clerking, traditionally a male profession, was quickly transformed into a field dominated by female labor. At the turn of the century about one-tenth of employed women were secretaries or clerks. In 1920 almost half of all white-collar jobs were occupied by women. During the longer period from 1899 to 1949, the income of this sector declined relative to that of other workers, indicating a gradual erosion of status and, no doubt, a differentially lower wage paid to women.[37]

Among the first to recognize that white-collar work was enervating and unrewarding were the pioneer experts in office management and organization. Their interest, however, was to intensify production schedules and complete the revolution in work that substituted efficiency for creativity as the criterion of success. In his popular business text *Making the Office Pay*, William H. Leffingwell admitted the alienating character of office work. But such problems could be overcome and even translated into higher production. "Physical or mental fatigue," he noted, "lack of interest, and the like, can often be overcome by instituting periodic exercise, improving ventilation, and giving rewards for excellent performance of work." His long list of hints designed to make workers happy in their jobs amounted to the suggestion that management provide the illusion of social and ethical meaning in work. Thus he suggested flowers, music, mottoes, exercise, small rewards, "conferences, [and] an organization which hooks up the social life of the employee with the work of the office."[38] If this sounded empty and cynical to a generation raised on the traditional ethic of work, one that expected that work itself would provide ethical growth, it was probably not intended as such. Leffingwell and scores of others who entered the factories, offices, and universities to rationalize and systematize labor simply had a different view of human nature. This they defined in terms of process and operating capacity. They still recognized a need for some form of enjoyment or fulfillment in work, but not for moral purposes. Such by-products were justified because they led to increased production and, therefore, to a more affluent society.

The revolution in work expectations had as suggested above, a particularly significant effect upon women. Woman's work, as tradition had it, was to occupy herself with home and children. From the exercise of this domestic function her sentimental, emotional, and salving personality would emerge. But what happened when women entered the factory? Social Gospel Minister Walter Rauschenbusch worried that work might alter womanhood. In his "A Prayer for All Working Women," published in May 1910, he asked: "Grant them strength of body to bear the strain of unremitting toil, and may no present pressure unfit them for the holy duties of home and motherhood which the future may lay upon them."[39]

Was the world of labor experienced by women a nightmare world ruled by a time clock in the shape of a three-headed dog that nipped late workers, as the author of "The Tragedy of the Wage Earner" indicated? Or did this modern world offer a chance to make the home into an extension of the "great factory for the production of citizens," as Robert and Martha Bruere suggested in their tract *Increasing Home Efficiency?*

Whatever their precise conclusions, many observers concluded that women in particular suffered from a confusion of work and social roles. Simply put, they did not know what society expected of them because society did not know. The result, according to Abraham Myerson in his book *The Nervous Housewife*, was an epidemic of neurasthenia. Insecure as workers or as housewives, women turned to invalidism as an escape. Rather than dissipate energy in an activity that they were reluctant to pursue, he continued, women lapsed into the lethargic, listless syndrome of mental disease.[40]

The most astute and extensive remarks upon the effects of alienation and the division of labor on women were made by Charlotte Perkins Gilman in her book *Women and Economics*. The repression of the work instinct and the proletarianization of workers suggested ideas around which Gilman grouped her arguments about the condition of modern women. A woman's status, as she described it, was defined by modern economic conditions. Women were barred from creative labor because their "work" was confined to their existence as sexual objects. This specialization, she continued, had distorted female personality and intensified emotions. "The nervous energy that up to the present moment has impelled women to labor incessantly at something, be it the veriest folly of fancy work," she wrote, "is one mark of this effect." Men, on the other hand, lived in the world of democratic industry where they expressed their creativity and self-development. Gilman desired real equality and, for her, this meant participation in the dynamic and rewarding world of human labor and creativity. By comparison, the circumscribed world of women appeared bleak and confined.[41]

If the symbol of human alienation was, as Gilman suggested, overspecialization and exploitation, what was to be done to restore balance to a society where the division of labor had become synonymous with progress? This question could be answered only after a fresh look at the nature of human personality and its relation to labor. If it was still desirable to preserve an autonomous, self-governing citizenry, then perhaps society would be obligated to restore the principal elements of the traditional work ethic, or even give up machine labor. If the work ethic did not contain the only practical definition of social ethics and their formation, then an alternative view was possible. If the individual was not an ethical being or a rational creature but, rather, a biological process located in a specific historical geography, then the problem lay, not in restoring the old order, but in finding a new one where each human mechanism could operate at its highest efficiency for the good of all.

The discovery of alienation, the realization that modern industrialism challenged the operation of traditional self-sufficiency and individualism, spurred on an abrupt turnabout in the assumptions of American social ethics. The promises held out by progress based upon industrial specialization were boundless in one sense, but it was frightening to contemplate the moral implications of this progress.

Some observers, such as Hamilton Mabie in his *Essays on Work and Culture*, ignored the signposts and argued that labor could still function as the force that created individualism. Work settled man's place in the world, for this could "be determined only by a complete unfolding and measurement of all the powers that are in him, and this process of development must have all the elements of the highest moral process." The effect of work well done was the growth of character. Or, as Charlotte Perkins Gilman put it in *Human Work,* for individuals labor is "an end in itself, a condition of their existence and their highest joy and duty."[42]

Another extreme may be seen in Gerald Stanley Lee's rhapsodic exposition of machine aesthetics. Workers seated by their machines, he noted, experienced the poetry of their calling, but in a different sense. "Modern religion is a machine," he continued, "Modern education is a machine." And modern man was entirely bound up with the fate of the machine. "The real problem that stands in the way of poetry in machinery is not literary nor aesthetic," he argued, "It is sociological. It is getting people to notice that an engineer is a gentleman and a poet."[43] Put another way, a man trained scientifically and placed in a proper job would find great happiness and efficiency. As one writer put it in 1912, the effect of machinery was to create a new form of social ethics. The modern manager, the modern leader, must be, he concluded, an expert in ethics, moral-economy and psychology. But he could not be a self-made man. Efficiency expert H. L. Gantt did not hesitate to sanctify this new industrial regime. Christ's, as well as Abraham Lincoln's teachings, he noted, would be fulfilled if only the ethic of efficiency, planning, and scientific management replaced the older self-governing work ethic.[44]

Given the background of Americans, steeped in the ethic of work, its dependent notions of craft and apprenticeship, and its values of self-reliance and individualism, it is understandable that the division of labor and industrial alienation were deeply distressing. Some reacted by trying to turn back the clock. But even for those who cast their lot with progress and specialization, there remained the ultimate goal of a brotherhood of hard workers building a Christian commonwealth.

6

Sport and Violence:
Reviving the Game of Life

In his ecstatic commentary on American democracy, the French sociologist Paul de Rousiers noted in 1892 that sport was a preparation for and even a surrogate for the strenuous economic life of the American nation because it demanded the same sort of fortitude and strength as raising cattle on a ranch or maintaining a business. From a very different perspective, social reformer Jane Addams came to much the same conclusion about the relationship between economics and the idea of sport. "A strike," she wrote, "is one of the most exciting episodes in modern life, and as it assumes the characteristics of a game, the entire population of a city becomes divided into two cheering sides."[1]

Much of the justification of sport and the interest in ritual violence and primitivism in this period rested upon the view that such practices could accomplish the same sorts of character-building ascribed to work. The frightening rise in the social statistics of immorality made such an argument all the more attractive. It was hoped that reenactment of the struggle for life would end mankind's alienation from the healthy expression of its instincts and restore physical struggle, personal will, and responsibility to their central position in the formation of character.

Symbolic of the most enervating aspects of modern civilization were the monotonous, routine, physical and intellectual labors that required intense attention and repetition. The proper antidote to this new form of life was thought by the advocates of sport to consist in retreat from the contemporary industrial world onto the playing field, where the traditional and proper relationships between individual effort, competition, and reward could be found. Celebration of sport as a moral refreshment updated and transformed traditional notions of the proper relationship of human nature to work and struggle. The justification of sport in this era paralleled the arguments in favor of mind cure. It

67

was celebrated as a physical reenactment of the ideal conditions that had traditionally created a healthy, self-reliant individual. Sport was work.

The vision of sport as a return to nature was, in one sense, merely a further convolution in the historical American celebration of naturalness and self-sufficient individualism. But there were new aspects in the debate about sport that derived from the fact that modern games had become codified and specifically symbolic, played out before large numbers of spectators. Thus if sport represented a retreat from the artificiality of civilization into a momentary but healthy struggle for life, it could be defended as a perfect preparation for competition in the business world.

What some observers saw as a need for physical exercise or a reenactment of the simple and basic rules of human conduct others described as a need to return to a more primitive and instinctual life. The phenomenon of primitivism actually encompassed a vast array of opinions and purposes in the late nineteenth century, but part of its significance was due to the comparison that could be made between simplicity and complexity, individual and society, and the natural state of humanity versus the civilized. Primitive man was thus sometimes defined as an individual completely at home and at ease in his world. Civilized man was unable to achieve genuine self-expression or feeling. Celebration of the primitive emotions, actions, and instincts of mankind was, perhaps, extreme, but it did, nonetheless, suggest a route to the rediscovery of the true self.

That the end of the century marked a revival celebrating sport and a return to nature has been widely noted by American historians. While the details of this revolution in sport and physical culture and the revival of martial values are of great interest, an explanation of the general impulse that lay behind them is more important. As historian John Higham has written, the transformation of colleges into football theaters or arenas of "organized physical combat illustrates a master impulse that seized the American people in the 1890's and reshaped their history."

A favorite way to express the quintessential experience of American culture was to picture it as a struggle of man versus nature. However the details of this mythic encounter were arranged, one of the most important elements of American self-explanation has always been the importance of direct, first-hand knowledge of struggle and hard work; this was no less true in the 1890s. In isolation—that is, in nature, in war, and in the hunt—the virtues of duty and the clarity of vision that derived from confronting danger were injected into the American character.[2] These traditional images and symbols of struggle and competition were underscored by the widespread acceptance of Charles Darwin's almost poetic description of struggle and competition in evolution.

In the ever-present idiom of nature versus society, Americans have had a useful explanation for the problems that beset them and the nation. Continued devotion to the model small community and natural harmony as opposed to urban personality gave hope that the relation between humans and nature could be restored, that the personality could discover its hidden strengths. By the late nineteenth century this idea devolved into a new meaning: the relationship could now only be achieved symbolically. This was what Charlotte Perkins Gilman noted about contemporary writing: "Current literature is full of this reversion today, this 'call of the wild,' this tempting invitation to give it all up and go back to the beginning."[3]

Under the regime of industrialism retreat to nature, in the older sense of fleeing to the frontier, was a physical impossibility. The wilderness that could be appropriated, owned, and transformed had disappeared for most citizens. The trials and tests of life in nature could only be invoked on the playing field, in parks, in military training, or, perhaps, in the purely mental feat of seeing one's dull and routine work as symbolic form of the struggle for life.

Through the judicious practice of play, even children could achieve a balance in their experience of civilization and nature. As Henry Curtis, director of the New York City playgrounds, wrote of the play movement in the United States, "It has been a rather social movement, arising from the realization that idleness bred delinquency." The play movement to which he referred first appeared in 1886 in Boston, when, as Curtis concluded, the conditions of work had undergone a revolution that demanded less effort or exertion, at a time when leisure had become a problem.[4]

Many of those writers who advised the practice of some sort of physical culture had, in addition to social order, their own class interests at heart. What Phillipe Ariès says of the origins of modern games in his book *Centuries of Childhood* also helps to explain the form and development of American sport after the Civil War. Speaking of another century, Ariès writes that a choice was made between games: "Some were reserved for people of quality, the others were abandoned to the children and the lower classes." During the late 1860s and early 1870s many games were imported into the United States and intended specifically for people of fashion, not for the masses. The growing popularity of one of these—football—at American elite universities made this sport a particularly important symbol around which the discussion of sport took place.[5]

University of Chicago sociologist William I. Thomas, writing in 1901 for the *American Journal of Sociology,* expounded upon many of the implicit aristocratic ideals expressed by sport or the "gaming instinct," as he called it, and its relationship to leadership qualities and individualism. "Our socially developed sympathy and pity may recoil from witnessing a scene where physical hunt is the object of the game," he wrote—but the hunt could also be experienced vicariously. This would gratify usually repressed human instincts. Thus such a sport as football could express in symbolic terms the instincts that had evolved through centuries of conflict in securing food and suitable mates. Football, like war, appealed to the deepest aspects of the human psychology. Thomas wrote that the Spanish-American War Rough Riders regarded military conflict as "the greatest sport they were likely to have a chance at in a lifetime."

The practice of sport, Thomas continued, was particularly apt as an outlet because modern conditions of work exposed Americans to situations that were frequently unsatisfying and degrading. In leisure time, those who had to accept this artificial and alienating work could refresh themselves in hunting and golf, or at the prize fight or theater, and "live through, in imitation or imagination, the instinctive, motor-conflict life of prehistoric times."[6] Those who could not find some such healthy release and who could not find a balance to the "artificiality" of modern life often became tramps and criminals. Unable to accept the "new arrangement" of work and leisure, they demanded a life totally of the instincts. While this might be understandable, Thomas sternly rebuked those citizens who collapsed into primitivism and antisocial behavior.

The impulse behind the ritual practice of active mastery over life no doubt reflected what one historian has called an anxiety over social roles, particularly among American men, who had been brought up in a tradition of self-reliance and who expected to achieve social mobility and success through economic competition.[7] Less the historian than the satirist, Thorstein Veblen mocked the playing field, calling it an arena for atavistic behavior. Veblen felt that he detected a link between the social hegemony of the upper classes and the violence in which they engaged and the sports they practiced. He felt that the sports of the leisured class were characterized by an ostentatious waste of time and money. They were a key component in leisure-class education, because success, for an athlete, presumed "not only a waste of time, but also a waste of money, as well as possession of certain highly unindustrial archaic traits of character and temperament." Here, as in much of Veblen's writings, irony has an ulterior motive. The symbolic enactment of warlike behavior (the slang of sport, he wrote, was often borrowed from warfare) was an attempt to preserve a dying class influence.

Even though some sports enthusiasts, including Theodore Roosevelt, might have agreed with Veblen's notion that sport was practice for the exercise of class hegemony (although Roosevelt certainly would have resented the tone of Veblen's remarks), they would probably have been upset by a second set of relationships that the sociologist found between athletics, economics, and social life. Veblen pointed to some glaring similarities between the behavior of the lumpen proletariat and the American upper classes. "It is," he remarked, "only the high-bred gentleman and the rowdy that normally resort to blows as the universal solvent of differences of opinion." Thus, in his view, both extremes of society exhibited the same tendency to atavistic and undisciplined behavior. This could be explained, Veblen continued, because neither aristocracy nor lumpen elements had a healthy relationship to work. Both made a virtue of their inability to adjust to modern conditions.[8]

Veblen's sarcastic remarks about the similarity of aristocratic activities and the underworld of tramps and rowdies was obviously intended to discredit the leisure class, which had no function, according to this analysis, except to convert its own uselessness into patterns of consumption to be copied by the middle classes. An aristocracy left over from a more primitive social arrangement where it did have a purpose had little left to it other than to invent and sustain a culture to be emulated by those below it. That sort of creativity and leadership was the source of its power and its corruption.

Where Veblen disparaged and others doubted, some writers rushed in to praise. The similarity between aristocracy and the social underworld, they argued, did exist, but Veblen misunderstood it. In contrast with Veblen, they stated that the extremes of society still managed to live the life of instincts. For different reasons, each group avoided the melancholy world of routine and monotony that was the lot of the middle and working classes. Each group was able to sustain a more primitive mode of existence.

Describing sport and physical exertion in terms of class rule inevitably invigorated the discussion of violence and primitivism. For Harvard philosopher Joshia Royce, and others who wished to evoke the abstract lessons of loyalty and moral education, sport presented a serious dilemma. Practiced properly, it could be moral behavior demanding the participation of the whole self, organizing the sportsman's "conduct in harmony with his nobler sentiments." To Royce, the loyalty in team sports was not an abstract goal. It came from the practice of persistence and self-control in pursuit of a specific form of victory—all according to the code of fair play. Like any form of effective moral training, athletics could develop the individual's sense of self-integration and lucidity. But, as he noted, a serious problem had arisen. Athletics, and especially football, had become professionalized—that is, designed for no purpose other than to please unthinking crowds. "The Harvard stadium," he told the Boston Physical Education Association, "is an admirable place when it is not too full of people. But when it is full of people it is a bad place for moral education of our athletic youth." Thus Royce agreed with Veblen that the playing field was an arena for acting out moral situations. He even saw some danger in the contemporary practice of sports. But he would never agree with Veblen's mocking remarks about the ulterior motives of athletics.[9]

Veblen's and Royce's commentaries are part of the important public discussion of football that recurred in the United States from the 1890s to the beginning of the First World War. This discussion involved a spirited dispute centering around several conflicting interpretations of the sport. Some asked if football had a specific class meaning. Was it a symbolic acting out of the basic elements of life— struggle, competition, and will power? Did participation in football select those virtues in an individual which would enable him to compete more successfully in business? To what degree was football governed by the same sorts of principles that ruled the marketplace? As the commentary and controversy thickened, the discussion focused more and more upon football as a game governed by the ethic of work.

College football was defended by arguments that appealed to both morality and a safety valve theory of exercise. In *Popular Science Monthly* in 1902, Calvin Woodward summarized these arguments, claiming that football had five important moral lessons to teach. It was done at a specific time and place and therefore encouraged prompt and steady behavior. In underscored positive elements of behavior. It discouraged lazy temperaments and encouraged self-discovery. And, finally, it promoted self-restraint, thus laying the foundations for gentlemanly behavior. In the same magazine somewhat later, Edwin Dexter of the University of Illinois argued more stridently in favor of college athletics. Football was no gentle game, and fathers and sons who were satisfied with "tiddle-dy-winks" were advised to avoid it. For the masculine majority, however, football was the equivalent of knight-errantry and the tournament. It was the "last safety valve to virile expression." Without it, society might explode.[10]

Several popular notions about human personality were captured here and elsewhere in the debate over football. The individual human was likened to a closed energy system requiring exercise or expression, the lack of which would cause the instincts to seek other, less constructive outlets. Secondly, the whole argument in favor of football implied a crude moral faculty psychology that described human personality as a collection of traits requiring specific, guided training. Physical effort stimulated mental development; qualities that emerged on the playing field could be practiced in economic and social life. Athletics was the "game of life."

The debate over professionalism can be seen as a further index to the social and cultural implications of sport at the turn of the century. In 1905, during one of the high points in the debate over football, President Eliot of Harvard proposed the suspension of intercollegiate competition for a year because of "intolerable" conditions and the "fundamental difficulty" of a game played in "bad spirit." Fifteen years before this Theodore Roosevelt had warned about professionalism in athletics. "The mere statement of the difference is enough to show," he wrote, "that the amateur, and not the professional, is the desirable citizen, the man who should be encouraged." Roosevelt opposed professionalism because of the adverse moral environment it engendered. When he compared professional football to prize fighting, he expressed a distaste, not only for pugilism, but also for its lower-class "patrons."[11]

Civic reformer Albert Shaw agreed with this sort of distinction. Amateur athletics, he argued, was a healthy reaction to a college life too exclusively devoted to education of the mind. Unfortunately, sports had gone well beyond this purpose since they had been instituted in academies of higher learning. Until recently, he stressed, "drunkeness, gambling, lavish expenditures, and scandalous practices" had no place in college life. But now, professional sports had brought them all into the ivy halls. During important games between keen rivals there were "disgraceful orgies," recalling the world champion matches between prize fighters.[12]

David Starr Jordan of Stanford University agreed that football had evolved into an unseemly professional activity. Like Eliot, he faulted the game because it was ungentlemanly and violent and because, he added, it required little true individualism. Worse, it had fallen into the hands of nonacademic men. Rugby would be a far better sport, he suggested, because it was more individualistic and therefore emphasized collective order and coaching less. Rugby would lend itself to the cultivation of "the gentler and finer qualities of sportsmanship."

Jordon's remarks, like those of Bostonian Charles Eliot Norton, were founded upon a strong, class-conscious attitude toward sport. Jordon did not reject physical training any more than Theodore Roosevelt did, but he was appalled at the moral and the social context of the sport. As Norton expressed it, sports heroes cut immoral figures; they recalled the violent, drunken democrats of American "border life." The most

74   DEFINING THE PROBLEM

flagrant violaters of the gentlemanly code—those who went from college to college playing football and posing as amateurs—deserved the
derogatory name "tramp players."[13]

If football was the game of life, it had to be the sort of game that,
rightly played, selected and strengthened the best personal qualities.
For such critics as Norton, Jordon, and Roosevelt, the worst qualities,
which often surfaced under extreme competition, were those associated
with the lower classes, and best symbolized by the term "tramp." Thus
football could be as destructive as modern work, with the same problems of overexertion, imbalance, ruthless competition, and alienation.
Properly played, football encouraged the proper expenditure of energy
within a controlled and civilized environment. Like creative work, it
could enrich the personality. As Roosevelt remarked in his appraisal
Value of an Athletic Training, sport could be of immense value to
merchants, lawyers, students, and scholars—all of whom were in danger of overcommitment to mental labor.

The symbolism surrounding football sometimes became more important to critics than the actual practice. If some saw the demonstration of aristocratic virility in success on the playing field, others, including Norton and Eliot, feared a degeneration and democratization
that would be dangerous and immoral. Perhaps there was also the
unexpressed worry that in any sort of democratic competition, work
or sport, the lower classes might prove to be superior.[14]

The mental and physical parallelism that underlaid the debate over
sport was based upon the same energy theory of human personality
that contributed to theories about neurasthenia. A popular way to
express this idea was in terms of a mechanical model. As Edward Hartwell wrote in 1898 for the *Report of the United States Bureau of Education,* the human organism was a "living machine for doing work"
that possessed certain evolutionary tendencies passed from generation
to generation through heredity. The point of this elaborate metaphor
was to demonstrate the human need for certain sorts of specific activities. Like any machine, the human organism required a proper balance between inputs and outputs of energy. Hartwell recognized that
physical training was one way to implant crucial habits. In this he was
reacting to the exclusive intellectualism of American schools, much as
educators in the early nineteenth century had been when they used
manual labor to diversify the training of their students. The Society
for Promoting Manual Labor in Literary Institutions, operating in the
1830s, he noted, set important precedents for the modern recognition
of the human need for exercise and balance.[15]

The mechanical metaphor that appeared to justify athletics lent a
distinct new vocabulary to the description of human qualities. Stand-

ards of efficiency, durability, and output were linked to the idea that the human body and spirit were mechanical in nature. The machine metaphor was also a way to tie notions of personal alertness, will, and efficiency to qualities necessary for success in business. Athletics was the dressing room for economic competition.

One implication of this thinking was, as A. T. Dudley wrote in the *Harvard Monthly,* that great creative scholars did not make good businessmen. Both the businessman and the athlete required trained impulses and a coolness and confidence that were almost instinctive. The best athlete obeyed the habits inculcated by hours of practice; he was "controlled so as to act at the right time and in the right manner."[16]

In this argument to justify sport, Dudley was suggesting that creativity and intelligence had little to do with success. Was there not the risk that, disguised as a theory of individualism and self-control, modern sports might produce precisely the opposite effect than the one intended? Were not team play, obedience to rules, and collective victory precisely the same, as Adriano Tilgher suggested, as "what is done by the division of labor?" Perhaps this similarity was what attracted Frederick Taylor, the efficiency expert, to consider the similarities of modern sport and industrial work. Was athletics important because of the heroism it inspired, or because of the cooperation, training, and collective work it demanded?

The sports and physical exercise discussion was a variant of the question of the cultural uses of violence. In much of the popular mythology of the frontier and even in the gentler pastoral imagery of American nineteenth-century writers, there was often an implicit celebration of violence or primitivism. The transformation of these two notions into social and political theory at the turn of the century coincided with a disappearance of the very environment where they might be expressed. Both violence and primitive simplicity were attractive traits to hold up against the mediocre, routinized, industrial life that was beginning to characterize American society. As Veblen suggested, there was a broad retreat in social theory into sport, militaristic atavism, or primitivism. The defenders of amateur football recognized that even the values and rituals they hoped to create on the playing field were threatened by commercialism and professionalism. Once the realization was made that sports could be compromised, it was even more difficult to imagine how violence and primitivism could be maintained in American life so that these experiences would remain agents of rejuvenation and individualism. Was it possible to escape modern civilization's propensity to fashion every institution into a model of efficient, industrial labor?

Several questions posed serious problems for critics, who could see no end to the advance of industrial society. What did violence and primitivism mean in the modern context, where the frontier was no longer a geographical site, but a myth? How could modern Americans practice either, in the context of contemporary urban institutions? Was there any group in the existing population that experienced a profounder, more essential reality than the ordinary citizen? What social impact would a symbolic reenactment of primitivism or violence have?

For several European intellectuals, primitive or violent action in industrial society implied revolution. Although their works touched base upon many of the same problems that disturbed Americans, they went further. In the works of the French revolutionary Georges Sorel, primitivism and violence emerged as central concepts. For him, the return to an elemental, clean expression of the inherent unreason of the self was the starting place for social regeneration and political revolution. Sorel preferred acting out his myths, not on the athletic fields of Harvard Stadium, but in the arena of class struggle. He went clearly and quickly to the central political meaning of violence, and, because of this, he highlighted the American discussion of this problem in a way that few intellectuals, with the possible exceptions of Brooks Adams and William James, did in the United States.

In his tract *Reflections on Violence,* Sorel took the arguments that Americans had used to justify sport and organized athletics and combined them with ideas that he found in American pragmatism. His theory of revolution was grounded in a familiar dichotomy: civilization versus spontaneity, the free-acting, self-willed individual versus the routinized, repressed, and socially defined self.

Sorel's analytical model focused on the paralysis of will that he and others felt to be typical in modern society. Underlying the modern incapacity to act lay the repressed, raw elements of irrationality and sponteneity. If they could be liberated from the daily routines of work and from habit, these fierce emotions could unleash the revolutionary violence that would restore individuals and classes to their true function. "In the total ruin of institutions and of morals," he wrote, "there remains something which is powerful, new and intact, and it is that which constitutes, properly speaking, the soul of the revolutionary proletariat."

Many American social commentators might have agreed with Sorel that spontaneity and irrationality, if properly expressed, could help liberate the modern personality that was too much encumbered by social custom and too specialized in formation to hold together the diverse experiences of contemporary industrial society. The pragmatic elements of Sorel's philosophy, through which he hoped to use social myth to validate a creative relationship between individual will and social reality, were familiar to any American theorist who had followed the major developments in philosophy, education, and sociology at the turn of the century. For William James and even for Thorstein Veblen, Sorel's proposal to judge a myth "as a means of acting on the present" would have been familiar, if not exactly comfortable.[17]

But precisely where Sorel seemed to borrow heavily from American thought (particularly James's), or where he might appropriately have lapsed into the sardonic humor of Veblen to poke fun at the social operation of myth, the French philosopher took his leave. He was eager to express the undemocratic implications of theories that Americans only occasionally considered. Fundamentally uninterested in restoring social balance or individual health, Sorel directed his study toward the release of mass violence, something that both James and Veblen abhorred. The liberation of human personality from the bondage of custom and politics was the moment before the apocalypse. It was a first step toward the complete and violent overthrow of the regime of industrial alienation. Rather than see in primitivism or instinctive behavior the symbolic reenactment of older, simpler, more direct forms of human behavior, Sorel saw in it a way of transforming the myth of violence into practical, political activity.

Sorel's anti-intellectualism also highlighted a tendency that had emerged in the American celebration of sport. His writings, for all their extremity, attacked materialism and mechanical theories. Sorel wished to break down the walls of ideology that shut man into a world of routine and machines. But social violence was also a trap, and he proposed no effective release from it. When the dust of social change settled, the same industrial system with its alienating features and its enslavement to the machine would remain. In their own manner, American thinkers fell into the same trap. In their praise of the football hero (the "natural man" on the playing field) they had worked out a model of physical and mental alertness that, ironically, found its best analogy in the uncomplaining industrial laborer.

William James sounded the depths of the various and contradictory arguments over primitivism, spontaneity, and violence in the United States, and his arguments enlighten the intellectual predicament of Sorel. His essay "The Moral Equivalent of War" is perhaps the principal document in this inquiry because it explicitly developed a number of key ideas that were only half-felt or understood by others. Ralph Barton Perry wrote that there was a primitivism that "always disputed for possession of [James's] soul." As James put it in a letter to philosopher L. T. Hobhouse, "Your bogy is superstition; my bogy is dessication." Dessication, routine, and mediocrity were at the base of what James, neurasthenic experts, and other social commentators diagnosed as

American nervousness. James agreed with the advocates of martial training and the enthusiasts of sport that physical activity could counter the flabby modern personality called for by reformers and institutionalizers. Mankind needed to exercise its instinctive pugnacity.[18]

To make his point more sharply, James quoted the militarist Homer Lea. Lea had written that, as social and industrial activities in America became more complex, "the self-deception of the people as regards their inherent military capacity becomes more dominant and unreasonable."[19] James detected this sort of weakness in "all the socialistic literature with which I am acquainted." Yet the philosopher had no intention of proposing warfare as a counterbalance to social degeneration. He desired a moral equivalent for the militaristic instincts of modern youth that would allow them to be expressed in a socially useful manner. To this extent James agreed with the proponents of sport. But he went beyond them by arguing that society should not merely create the circumstances for the symbolic satisfaction of the instincts, but, as Sorel suggested, these should be turned to a practical end. "The military ideals of hardihood and discipline" might be wrought into the youthful population if, he wrote, young people were drafted into civilian armies where they could learn "the permanently sour and hard foundations" of the higher ethical and intellectual life.[20] The social and moral values that would flow from this ethical equivalent of man's quintessential but destructive nature could breed a healthy society.

In another essay, *Talks to Teachers on Psychology: And to Students on Some of Life's Ideals,* James revealed how keenly aware he was of various contemporary expressions of this same idea. Speaking of the strength of the British Empire, he argued that the English kept themselves strong through exercise and sport. In the same essay he returned to the problem of American nervous disorders. Europeans were right to remark upon the worried and tense faces of our citizens, he admitted. But the causes of this strained physiognomy were not climate, beautiful women, or even the industrial brainwork that Beard had noted. They were the secondary social and psychological attitudes surrounding labor and advanced civilization. Nervousness came from the "absurd feelings of hurry and having no time, in that breathlessness and tension, that anxiety of feature and that solicitude for results, that lack of inner harmony and ease, in short, by which with us the work is so apt to be accompanied."[21]

The evolution of modern society, as James understood it, had created a divided personality; the artificial demands of success and competition did physical damage to the individual. Modern industrial society was a world of alienated experience. James's antidote was a moral equivalent that would allow the expression of mankind's instinctual and secret life. But what American thinker was willing to follow him to this extreme in seeking to readjust society to the demands of the human personality? Surely not the advocates of football, who confined their attention to life on the playing field.

II

Revival of Old Ways

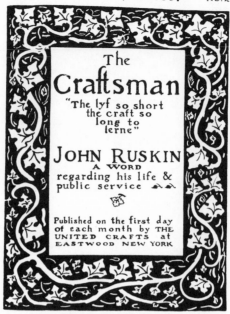

VOL.I   November, MDCCCCI   NO.2

The
Craftsman
"The lyf so short
the craft so
long to
lerne"

JOHN RUSKIN
A WORD
regarding his life &
public service ◢◤

Published on the first day
of each month by THE
UNITED CRAFTS at
EASTWOOD NEW YORK

Price 20 cents the copy

Cover of the second issue of the Craftsman, *1901.*

Carlisle Indian School, Carlisle, Pennsylvania, 1903.

7

Reviving the Work Ethic:
The Arts and Crafts Movement

The rapid industrialization of the United States complicated and frustrated efforts to restore a proper balance between expectation and achievement, work and fulfillment. Discovery of industrial alienation and the destructive effects of modern laboring conditions posed a grave problem, which some Americans felt could only be solved through institutional rearrangements. The result was a focus on the environment of work and an effort to recreate there the conditions that had once induced a healthy relationship between labor and moral character. Whatever the precise formula for a revival of craft industry—rural life, manual labor, or vocational training—one assumption reigned: the ideal personality emerged from the moral and social compulsions of a handicraft society. The age of preindustrialism, it followed, was the optimal environment for the traditional work ethic. If such conditions did not prevail in 1900 in America, it was the duty of society to restore them through special training institutions.

The arts and crafts movement that flourished in the United States at the turn of the century was founded upon the desire to reassert traditional notions of work and manufacture. It existed as the afterglow of a preindustrial society, now shrunk to a small and insignificant element of a booming industrial world. Confined primarily to devotees of handicraft or American Indian arts, the movement nonetheless posed an important question about modern society and gave an impossible but fascinating answer to it. Could a humane society be founded on the basis of machine work? The response was a hesitant "yes," with the provision that the aesthetics and moral standards of manual labor be put into the modern workshop.

The movement expressed a deeply felt sense of the loss involved in the disappearance of aesthetics from labor and production. It attracted more than its fair share of attention from American intellectuals, who had already been fascinated by the earlier political and aesthetic movement in England of the same character. Much more than a revival of hand labor or hobbies, the arts and crafts movements in England and America expressed an extreme but insightful solution to the dilemma of industrial alienation. Whatever concessions it made to the necessity of progess and industrialism, the American movement particularly applauded any effort to revive manual labor. It celebrated the ideal of a traditional America where work and individualism were linked in social harmony.

Mary Ware Dennett, writing for *Handicraft,* one of the principal journals of the American movement, noted that labor exploitation and intensive agriculture had practically destroyed the older bases of craft by 1900. One could not avoid concluding, she noted, that this development was "an economic, moral and religious problem, and that its solution [was] immediately a matter of life itself." Ellen Starr of Hull House (which became an immigrant arts and crafts center) agreed with this agenda: "The soul of man in the commercial and industrial struggle is in a state of siege. He is fighting for his life." The ugliest characteristic of modern industrialism, she continued, was the segregation of aesthetics from work and production. The result was an empty life for workers and the manufacture of ugly, utilitarian objects. Only a return to the older relationship of art and work could unite man with the product of his labor; the artist in each individual could be liberated only by freeing his moral and aesthetic senses.[1]

The major proponents of the arts and crafts movement subscribed to this view of work. To them the lack of aesthetic enrichment was the severest criticism that could be leveled at industrial activity. Work, they contended, had become separated from pleasure. Mass production was hostile to any standards other than profit or usefulness. The resulting industrial ugliness had grievous moral effects upon the worker and society. Industrialism and degraded taste (which went together) were visible symbols of exploitation. The struggle against domination by a machine culture was, therefore, also a fight to regain beauty and individuality.

With this severe stricture against the regime of machines, it is not surprising to find that the arts and crafts movement was strongest in such places as Boston (and New York and Chicago, to some extent), where both traditional craft and industrialism were strongest. In view of their important and traditional role in determining artistic standards, particularly in home furnishings and architecture, middle-class women played a leading part in the movement. Charles Binns, in his history of arts and crafts in America, cited the International Exhibition in Philadelphia in 1876 as a beginning of the movement, because it was there that the decline in traditional American craft became apparent. After 1876, he asserted, women in particular had become active in reviving china painting, pottery and metal work, book binding, weaving, and printing. At the Chicago World's Fair in 1893, the woman's building demonstrated the enormous progress of modern craft.[2]

Women were particularly active in the most important American arts and crafts group, the Boston Arts and Crafts Society. The non-artisan, sustaining membership of the group was heavily weighted with names from the city's elite districts. The most frequently given addresses in membership lists were located in the fashionable Beacon Hill area of Boston. Among the members were Mrs. Charles F. Adams, Mrs. John Jay Chapman, Mrs. Alice Longfellow, Mrs. Francis C. Lowell, and Mr. Charles Eliot Norton. Publications of this and other groups attracted important writers of the day, including John Spargo (later a leading socialist intellectual) and the scholar and social critic Vida Scudder. Frank Lloyd Wright and Louis Sullivan often contributed to movement publications.[3]

The presence of Charles Eliot Norton in the Boston society suggests the ties between this group and the English Pre-Raphaelites, for Norton was not only a well-known Dante scholar and editor of the *North American Review*, he was also John Ruskin's literary friend. Not surprisingly, one of the activities of the arts and crafts movement was the organization of "Ruskin Companies," groups set up to discuss the works of the distinguished English art critic. As Norton himself suggested, Ruskin's thought bore directly upon a relationship that society had to readjust: the role of aesthetic and moral criticism in industrialism.[4]

In Ruskin's works, aesthetic judgments coincided with his moral and political evaluations. This mixture of aesthetics, politics, and social criticism was precisely the harmony that the arts and crafts movement hoped to suggest for American society. The moral universe of Gothic art that Ruskin celebrated seemed to be much the sort of Christian Commonwealth that the American proponents of craft desired.

Thus there were two important sources in the arts and crafts movement. One, indigenous, was based upon the association of handicraft and manual labor with moral satisfaction in work—in other words, the intellectual expression of the work ethic. The other source was primarily British (although there was some cross-fertilization from America). This tradition began with the works of essayist Thomas Carlyle, continued through Ruskin, and terminated in the writings of William Morris, who united both the theory and practice of the English craft movement.

In the United States it had long been assumed that physical labor and mental prowess had a special relationship to one another. In the early nineteenth century Theodore Weld, agent for the Manual Labor Society (which had been formed in 1831), traveled through the country promoting the cause of physical labor in "literary institutions" and gathering information for an invaluable survey, which he published. Weld's report revealed a strong interest in manual labor in this decisive period of initial industrialization. American educators and intellectuals sought to promote harmony between hand work and mental labor. Quoting Benjamin Rush, Horace Bushnell, Sylvester Graham, and scores of lesser-known medical men and educators, Weld demonstrated how important the idea of physical culture had become in American schools and colleges. Weld could also point to several schools that had been founded specifically to teach manual labor: the Oneida Institute, the Manual Labor School of Greenfield, Massachusetts, and the Maine Wesleyan Manual Labor Seminary.

Weld also revealed the degree to which teaching the work ethic was a preoccupation of American educators. It was a symbol, as it were, of a healthy psychological balance between mental and physical activity. Like the doctors who discovered neurasthenia forty years later, American educators, even in this early period, felt that a disharmony in mental and physical training could lead to physical and mental degeneracy. As one professor wrote, "The Christian church at the present day is losing a great amount of power by the feeble health of her ministers. To meet a clergyman, indeed, especially of the younger class, is come to be almost synonymous with meeting an invalid." The fear of intellectual overspecialization suggested in this quotation was grounded in a psychological theory that assumed a parallel between physical and mental faculties. As Weld put it: "The experience of every day demonstrates that the body and mind are endowed with such mutual susceptibilities, that each is alive to the slightest influence of the other."[5]

Manual labor and hand work could, presumably, help to close the growing distance between the experience of manual workers and middle-class professionals in the 1830s. In large measure, this was a prescription directed to middle-class children in literary academies, who seemed to be unfamiliar with the elementary processes of production. While this restorative view of physical labor was not precisely the same as the aesthetic judgments of Ruskin or Carlyle, it was part of the American heritage that a later generation called upon in examining the problem of industrial work.

In their history of arts and crafts Edward Pressey and Carl Rollins acknowledged such divergent origins of the movement as it appeared in 1900. As they put it, moral and aesthetic interests compelled modern critics to consider "the character of the work of its hands, and the moral standing of a majority of its indiivduals" in judging a society. Intellectually, the movement began, they argued, with the English political essayist Carlyle, whom they called the first modern prophet of work to understand the nature of industrial exploitation.[6]

Certainly, Carlyle was not the first critic to notice the destructive effects of industrialism, but most American historians of the arts and crafts idea agreed with Pressey and Rollins that he was the founder of the tradition of criticism that flowered in the Pre-Raphaelite movement. Carlyle's cultural criticism, as Raymond Williams has noted, was no mere antagonism to industrialism; it was a crucial step in the emergence of a modern intelligentsia. Thus the arts and crafts movement was merely one expression of the grand nineteenth-century debate over the function of intellect in modern society. In concrete, practical ways these artists and critics hoped to demonstrate what their more literary allies were arguing. More extreme than its American counterpart, the English arts and crafts movement developed a sweeping solution to industrial alienation, the division of labor, and the appearance of classes and class struggle. To reestablish the aesthetic and moral hegemony of hand labor, they proposed to throttle mechanical innovation and master the machine.

The English influence was brought to America primarily through Ruskin rather than through Carlyle (who was seen primarily as a pioneer) or even through William Morris, whose explicit socialist ideas often disturbed Americans. Ruskin's social conservatism and his attack on modern industrial aesthetics—his reassertion of the affinity between work and art—were, as arts and crafts historian Oscar Lovell Triggs emphasized, the most interesting and important elements of his thought to Americans. To the American Fabian W. D. P. Bliss, Ruskin was the discoverer of a modern moral and religious theory of art. Society, according to his dictum, should be "a cooperation or communism of artists, submitting themselves humbly to the law of love, and in the joy of beauty working to produce the highest and the noblest that is in them." Bliss quite rightly added that this "communism" was not politically radical but was based, instead, upon a revival of the medieval guild idea. He might also have added that the American interest in reviving apprenticeship systems was what made the guild notion particularly attractive.[7]

For Ruskin the definition of work was disarmingly simple and dogmatic. As he wrote in the *Crown of Wild Olives*, labor could be defined only by the product that resulted. But this simplicity had a moral proviso; only judgments based upon usefulness and beauty could truly define an object. Work, properly done, generated objects of social and individual value. That which was done for gain or in ignorance of its function was evil. Labor was sound only when performed by a person who knew he was "doing what he should and [was] in his place." If the process of work were immoral or alienating, then the product and life that resulted would be ugly. Thus Ruskin combined the traditional work ethic and the calling of Protestantism, which Americans had long honored, with aesthetic judgments about objects created by work. It was a harmonious system that implied social, psychological, and moral well-being that could be detected by aesthetics.[8]

Ruskin's specific contribution, beyond pointing to the central position of aesthetics in talking about work, was to focus attention upon the Gothic period, which was, for him, a time when style embodied and expressed the perfect work relationship. Ruskin, Morris, and other Pre-Raphaelites celebrated what they called the organic art and architecture of medieval Europe that appeared prior to the Italian Renaissance. The Gothic revival in art and architecture, which they helped to create, was strengthened by the mid-nineteenth-century English rebellion against classicism. This aesthetic movement pointed to Gothicism as a style that expressed organic designs and relationships or, as the American architect Louis Sullivan was to put it, as an intimacy between form and function. Classicism, on the other hand, was monumental, ornate, and impersonal.

The Pre-Raphaelite artists were also important to Americans because they suggested organizing labor into craft guilds. The English movement proposed the formation of small, communally organized bands of workers who would perform the tasks of design, creation, and execution. In recreating the social forms of medieval work, the problems of modern industrial alienation would be abolished.

The political implications of the neo-Gothic in art could be turned to conservative or socialist purposes; they might be called to support an anti-industrial or a postindustrial position. In England the movement flowed in two distinct and contradictory directions: the Roman Catholic, Anglo-Catholic revival, which was very conservative in orientation, and the Fabian and socialist movements. Ruskin, who belonged more in the first group, nonetheless bridged the gap between radical and conservative by proposing that society be judged on aesthetic and moral grounds. His notion of the structural coherence of the art, architecture and economy of a society during an historical period could be the foundation of any larger critique. In America this sort of organicism provided the overriding assumption in Henry Adams's *Mont St. Michael and Chartres*, a work that celebrated the coherence and order of medieval architecture, society, and theological literature.

Ruskin's ideas were accepted only piecemeal in the United States.

He had several important followers in America, including Charles Eliot Norton, and he was read and praised by such writers as novelist William Dean Howells. His tastes in architecture were widely noted. But his conservative, almost anti-industrial orientation was rarely welcome. Critics and architects like Louis Sullivan might agree with his insistence upon the moral qualities of artistic and social arrangements, but few could follow his rejection of political and economic liberalism. His romantic view of nature and culture was immensely attractive, but at heart it was too nostalgic and too archaic for Americans. His ideas were, therefore, most important because of what they shared with other English writers who also demanded that modern intellectuals look to the organic relationships of a society before they criticized its organization.

William Morris, the English poet, craftsman, and socialist theoretician, offered another variant of neo-Gothicism, which was more in the spirit of the late nineteenth century and certainly better tuned to the specific social problems of modern industrialism. As one American craftsman and historian of the Gothic movement noted, his style was a protest against the decadence of Renaissance art in the name of "expressiveness, inventiveness, freedom and individuality." To the problem of modern industrial alienation, Morris brought a theory based upon individualism as it emerged from work and craftsmanship. Man must assert control over the machine, he wrote. The worker must reclaim his soul through the creation of variety and beauty. Like Ruskin, he proclaimed that the essence of the work ethic could be seen in the dynamic relationship between labor and ethical self-development.[9]

Morris's contribution to the English guild movement intrigued American writers. As Oscar Triggs said in his commentary on the origins of arts and crafts, the guild idea could transform the factory into a school for citizenship. "The present factory, with its monarchical order and intense division of labor, will give way," he wrote, "to the guild or small co-operative society, which shall be integral as to its work, human as to its motives, artistic as to its ends."

Although Morris's socialist proseletizing displeased many American writers who feared that the political thrust of the Gothic movement would be snatched up by radicals, he nonetheless forcefully demonstrated the practicality of the craft ideal. In his laudatory appraisal of Art Nouveau Claude Bragdon wrote that the return to natural forms and the discovery of natural law had flowered into a remarkable art. With Morris in England and Louis Sullivan in America, the new organic aesthetic demonstrated the continuity between ethics and art, work and creativity. Bragdon concluded: "Mr. Sullivan possesses in an eminent degree what I have called the Gothic mind; he is strongly individual, a lover and a student of nature, and at once a logician and a mystic."[10]

The ideas of Ruskin, Morris, and other Pre-Raphaelites were a constant inspiration to Americans like Sullivan who sought to return to the aesthetics and ethical environment of a craft world. But few Americans were willing to pursue the conservative implications of Ruskin's theories or the socialism that Morris preached. Nor would they go as far as the English toward rejecting modern mechanical civilization. The American arts and crafts movement spoke in constant praise of handicraft and manual labor and was tempted by thoughts of returning to a more primitive mode of production. Yet almost no one questioned industrialism, progress, or the machine itself. The ambiguity and even the contradiction of this position invaded Louis Sullivan's call for a democratic and individualistic urban architecture, to be inspired by the forms of nature but produced by machines stamping out modern materials. What he desired was a craft-designed but machine-made democracy.

This paradox in American thinking about arts and crafts was resolved by the turn of the century argument that manufacture and industry could be efficient and morally regenerative if they were kept on a small scale. "Notwithstanding it is the purpose of everyone to obtain goods at the lowest price," wrote an observer for *Articraft*, a small movement paper, "there are quite a number of people who consider the ethical side as well. To favor handicraft work is to believe in a new industrialism, an industrialism which means the exercise of a higher form of intelligence upon the part of the workman."[11] Faith in the restorative nature of small-scale enterprise thus became an invariable premise of the American arts and crafts movement. It was seconded by the contemporary antimonopoly impulse in political movements like Populism.

Gustave Stickley, one of the leading American practitioners of craft, dismissed the need for large size and scale in manufacturing. Architect Frank Lloyd Wright noted in *Articraft* that the machine could become democratic; it could be enlisted in the creation of art. Both Stickley and Wright were more interested in a return to nature and natural forms. They sought to restore some of the economic and social relationships of a previous era. But, like other American craftsmen, they refused to turn their backs upon industrialism.[12]

American members of the arts and crafts movement who accepted industrialism necessarily emphasized the social and psychological rewards of limited experiments in handicraft and small enterprise. As Triggs put it, "whenever a man expresses himself under conditions of freedom and self-control, he is an artist—whatever his occupation or field of activity—and he receives the rewards and gains of the artist: the reward of pleasure, the gain of an enlarged personality, and an increasing personal force."[13] Louis Sullivan's dream of an individualistic but machine-made aesthetic could be realized—in theory at least—if one rejected the contemporary culture of industrialism and fit manufacture to the Jeffersonian scale of values.

The principal journal of the American arts and crafts movement was the *Craftsman,* a monthly publication devoted to the art, the architecture, and, especially, to the theory of the movement. Its editor, Gustave Stickley, like his English counterpart William Morris, was a recognized furniture-maker; to him, this simple but important art expressed the essence of the revival of craft. As he noted, the craftsman's task was to provide a democratic art expressly for the middle classes. This art was not, however, to be exposed to professional criticism. "It should be brought to their homes and become for them a part and parcel of their daily lives," he continued. "A simple, democratic art should provide them with material surroundings conducive to plain living and high thinking, to the development of the sense of order, symmetry, and proportion."[14]

Stickley's magazine was an important center for the integration of influences and styles in arts and crafts. In its pages he and other writers attempted to outline a general aesthetic and political theory that could unite English neo-Gothicism, the Art Nouveau of France, the craft American artists like Tiffany, and the mission furniture revival of the Southwest United States with an ethical critique of work and industrialism. Including medieval, oriental, and American Indian art forms, proponents of craft hoped to discover a basis for a democratic art inside modern industrialism by stressing natural materials and geometric or primitive design.

Stickley hoped to create such an art upon an evolutionary aesthetic, not a reactionary or a revolutionary one. The progressive impulse in society, he wrote, lay with the workers and middle-class citizens, not with the great owners of wealth. "I realized that the twentieth century, then a few years distant," he wrote, "was to be, like the thirteenth, distinctly an Age of the People."[15]

The structure underlying Stickley's thought was his faith in the traditional work ethic or, as he put it, the harmony between labor and ethical, aesthetic, and political development. To him the cause of modern "social unrest" could be found in the decline of older forms of work and the rise of a national spirit of speculation. "It is a truth," he wrote, "now so universally recognized as hardly to need repeating here, that the most solid mental and moral development results from learning to use the hands dexterously and well in some useful productive employment." The industrial division of labor had broken up fundamental institutions like the home into functional units. Traditional duties of education had been taken over by the state. The removal of work from the home environment to the factory caused unnecessary large-scale production and social conformity. The result was a kind of decadence to which Stickley contrasted the purity and simplicity of the medieval organization of work.[16] Thus primitivism in social relations and mechanical skill was a viewpoint from which to judge modern society.

Like Henry Adams, Stickley portrayed medievalism as a unity of art, ideas, and social organization. But unlike the novelist-historian, he did not lament the decline of this particular organic idea. He still looked to the future. Through the practice of craft a new age of artistic brilliance was still possible.

Stickley's orientation toward the future also made him optimistic about machine-made art forms. Agreeing with Louis Sullivan, he emphasized the democratic and individualistic possibilities of a modified industrial society. But two revolutions were necessary before modern alienation could be ended. Society had to restore work to its primary and healthy function by reviving and encouraging handicraft and manual labor. Moreover, art and aesthetics had to copy the simplicity of nature, as did the organic designs of Louis Sullivan's architectural ornament and the frozen natural shapes of Art Nouveau. The revolution in taste, pursued in every product created by society, would enrich the life of each citizen.

A second center for the development of the American arts and crafts idea was *Handicraft* magazine, published intermittently between 1902 and 1912 by the Society of Arts and Crafts (later the National League of Handicraft Societies).[17] Unlike Stickley's *Craftsman,* publications of handicraft societies were concerned not so much with the spread of new artistic styles as with organizational and practical problems of handicraft artists. The ideological and social orientations of the movement determined the nature of articles and letters published by the magazine. There was a strong rural, often New England, bias expressed by authors who envisioned craft as the decisive element in the strength of the traditional American village. There was an explicit attack upon the modern division of labor which seemed to many writers to be the most destructive aspect of industrialism. Finally, the preponderance of women in the movement, as officers of local craftsman clubs and as participating artists, expanded the definition of craft to include jewelry-making, weaving, and other "household" occupations.

Arthur Cary, in his short survey of the first years of organized crafts in the United States, wanted to dissociate the movement from any bohemian taint. The ideal artistic community, he wrote, did not consist of eccentrics, but rather, could be found in a rural village of self-respecting craftsmen and workers. In her appraisal of the aesthetics of the movement, Mary Ware Dennett agreed with this rural utopianism. Praising Tolstoy and the Russian anarchist Kropotkin, she argued that the best possible context for a craft revival was the small town. Sequestered from the demands of industrial work, each person could develop mental and physical abilities far beyond the limitations that machine-tending placed upon growth. The aesthetic of craft, as she noted, was closely related to rural life. No amount of intensive effort or intelligence could ever make a machine produce anything more than it was designed to. Only by practicing a craft in a rural setting could the artistic tendency of a person be released from mechanical captivity.[18]

The rural orientation of the handicraft society was explained in an article that appeared in October 1902 entitled "The Movement for Village Industries." The author, Sylvester Baxter, wrote of the spread of village industries in the small towns of the Connecticut Valley. In such places a perfect combination of art and democracy had once prevailed. Mary Dennett extended this notion. Only the "great guild period of the Middle Ages, where there was the most convincing example of this natural union of art and democracy and the marvelous beauty and spontaneity of the Gothic work," she wrote, was superior to the village society of New England. By identifying these two utopian visions—the medieval guild society and the democratic craft world of New England—she demonstrated how the neo-Gothic ideal could be merged with the American heritage of handicraft.[19]

Like many other social movements of the day, the arts and crafts societies expressed a utopian vision of the American past—the way of life it hoped to reestablish. The antiurban bias that was a part of this vision was, in one sense, part of a general American protest against the effects of late-nineteenth-century urbanism. Walter Crane, one of the theoreticians of the movement, believed that urban living had become a major obstacle to the creation of an aesthetically tolerable civilization. Modern industrial culture, from its utilitarian work habits to its joyless toil and lack of poetry, he wrote, dictated against the creation of art. "From the close relationship and cooperation of generations of good craftsmanship in all the arts of design, and by their associated and harmonious labors, has been reared the house of art in the past." Such conditions certainly did not prevail in the cities of modern America.[20]

Closely related to the arts and crafts movement was the village improvement idea. Charles Eliot Norton, for one, found both movements compatible, and worked for each. The village improvement idea had begun in the 1850s in New England, and was devoted to ameliorating the aesthetic surroundings of small towns in Massachusetts and Connecticut. It proposed to make life in such villages more pleasant by ending their cultural and economic isolation. Norton felt that, in addition to making towns more pleasing by planting trees or landscaping, craft societies would help restore the small town's economic integrity. Although by 1900 this effort to improve rural life had become part of the general movement to improve agricultural methods and rural social life, it reflected precisely the same sort of ambiguous attitudes toward industrialism that influenced the arts and crafts movement.

To practicioners of handicraft, the most insidious, the most baffling and insoluble problem of modern industrial life, was the division of labor. Modern civilization and production—even progress itself—advanced upon the economic law that stated that divided tasks were more efficient than those performed as part of a craft. The arts and crafts movement was hostile to this division of labor that had resulted in divided tasks and repetitive work, but it could not envision an end to industrialism. The contradiction was obvious and, ultimately, fatal to the movement. As H. Langford Warren wrote in *Handicraft* in 1903, "Commercialism has its place, the subdivision of labor has its place, the machine has its right and proper place. But we need to recognize that these things have also their limitations." Warren rejected socialism and ruralism and called for a new and heterogeneous economic system where there could be industrialism and hand labor.[21]

This characteristic proposal settled nothing at all. The contradictory attitude of the arts and crafts movement toward the machine deeply confused its political and social attitudes toward industrialism and modern society. Did the modern craftsman reject the machine or not? Was everyone to become a manual worker? In June 1910 Frederic Whiting tried to answer precisely these questions. The movement should stop attacking the machine, he wrote, and concentrate upon the evils of specialization, which, he said, have "deprived us of the old all-round craftsman who knew his craft as a whole and saw, in each task which came to him, a challenge to his knowledge and capacity."[22]

The failure to answer the question of how to reconstruct society and end the evil effects of the division of labor ultimately reinforced the nostalgic utopianism of the movement—and limited its influence. Unable to see much relevance in the economic ideas of Marx or even of William Morris, the American craftsmen continued to view manual labor as a single form of virtuous work in the midst of growing commercialism and exploitation. As a result the movement as a whole never fixed upon a precise attitude toward industrialism or upon the place the revived medieval guild should have in modern society. Arts and crafts, in other words, had no impact upon the vast majority of industrial and white-collar workers who had neither the leisure nor the talent to pursue a craft.

That the arts and crafts movement existed at the periphery of the industrial system it hoped to influence is indicated by the high percentage of women who were artists and officers in local craft groups. This trend indicates, indeed, that the movement may ultimately have been more involved with questions of leisure than with work itself.

The preponderance of women in the movement may well have stemmed from the same phenomenon that caused such magazines as the *Ladies Home Journal* to suggest that women should become experts on the aesthetics of interior design. Elizabeth B. Stone, writing for *Handicraft*, had another explanation. The arts and crafts movement, she suggested, gave the modern woman and, especially, the housewife an important function. "Under American conditions," she wrote, "might not the housewife be a most potent factor in the work?" Was she not responsible for choosing what was produced by industrial labor?[23] Stone thought she had found an answer to the dilemma posed by Charlotte Perkins Gilman in her discussion of the alienation of women. Women, by controlling consumption in the home, might gain an important function in a society that had, through specialization, transformed them into sexual objects.

However indecisive or contradictory the arts and crafts movement may have appeared, particularly as it attempted to confront its own motivations and the political and economic effects of reintroducing craft as a central mode mode of production, it raised a crucial and difficult question, which, ultimately, it could not answer. It regarded the modern division of labor as being responsible for a grave social and economic crisis. It argued that work could express a healthy relationship between man and his labor, but important changes were required. Work was the physical and psychological mechanism that released social creativity. It instructed each member of society in the duties of ethics and the principles of aesthetics; it therefore made a healthy social life possible. The movement also assumed that ideal conditions of work had once prevailed in two societies—medieval Europe and Puritan New England. The larger question was how work could be restored to its central and ethical function in an industrial society. The answer, ambiguously given, was that it could be restored through the revival of handicraft and, especially, handicraft aesthetics. By looking backward and restoring archaic forms of work, the alienation of modern society might be ended. Return to a simple life by a few might provide guidance for everyone.

Because of its ambiguity about modern industrialism and its half-hearted covenant with an idealized past, the arts and crafts movement had only a slight impact upon the outcome of the modern discussion of the division of labor. It marked a path that was impossible to follow in a day of rapid industrialization and immigration. It was undesirable for all but a few to return to an older way of life. Therefore its appeal was felt most strongly either by artists and craftsmen themselves, or by those in society (particularly middle-class women) who had the greatest amount of leisure time. The twin ideals of craft and community were not without meaning in this era. Perhaps they could be attained by other means. It was possible that the older relationship of work could be restored and the lessons of the New England village retained. But the literal return to the archaic labor forms of hand work advised by arts and crafts theorists (whatever their other attitudes toward industrialism) was impossible. It might be possible to reconstruct the lost utopia of unalienated work and individual creativity, but not this way.

8

Reviving the Work Ethic:
Manual Training

The vast army of criminals and social parasites that tramped through modern American society at the turn of the century existed, wrote one observer for *Craftsman* magazine in 1905, because of a crisis in education. Quoting criminologist Arthur MacDonald, the author continued, "Teaching of practical morality in such a way as to form good habits in the young is doubtless the surest preventive from a criminal career." But how could morality that had once developed automatically as the result of a balanced, rural craft society be taught? To many American educators and psychologists, the answer lay in instruction in manual labor.

In 1911, slightly after the height of interest in manual training, Arthur Payne explored the relationship of this instructional device to the arts and crafts idea in *Handicraft* magazine. "Since the adoption of manual training into the schools of this country," he wrote, "we have been informed upon its educational values, later of its ethical values, but the arts and crafts movement has showed to us its art and its social values." What Payne suggested about the manual training movement was true. It attempted to fulfill the same social purpose that arts and crafts did, and it was based upon the same general social and psychological theory of the work ethic. It envisioned, although less explicitly, the same lost utopian world of handicraft.[1]

Unlike the craft movement, however, manual training was intended to be a universal system. Manual training advocates did not suggest restoring single skills or older forms of work, for they acknowledged, implicitly, at least, the continued existence and even predominance of alienated forms of labor in modern society. Given the slim moral and psychological rewards of most industrial work, the manual training movement nonetheless promised to train students in the work ethic by focusing instruction upon the broader principles of craft and industry.

The student would carry these lessons to the tasks he performed in the factory or office. He would personally enrich his work with the ethical and social ideas and the feeling of community that he had learned in school.

Manual training was thus intended to fill the moral and social gap created by the disappearance of handicraft and apprenticeship. Instructing students in the techniques of craft and hand labor would provide them with a sense of the old work ethic without changing the actual conditions of modern labor. As a halfway measure between the revival of old work methods and the outright rejection of instilling the work ethic through rote instruction, manual training was an important attempt to deal with modern industrial alienation. Its widespread popularity among educators in the late nineteenth century reflects the persistence of traditional definitions of the wholesomeness of labor. Although it paralleled several of the elements of progressive education, manual training provided a more literal instruction for future citizens in the virtues of work. Unlike the vocational education movement that later absorbed it, the manual training movement was not designed to prepare students for specific occupations. It existed primarily to teach moral and social lessons.

G. Stanley Hall, who, together with William James, was the most widely known psychologist of this period in America, recognized alienation from modern labor to be a major educational predicament. Hall believed that modern industry would continue to spawn such problems and that this meant continuing problems in adjustment and instruction. One way to compensate for the lack of moral and social training in society—one of the worst results of modern labor—was through manual work in the schools. The American manual training movement, he noted, had two immediate and practical predecessors: the Russian system of manual instruction, which was predominant in the United States, and the Sloyd system, which was introduced from Sweden in the 1880s. Hall criticized both systems from the standpoint of their psychological assumptions, but he admitted that they represented major attempts to instill socially necessary moral virtues.[2]

What Hall referred to as the psychological and moral basis of manual training was the aim of its apostles to instruct in the techniques of craft. They sought to provide the social and moral environment of the ideal working society. Because they assumed that there was no way to save older forms of production except through an attack upon industrialism itself, they proposed that the schools take over the function that the workplace had once possessed.

The Russian system, which Hall mentioned as the leading influence in American manual training, was brought to the attention of American educators and the public in general at an exhibit at the Philadelphia Exposition of 1876. As Issac Clarke, advocate of technical art instruction in the schools wrote, "The Centennial Exhibition taught the people of this country how beauty enriches all the appliances of life; the study of drawing in the common schools will teach their children how things are to be made beautiful and these thousands upon thousands of home missionaries of the beautiful will create everywhere such a demand for the element of art in all manufactures, that either producers would comply or foreign goods would capture the market." Thus the teaching of manual skills (in this case, drawing) would lead to the aesthetic enrichment of the whole society and, eventually, to a transformation of production. Before the centennial, he continued, the American practical and fine arts had been in a state of decadence, but after 1876 a period of renaissance began in which manual training played a key role.[3] Thus the rise of manual training paralleled the growth of interest in arts and crafts.

American advocates of manual instruction acknowledged other important European theories in the development of training in physical dexterity. W. D. P. Bliss, in his short history of industrial education, noted that the technical and trade schools from which the manual impulse emanated were founded in Europe in the early nineteenth century. European educational theories, he continued, were also largely responsible for modern instructional practices that stressed motor training. The works of Friedrich Froebel and Johann Pestalozzi (who prescribed manual training for vagabond children) were, he noted, instrumental in linking physical activity and even play with ideas of educational development.[4]

Writing for the premier issue of *Monographs of the Industrial Education Association* in 1888, Daniel Coit Gilman found an even older European precedent. The origins in dexterity training for moral and ethical purposes, he suggested, existed in the first documents of modern British social theory. John Locke, he argued, had discovered the first principle of manual training in his *Thoughts on Education* in which he discussed the effects of physical exercise upon mental growth. Locke had discovered that "constant bodily labor" stirred up force and vigor in the personality. Gilman went on to claim that this central notion had been accepted by most important English philosophers since Locke, including John Stuart Mill and Thomas Huxley.[5]

The centrality of the manual training theory to English economic and social thought and the existence of similar theories that had developed in other industrializing areas of Europe, such as Switzerland, France, Germany, and Italy, indicates the relationship of this theory to the rise of the work ethic. However, by the 1880s it was precisely this ethic which seemed threatened by the rapid development of modern manufacturing and the intense division of labor in shop and office. To restore the functioning of this ethic, theorists of manual instruction isolated one important element—hand labor—and constructed their whole theory to rest upon it. By teaching this one crucial function that underlay the older work system, they hoped to restore its integrity.

Examples of manual training used in schools or in reformatories as part of rehabilitation programs were important precedents to the manual instruction movement in the American public schools. By the middle of the nineteenth century several sorts of manual training institutions had appeared in New England. In 1835, for example, girls in the second and third classes of Massachusetts grammar schools were taught sewing and knitting. While this was certainly no full-fledged program of manual instruction, it was an early example of practical activity in the schools designed to teach the principles of work while providing useful domestic skills.

By the late 1840s Massachusetts had also set up a boys' reform school that employed manual training in rehabilitation. In 1856 a similar institution for girls was organized. By the 1880s Massachusetts educators were convinced that teaching rural arts and handicrafts was a principal means to overcome delinquency and crime.[6]

Industrial education and manual training drew support from several sectors of the American public. Educators also supported these innovations because they followed major new educational and psychological theories that stressed habit formation and socialization through participation in creative physical activity. As early as 1875 an official group within the National Education Association constituted itself in order to promote the cause of manual training. In 1893 a competing group, the American Manual Training Association, was formed because of dissatisfaction with the N.E.A. organization. An important development, even if only symbolically, was the absorption, in 1897, of the Chicago Manual Training School by the University of Chicago School of Education. This move suggests the importance of the manual training idea in one of the principal centers for the development of modern progressive education. To many educators, by the turn of the century, what William James said of the movement was true: "The most colossal improvement which recent years have seen in secondary education, lies in the introduction of the manual-training schools."[7]

One motivation of educators in adopting manual training was surely their belief in its efficacy as a means of Americanization. Teaching craft skills was part of a vast effort to acclimate immigrants, freed slaves, and Indians to the industrial civilization that was, inevitably, to be their environment. Thus training in the principles of the work ethic through manual instruction was a leading element in preparation for American citizenship. W. J. McGee, in the official catalogue of the St. Louis Exhibition of 1904, described the extensive Indian School exhibit as a demonstration of the means whereby America could share the "white man's burden" and bring civilization and order to its new colonies. The school exhibit illustrated the education policies of the United States Bureau of Indian Affairs and "the most approved methods of raising aboriginal tribes to the plane of citizenship."

The central activity of the model Indian school, he continued, was manual training, "since experience has shown that among all aboriginal peoples the hand leads to the mind." The ideal regimen for younger students divided their time between kindergarten, which was designed to organize and direct spontaneous play into useful activities, and industrial training. Advanced grades received specific and intensive manual and vocational work.[8]

Other supporters of manual training expected somewhat different results. Manufacturers, for example, hoped for the development of specific, useful skills. Early labor leaders, like Terrence V. Powderly of the Knights of Labor, hoped that the trade school and manual training would replace the declining apprenticeship instruction that had been associated with the craft industries organized into unions in the 1830s.

Differences between these narrow or specialized aims of powerful interest groups and the more general and sometimes contradictory purposes of educators symbolized rather different expectations inside the movement and, ultimately, broke it into two parts, one of which followed the general desires of businessmen and unions for specific vocational instruction. The other was absorbed by the complex of educational theories and practices grouped under the general name "progressive education." But in the late nineteenth century manual training appeared to be a perfect and universal answer to the problems created by a declining work ethic. Without sacrificing industrialism, without returning to an era of craft, citizens could learn the inspiration and ethical delights of creative work. Manual training, in addition to being a means to direct some students toward an occupation, would, as a central activity of the common schools, instruct every child in the older meaning of work.[9]

Many of the arguments in favor of manual training were based upon the same fears of industrial alienation that had spurred the arts and crafts movement. Many of the supporters of manual instruction perceived that modern factory labor separated a worker from the product of his creation and from any aesthetic or moral reward. It reduced the function of work to survival. Thus the aesthetic, the moral, and the social areas of human environment suffered from the impoverishment of progress. Those who proposed manual labor as a regenerative experience almost invariably hoped that craft technique taught in the public schools would stimulate the artistic, ethical, and community sense of the student. Thus the traditional flow of benefits was reversed. The worker would now regenerate work by bringing his awakened sensibilities into the factory.

In a report for the United States Commissioner of Education in 1888, Isaac Clarke wrote that the teaching of drawing and artistic techniques in the public schools would have several beneficial effects. It would provide students with useful skills; teaching craft to each student would help overcome the growing snobbery (as he put it) about work that was developing among upper-class Americans who disparaged and avoided physical labor. In this vein he praised the work of educators such as Felix Adler, who had organized kindergartens in New York City around the relationship between play, work, and aesthetic creation.

An even more extensive plan of manual training was needed to enrich each year of schooling. As Clarke argued, instruction in drawing and art techniques would provide practical mental discipline, unlike the more common but impractical discipline in abstract grammar and mathematics. In conclusion he noted that teaching art in the schools could overcome the estrangement of modern work. For those whose destiny it was to labor, he remarked, society should provide training which would make them effective and render "their work a joy, and their lives happy and contented, instead of dark, gloomy and wearisome."[10]

Writing somewhat later, for the Massachusetts Board of Education, Leslie Miller, principal of the Pennsylvania Museum and School of Industrial Art in Philadelphia, noted that artistic training in the public schools could accomplish what the arts and crafts movement had proposed as it goal. Teaching art in the public schools would vitalize and inspire the creative instincts of young workers. It would "rehabilitate home and village industries," and "counteract the terrible centripedal force of the cities." It would provide a clear and consistent opportunity for the contemporary age to get "the full benefit of all that is best in the experience and attainment of the past." Teaching the process of craft in the public schools rather than attempting to deflect the course of industrialism by trying to revive apprenticeship or guild systems would achieve identical results: an end to alienated labor and unaesthetic production.[11]

Despite the realism and practical bias of the manual training movement, the argument in favor of such instruction rested heavily upon what were, undoubtedly, utopian assumptions about the work ethic. Proponents of manual training hoped to establish a proper relationship between mental and physical aspects of personality and between effort and ethics through a ritual or symbolic reenactment of the past. By artificially creating the rhythms, motions, and principles of work, and by exposing the student to these, it was hoped that the vast problems of modern labor could be overcome. In this sense the advocates of manual training were even more ambitious than the practitioners of arts and crafts who, despite their emphasis upon simplicity and universality, were generally associated with a relatively esoteric movement in the fine arts and literature. Manual training was supposed to save everyone.

The school was to be the locus for teaching the manual arts. As Lois Coffey of Teachers College, Columbia, wrote, modern industry had destroyed the possibility that any individual on his own could understand modern work. With labor removed from the home, no child could hope to understand the important social and aesthetic elements of labor. But these things could be taught in public schools. Coffey's expectations for the accomplishments of such instruction were grandiose. Teaching manual training would allow children to understand the "dignity of labor" and bring them in contact with the "great thought of the world, as expressed in music, literature, painting, sculpture, and work in clay and metals." Students would become "independent workers" with an insight into the meaning of human history.[12]

Although the main emphasis of this training was to be the instruction of children, other elements in the population were also to receive manual training. Workers, through programs of continuing education, could also be given what amounted to apprenticeship training, transformed and updated for modern industrial society. Herman Schneider, dean of the College of Engineering at the University of Cincinnati wrote that, once enrolled in adult manual training classes, the worker could learn a more positive attitude toward his labor. He would realize the contribution of his own labor in the whole creative process. Because of this new understanding he would be happier and better adjusted, and he would stop patronizing movies, dance halls, and amusement parks, to which he turned as a release from enervating work.[13]

How manual training might operate to regenerate lost souls was no mystery to those steeped in the traditional ethic of the calling. To Populist Henry Demarest Lloyd political democracy, the preservation of individualism, and the solutions to the problems of modern labor were all dependent upon work. As he wrote in a book entitled *Man, the Social Creator,* one enormous problem of modern society was saving the individual: "The proof that an individual has been regenerated is that he proceeds to regenerate things about him—and that's Democracy, and that's the Religion of Labour."

Lloyd's theory of the divinity of labor underscores the religious origins of the nineteenth-century American work ethic: "To labour is to pray; work is worship," he wrote. The idea of a sanctified political economy was a notion that Lloyd also discovered in the writings of Emerson and Carlyle. Like other advocates of manual labor, Lloyd hoped that by reproducing the perfect harmony of labor in the schools, society might help restore the practical democracy of work. "The Manual Training Schools," as he wrote, "put the son of the millionaire by the son of the stoker at the forge and the lathe." This symbolic democracy reinforced Lloyd's notion that private property should be preserved but made more equal.[14]

Lloyd's hope that physical labor might become the source of individual and social regeneration and his belief in the religion of work disguised the ambiguity of his position. Manual training and work were substitutes for politics, organizing the experience of each citizen, helping to create the sentiment of equality, and acting as a primary educative and selective device whereby society might recognize a person's virtues through his ability, rather than by his class identity. In other words, manual labor—the religion of labor—would reestablish the hegemony of the calling or, as Emerson had called it, the "election by education." In the face of the spreading consolidation of corporations, this was, at best, a wild hope.

The disjointed place of work in modern society attracted several Protestant thinkers to the manual training idea. In a speech to the first annual convention of the Religious Education Society in 1903, Reverend Francis Clark suggested that manual training could accomplish the same deeds that traditional moral instruction did, and more effectively. Work was the basis of all knowledge, he wrote, including religious insight. Thus young people should be apprenticed to Christianity: "Like every other kind of industrial training, it must be gained by practice." Just as carpenters and painters learned skills by repetition and trial and error, so practical Christianity could be "learned only by doing it." Clark advised young people's societies to offer technical training for young Christians. There the student could learn the work of modern religion or what he called the "industrial or manual religious training."[15]

Clark's concept of an active Christianity rested upon more than a clever use of manual training as a metaphor for traditional activities. He proposed a rapprochement between the concept of work and Christian regeneration during an age in which they seemed to be growing apart.

He assumed that the social and political repercussions of the endeavor societies, which he organized, would have the same effect upon the development of young people that industrial training did in the public schools. He was, in effect, only expressing more bluntly and explicitly an idea—that the revival of the work ethic could reestablish the secular Christian utopia of the early nineteenth century—that was becoming a ritual expression for social critics and educators at the end of the century.

Even more secular expressions of support for manual training stressed the religious character of work and the hope that manual labor could stimulate the moral and social faculties. To some enthusiasts manual training could be as effective as religion once had been in organizing society. As Charles Henderson wrote in 1900, the practice of manual instruction in the school could replace the training once provided by the family. Poverty, pauperism, and the problems of immigration could all be alleviated if only this new form of education were universally applied.[16]

One proof of the effectiveness of manual work in neutralizing the destructive effects of urban life was reported by *Craftsman* magazine in an article on efforts among "Hebrew" children to prevent them from becoming peddlers. Manual instruction among groups such as this was called the "equivalent of Life-saving." The central problem of urban existence, continued the article, was the immigrant and his foreignness. Practical hand labor and instruction in the work ethic could speed his transformation into an American citizen. As support for this argument, the author cited Kropotkin, who had written widely on the crisis of modern work, and Theodore Roosevelt, who was a long-time supporter of manual instruction. Thus his definition of manual training embodied the hopes of a nostalgic handicraft movement and the sort of symbolic primitivism advocated by Roosevelt in the *Strenuous Life*.[17] Because of this stress upon physical realism and practical labor, the psychological effects of manual instruction seemed analogous to the effects of struggle and even of violence. It was a perfect solution for ending modern industrial alienation and man's division from the brute but vital struggle for survival.

Manual training, it was claimed, would be successful because physical labor generated specific mental and social effects. The proper sort of practical work could create, one author wrote, "a mental reaction that is ethical, bringing about a definite largeness of life, and approaching nearer to complete living." Since such work no longer existed in the factories, it could be taught in the schools. "In the forces which in the past have made for the progress of man," wrote one manual training advocate, "may we not with some reason expect to find the master-forces of education?"[18]

All of this argumentation implied, as G. Stanley Hall had perceived, a particular psychological theory. Herman Schneider of the University of Cincinnati (where much of the early work on an adult education was done) noted that manual training related to specific psychological problems raised by modern machine-tending. Following William James's distinction between active and passive, habitual and creative mental states, Schneider wrote that modern industrial work generally demanded only the development of habit. Thus it repressed the other, creative, aspects of the worker's personality. "In some of its phases," he wrote, the machine "controls the individual and tends to cause him to deteriorate; it ought to be controlled by him and help to build him up. It is the old story of Frankenstein."[19] Despite these severe strictures Schneider, like most advocates of manual training, accepted machine work as inevitable. But alienation was unacceptable, and to eliminate or prevent it, the author proposed a permanent and continuing education for workers.

The arts and crafts movement with its strong utopian bent, and the more practical, manual training enthusiasm, were motivated by the same psychological theories and by similar interpretations of history, which idealized family manufacture, village life, and hand labor in the early age of American industrialism. The keystone of this utopia was apprenticeship, which both movements sought partially to recreate. But manual labor advocates merely hoped to instill social relationships and harmony through instruction in the principles of craft work. Like many reformers of the late nineteenth century, they chose the school as the medium for their experiment because it was the logical place to start the instruction of Americans in the work ethic. They felt the schools could and should absorb the functions of instruction, discipline, and socialization once performed by the family and the community.

The history of the manual training movement in the United States records the triumph of this idea by 1900 and its eventual rejection somewhat later in favor of vocational education. Before the turn of the century manual training was, particularly in Northeastern states where it was most extensively developed, designed to Americanize immigrants, uplift the poor, integrate social classes, and provide moral and aesthetic experience. Schools, kindergartens, and penal institutions were the locations of these great expectations. Play, reform, and moral progress were all bound together in this method of teaching the work ethic. One historian has written that by 1900 "most educators looked to manual training to correct the disharmonies brought by technology and urbanization."[20]

The pressure for concrete results and more specific teaching of social discipline ultimately split the advocates of manual instruction into two camps. The first emphasized technical training for specific work, hoping to help ease individuals into the sort of employment for which they were best suited. Vocational training, then, stressed the selective and occupational aspects of instruction.

The other tendency clung to the importance of moral and, especially, social training, which, they argued, were inherent in hand work. For this band of reformers progressive education and, particularly, the theories of John Dewey were most hospitable. Here too prevailed the notion that children must be educated in primitive forms of labor and social organization so that they could understand the evolution of the past into the present. And Dewey, as we shall see, was deeply interested in manual training because it was justified by principles very close to those which he developed out of his psychological and pedagogical experimentation.

In the context of modern educational practice, manual training appeared as a specialized and, sometimes, overly particular version of modern learning theories. Even its supporters sometimes admitted that manual arts did not always bring about the proper socialization of students. Colin Scott, head of the psychology department of Boston Normal School, wrote that educators were often able to teach skills or the use of tools, but they frequently stumbled on the larger questions of organizing work. Instruction in the operation of the group or community must be useful in "adult industry and culture." Work should therefore be mixed with play and other forms of socialization. Above all, the future worker should become aware of how his activity related to the whole productive process.[21] Appraisal of manual training programs in the schools had to measure the degree to which they prepared the future worker for life. Did manual labor really create the desired system of social ethics that its advocates promised?

John Dewey's response to this question illustrated the important differences and similarities between manual training and his own educational theories. It also illuminated the degree to which both grew out of the assumption that mental development was related to physical activity and habit formation. Although Dewey's psychology was a good deal more complex than anything understood by most advocates of manual training, he shared with them (and the English philosophical tradition upon which they relied) a belief in the fundamental proposition that action was an integral part of thinking. He strenuously rejected any faculty psychology that argued that specific parts of the mind needed stimulation for the proper development of intelligence; nonetheless, his theory of the motor element in sensing and thinking shared something of this orientation: learning could not be abstract; it must be related to life and physical activity.

Dewey's educational theories also contained an implicit notion of utopia. The philosopher called his interest in the past and, particularly, in former stages of labor systems a recapitulation of human experience. It is clear that, for him, the manual labor stage was a permanent reference point in the development of ethics and community. The era of handicraft corresponded perfectly with the stage of direct motor experience in the education of the child. The age of handicraft—which, in the arts and crafts movement, was a lost utopia, and, in the manual training movement, the perfect model of industrial activity to be taught to each student—appeared to Dewey as the primary stage of education and the foundation for more advanced forms of learning. As he suggested in *Manual Training Magazine* in 1901, manual instruction was the necessary background to the fundamental disciplines of history and geography. It was, therefore, to be granted a central position in the school. More important than reading, geography, or the study of myth was the teaching of manual exercises, which imparted to the child "that which he is the heir of all the ages, and through which he recapitulates the progress of the race." The child should learn through activity. The tasks that he should engage in were those which, historically, led to invention and progress.

Despite his support for training through activity, Dewey criticized the mechanical-psychological theory behind manual instruction because he felt it implied a simple-minded faith in the calling. This and the notion of apprenticeship, he wrote, were, unfortunately, tied to a primitive faculty psychology. Both assumed that the individual was born with inherent abilities and talents related to a potential station in life. Apprenticeship systems and notions of the calling were thus historically linked to static, hereditary, class societies. Insofar as manual training depended upon such an unstated bias, it was of limited value to modern democratic society.

Dewey rightfully sensed the conservative assumptions of the manual training movement with its idealization of an older, nonindustrial, social model. He stated that it failed to concentrate upon the process of socialization, which was the real key to a democratic society. It substituted mechanics and motion for community. The result was a theory of learning by doing that stopped at the threshold of ethics. Because it was too dependent upon individual instruction and because it ultimately called for the stimulation of inborn mental faculties and abilities, it failed to emphasize the importance of social integration to modern democratic society.[22]

If modern society destroyed the natural education of the early nineteenth century, as Dewey surely believed it did, it was partly because of complexity and growth. However, one could not deal with contemporary problems, particularly those which derived from industrialization, merely by reproducing traditional forms of work in the schools. Rather, the proper work relation should be understood as part of the process of history. It should be highlighted as a central experience in social progress. Manual labor was only a first stage in the development of modern society. It could not eliminate the problems that beset modern education or society by itself, for it depended too exclusively upon a concept of work and personality that was frozen at an early stage in the development of American history.

9

The Work Ethic and
the Public Schools

The responsibility for a positive response to modern industrial and social alienation in America fell upon education rather than upon politics or economic reorganization. Within the broadest definition of education—including public schooling, vocational education, and prison reformation—diverse theories for adjustment to industrial society were developed and implemented. These ranged from efforts at teaching traditional morality through admonitions to work hard to efforts at altering behavior through medical or psychological means. Thus defined, education and pedagogic theory contained both older and newer theories relating to work, personality development, and social adjustment.

As a central component of modern social reform, education inevitably bore the pressures and ambiguities of the divergent aims of its many theorists. The history of education in this period is thus rich and, often, contradictory, because it was the terrain upon which paraded competing theories of personality, industrial alienation, and labor. In the United States education and not politics was the principal arena in which the issues of modern industrial capitalism were joined. The nature of society and property forms were not often questioned in this great debate; at issue was the formation of personality in the environment of industrialism.

By 1900 it was becoming difficult to justify social position and wealth simply by invoking the older work ethic or the calling. Hard work did not justify the rapacious methods of the robber barons. Instead, differences of education and inherent personal capacity were advanced as two important explanations for gradations and differences in a society of unequal rewards. What served as explanation was also a means of adjustment. Theories that measured and accounted for differences in personality were also quite often elaborate rationalizations for the social distinctions they were designed to explain.

Educational reform in this period was determined, in part, by the existence of industrial labor. Much effort was spent in trying to adjust citizens to this new reality. In the drift toward behavioral and biological determinisms in educational theory, there were, however, important and instructive exceptions, the most important of which was John Dewey. And even though Dewey resisted this tide, two important qualifications to his exceptionalness must be made. The philosopher occupied a transitional role in educational theory. His works were firmly grounded in modern biology and psychology but, at the same time, he sought to preserve the essential ethical and social organization of the homogeneous community—that is, the secularized, New England society of the nineteenth century. He hoped to use modern educational methods to inculcate the ethical norms and social integration that had, apparently, prevailed in this simpler society. Also, because of his inability to extricate himself from the general drift of educational theory toward adjustment, Dewey was unable to save his theories from "misinterpretation." He shared too much with the developing definition of human personality in mechanical terms to resist this temptation completely.

The reform agenda of American education and the practice of modern pedagogues is well known and has been justly criticized from a variety of viewpoints. Much of what was done in the schools during this time was idealistic at best, and often manipulative. But the fact remains that educational theory was one place in which industrial alienation and the problems of the work ethic were discussed with forthrightness, a quality sometimes missing from politics and sociology in this period. Because American schools have been traditionally decentralized and more open to experimentation than many other institutions, they have been used as vehicles for adjusting individuals to new social circumstances. But also because the school systems have been decentralized, new theories announced in textbooks or in university courses at leading pedagogical institutions quite often never made it into the classroom.

The "legend" of American schooling upon which modern reform movements depended rested upon two key assumptions: first, that the experience of education was universal, and second, that the school had been a major instrument of social mobility, particularly for immigrants. Recent appraisals of these assumptions have cast doubts on their accuracy. Certainly not all children were able or expected to benefit in like manner from education. Nor did immigrants necessarily achieve mobility through learning. On the contrary, early school reform in the nineteenth century may sometimes have been a disguise for the erection of class-biased institutions financed through public funds.[1]

During the 1800s the school and the related reform school increasingly assumed the task of preventing crime and teaching morality. As the century progressed the schools assumed the roles of moral preceptor and vocational expert. The weight of these demands sometimes led to excesses, bureaucracy, or even cruelty. But, as an important means of adjusting citizens to conditions of modern work, education should not be underestimated. In the classroom the ethic of internalized individual work and labor was transmuted into the preparation of the citizenry for a new mode of collective existence.

The school legend is not destructive because education failed to achieve any of these goals, because it lacked universality, or because it did not select the proper candidates for mobility. More fundamentally, it is questionable that the school should ever have been the place to begin social reform. The major premise of pedagogic reformers described a malleability of pupils and a flexibility in society that in practice have been consistently betrayed by failure.

Perhaps the most interesting overtone to the word "education" in the late nineteenth century was its association with the principles of the work ethic. Beginning even before Horace Mann in the 1840s, running through Dewey and finally ending in the explicit recognition of the selective purposes of public instruction, a leading definition of learning has been preparation for career. For Mann the common school (and the reformatory and the mental institution) was obliged to supplement traditional institutions such as the family, church, and small community, which had fallen into pernicious ways. Education, he felt, could teach moral order and provide the ethical context that other forms of training could not. Mann expressed this larger aim on the basis of several observations. There was, he noted, a critical need to eliminate the growing wave of viciousness and crime "which now sadden and torment the community." Public instruction would create law-abiding and docile workers. Toward this goal, the school should attempt to overcome the separation between family life, the work situation, and individual desires and aims. To instill obedience and respect for the law, the schools should teach the work ethic. The end result would be a creative and responsible community.[2]

Ethical instruction such as Mann suggested was a principal emphasis of educational theory in the nineteenth century. As much as later progressive educators challenged the manner of teaching this ethic or the political conservativism of their predecessors, they too agreed with the larger moral purposes of the school.

Early-nineteenth-century educators justified their activities upon a faculty psychology, however, which troubled progressive educationists. The notion of mind as consisting in a body of undeveloped abilities was a justification for strict discipline, which was intended to strengthen the abstract faculties. This was a principal rationale for rote memorization or the study of Latin and Greek. When William T. Harris, future United States Commissioner of Education, addressed a meeting of the Americans Charities and Corrections Conference in 1885, he expressed the range of expectations of such study: "There is grammar," he said, "the science of the organization of language showing how reason reveals itself in its special creation, human speech. The framework of reason is logic, and logic is revealed in the laws of syntax and etymology. Self-knowledge of an intimate kind, therefore, is reached in the study of grammar." Moreover, because language is a social production, he continued, knowledge of its origins leads to insights into human organization, and therefore prevents the spread of crime.[3]

Although the logical steps in this argument are unexpressed, they were surely familiar to his audience, which was filled with educators, charity workers, and penologists who subscribed to a faculty theory of education. One assumption in this theory was that strengthening the moral faculty or abstract ability in one area could regenerate the whole personality.

Harris served from 1889 to 1906 as education commissioner; from his post he was able to exercise considerable influence on the direction of the debate over public education. He often disagreed with the new progressive theory, specifically with the educational orientation of John Dewey. His sympathies lay with the moral educators who sought to inculcate "regularity, punctuality, silence, and industry" as well as art and ethics. The problem of modern society, he noted over and over, was that it only educated the lower half of the human self and never appealed to the higher, moral nature of the student. The forces that perpetuated this unfortunate situation were immigration, "the possibility of rapid acquirement of wealth," the necessity for frequent changes in vocation, local self-government, the growth of science and literature and "the diffusion of knowledge."[4]

As much as any other contemporary theory, moral instruction such as Harris suggested was designed to continue the traditional relationship between work, citizenship, and education. Henry Suzzallo, philosopher of education at Columbia Teachers College, regarded the direct inculcation of morality and proper behavior as the specific purpose of the modern American school: "The conditions of our American life," he wrote in his introduction to George H. Palmer's "Ethical and Moral Instruction in Schools," "have changed marvelously during the past century, and we are now feeling the full momentum of the consequences of these changes. The moral weakness of men before the pressure of temptations arising from our modern life has become painfully apparent." Since Suzzallo had no intention of challenging either the traditional social or moral order or what remained of it in modern society, the problem as he saw it was to strengthen moral values and self-reliance. There were two ways to accomplish this. There could be direct moral instruction, or students might be exposed to an environment that selected for certain ethical values.[5]

The traditional and direct teaching of morality and virtue had long been a part of the American classroom in such books as the *McGuffy Reader*. But there were many arguments against the suitability of this overt method at the turn of the century. Felix Adler of the Ethical Culture Society of New York undertook the revision and updated this approach. In his proposals for a modern school curriculum Adler suggested using specially rewritten fairy tales for students in lower grades. Later on, high school students could benefit from the study of actual, existing problems or hypothetical situations demanding ethical choices. The educational course he advised would then terminate with a year's study of what he called "vocational ethics." Thus, beginning with new versions of *Sleeping Beauty* and *Little Red Riding Hood*, Adler hoped to awaken the student to specific attitudes toward charity and prejudice, and to instill proper respect for superiors and equals.

The essential problem for those who hoped to reinforce the moral sensibilities of the student was, as education commissioner Harris noted in 1892, how to substitute "the internal authority of conscience for the external authority of the master." Harvard philosopher George Palmer suggested that the "moral crisis" could be solved, or at least diminished, by a different approach to moral schooling. Children should no longer be instructed in the strict New England manner, which, he suspected, could cause excessive self-consciousness. Students should be taught the habits of right conduct without forcing them to acquire the morbid habits of introspection.[6]

Although Adler's modernized version of the parable was attractive to some educational experts as a way of solving this problem, the bulk of those concerned with moral instruction were more deeply influenced by theories of environmentalism, which, by the late nineteenth century, were becoming a primary element in modern social and educational theory. Even Adler enthusiastically subscribed to manual training as one means of generating the proper environment for teaching ethics. As he wrote, manual training should be introduced into the public schools so that rich and poor might learn to work side by side. Thus education might unite the middle and lower classes at the base in such a way that they would "never thereafter entirely grow asunder." In the end, then, many moral educators agreed with the progressive theorists that the natural environment of the child was not that of books, but of work.[7]

The problems of American education during the nineteenth century were, in many ways, unique; thus the inherited cast of mind by 1900 bent pedagogic theory in unique ways. Nonetheless, European educational theories had an important impact in this country. In fact, American education became a sort of laboratory for the testing of pedagogic ideas first developed in France, England, Switzerland, and Germany.

The main assumption that bore upon this experiment, received from Rousseau to Pestalozzi—through Herbart, Froebel and Montessori—was that instruction could alter the behavior of the child. Education was, accordingly, the medium in which the student prepared for adult life. Whatever their different emphases—and sometimes these could be significant—these Europeans agreed that the child's personality could be changed. Inevitably, the school became the realm for their favorite reform schemes.

The universal application of education also meant that schools could instruct future citizens in skills that had formerly been learned elsewhere. Because this education was extended downward (first to the middle classes and then to industrial workers), European reformers such as Herbart, Spencer, and Froebel stressed the practical, empirical, even tactile experience of learning as opposed to the formal linguistic instruction that was associated with aristocratic learning.

It would be incorrect to describe the history of educational theory in the nineteenth century solely as a response to the development of industrialism, but, consciously and unconsciously, this enormous social and economic process deeply touched pedagogic thought. Educational psychologies based upon activity, change, and progress proved far more attractive—especially to those societies that were rapidly changing. The older faculty psychology, which was associated with traditional, static, and aristocratic education, was itself indicted by the changing process of life in advanced societies.

The implicit universality in leading European educational theories attracted many American pedagogues in the late nineteenth century. But a number of specific theoretical developments were equally influential. Several educators, including Froebel and Pestalozzi, had demonstrated in the early nineteenth century the importance of practical activity in early education. Philosopher and sociologist Herbert Spencer put such ideas into the larger, industrial framework in his important writings on education. Although elements of Spencer's educational theory recall traditional faculty training, the major thrust of his arguments was toward empirical training. The test of educational efficiency, he wrote, could be measured. If it prepared young people to live in a modern industrial society, it was beneficial. If it merely added to abstract knowledge, it was not.

The task of the educational theorist for Spencer and other educationists of his day was to discover which fundamental process incited learning. Spencer felt he had found this in science. The educationist's alchemist formula was, for him, the study of science and biology. These areas should be examined empirically so that the student could encounter the "rude empirical influences respecting human nature." Subsequently, the student would be led to apprehend elementary facts of social life—the relation of supply to demand, for example. He wrote that the study of science "generates a profound respect for and an implicit faith in, the uniformities of action which all things disclose. By accumulated experiences, the man of Science acquires a thorough belief in the unchanging relations of phenomena—in the unchanging relations of cause and consequence—in the necessity of good and evil results"—in other words, universal scientific truths. Spencer's effort to inspire the empirical teaching of cause and effect had an ulterior motive, which included his particular view of human and natural evolution. In defense of entrepreneurial individualism, the English philosopher and sociologist linked the developmental character of learning to a theory of practical and pragmatic instruction.[8]

The works of Jean-Frederic Herbart were less directly political than Spencer's, but he agreed with the English philosopher that education should be based upon a proper inductive psychology. He also stressed the developmental and tangible features of education. Instruction, he argued, should recapitulate (as the child's own mental and physical growth did) the development of human capacity and progress. To produce good citizens, discipline, and high moral sense, educationists must train the practical ethical sense. Although Herbart opposed the faculty-based traditional education, like most nineteenth-century educators, he emphasized one specific form of learning as the paradigm of all education. For Spencer this had been the study of biology. For Froebel it was the manipulation of objects shaped into cones and spheres. For Herbart it was the study of mathematics and poetry.[9] All of these theories proposed to lead the student to detect and acknowledge the order and structure in nature and society.

During the 1890s American educators found that such ideas bolstered their own approach to instruction, which also proposed to uncover or impose order and harmony in an environment of rapid social and economic change.) Most of the elements of the "new education" that appeared in the United States around the turn of the nineteenth

century were thus found in the works of major European educationists published before 1865. Nonetheless, these ideas made their way
slowly and incompletely into the American context. For example, it
was not until the psychological works of William James and John
Dewey that faculty psychology ceased to predominate as the essential
theory behind American education, and it would be inaccurate to suggest that rote learning or mental discipline disappeared from American
schools even then. Moreover, the universal and unchanging agreement
among most educators that the purpose of instruction should be moral,
acculturative, and disciplinary makes it sometimes difficult to discover
precisely what was new in a new educational theory.

Nevertheless, by the end of the century there was a strong propensity among American educators to discard the mental discipline of traditional pedagogy and substitute a more developmental and empirical
approach to instruction. That this opinion coincided with a rapid consolidation of modern industrialism and the sudden discovery of severe
national economic and social problems merely intensified the drive
for a more adequate theory and practice of education.

To the most astute educational writers, new theories of learning
posed two very serious problems. The first stemmed from the psychological discoveries of William James. If, as James implied—and Edward Thorndike proclaimed—the human mind was organic in nature,
and if its responses were based upon habit, instinct, and perception,
then, it might be asked, what was the function of the individual personality and the individual will, the exercise of which had been the
principal object of almost every educational writer of the nineteenth
century? James had an elaborate answer: Will was the creative, inductive, scientific, and, at the same time, the ethical center of human activity. But not everyone was convinced by James. The implicit emphasis upon the effect of environment in his theory became, in the hands
of Thorndike and later, in those of the behaviorists, a form of reductionism that James never countenanced. For them the personality was
bound by the limitations of heredity and the accidents of the environment. There was little room left in such a scheme for a controlling
moral center.

Another problem posed by the new education related to the crisis
of work. If, as it was often assumed, education was to be universal,
and if it could dramatically alter the direction of individual development, who should wield this enormous power and for what purposes?
If the school could reorganize society, did this not mean the old internalized work ethic was dead? Did this not substitute education for
work as the determinant of social hierarchy? How, under such circumstances, could society resist using education to answer the demands of

the industrial system, whatever they might be? What was to prevent education from reinforcing alienation and social schism?

John Dewey answered these questions by suggesting that the schools express the universal ethical and social experience of cooperative labor and discovery. They should integrate the experience of the individual student with that of his contemporaries and his ancestors. Dewey's theories resembled those of Spencer and Herbart, particularly because he stressed the recapitulation of social evolution. But Dewey had no firmly established order or social model as the goal of his theories. The continuation and expansion of education, the accumulation of knowledge, and the enlargement of possibility were his aims. The function of instruction was, therefore, to demonstrate the ties of isolated thoughts or activities to the larger social, industrial, and ethical context. In a much disguised way, this was precisely what the traditional work ethic was supposed to accomplish. And, as we shall see, manual labor and handicraft were, for Dewey (much like shapes and forms had been for Froebel), the essential integrative education tools and the primary form of instruction.

Materialism (that is, the definition of human personality in scientific —behavioral and biological—terminology) warred in Dewey with a deep suspicion of all single determinant factors in human affairs. For the philosopher, modern society presented an opportunity for the continuous shuffling of social positions. Unlike some contemporary educators, Dewey opposed using universal education to adjust the children of working-class parents to a limited future. Instead, he perceived the greatest problem of modern society to be the growing separation between citizens based upon the diverse tasks they performed. Middle-class children were isolated from the enriching experiences of cooperative manual labor just as poor or immigrant children were prevented from understanding the meaning and importance of the isolated assembly-line tasks of their parents and friends. And both were separated from each other by a gulf of suspicion and ignorance.

Dewey superimposed the traditional wisdom of the work ethic upon a biological and materialist conception of personality. Into an implicitly behavioral model of educational experience, he injected a nostalgic vision of community that resembled the arts and crafts description of the handicraft society as an ideal community, and this is what clearly distinguished his educational philosophy.

Dewey criticized contemporary American educational institutions at the turn of the century because he felt that they supported an existing hierarchical class system. In fact, he felt they exacerbated the divisions between citizens. The mode of instruction that reflected social inequalities, he remarked, was based upon an inappropriate and outmoded psychological theory. Modern industrialism, if understood properly, was a world of continuous change, yet some schools attempted to prepare children for a permanent, unchanging niche in society. "It is an absolute impossibility to educate the child for any fixed station in life," he wrote. On the contrary, any attempt to anticipate specific future occupations of the student would result in no valid preparation at all.

As for the faculty psychology upon which this conservative system was based, Dewey rejected its premises and practices. There were no special mental, moral, or manual faculties of mind with specific functions. Therefore the mental activity involved in intellectual tasks was much the same, he argued, as that for manual tasks. Neither the study of Chinese characters nor the learning of a manual trade required any special, isolated, original mental abilities. Faculties, he concluded, simply meant that "particular impulses and habits have been coordinated and framed with reference to accomplishing certain definite kinds of work." With this explanation, Dewey refuted a theory that had assigned specific mental abilities to diverse categories of work. He dismissed what he felt was a class interpretation of intelligence.

Unfortunately, as Dewey found, American schools often reflected the traditional value-loaded distinction between mental and physical, intellectual and practical education. The implications of this separation for social ethics were severe. Even those conservatives who lamented the lack of strict moral training in education recognized the "failure to conceive and construct the school as a social institution, having social life and value within itself." The school must become, he argued, a real social institution—like the family, for example. In this institution the moral compulsions felt by the child derived from the totality of social life that the family reflected and created.[10] So too, must the school operate.

With this "well-ordered family" as the model of the integrative functions of work and cooperation, Dewey had not strayed from an essential and traditional assumption of American educational reformers. But the practical means to bring this model into the classroom proved to be revolutionary.

Dewey was able to join traditional family life and the work ethic to his program of instruction because of his psychological interpretation of the stages of human development. In his fascinating discussion "Interpretation of the Savage Mind," he carefully enunciated a theory of the relationship between psychological and social character and the prevailing mode of production. To Dewey the savage mind was not a primitive, unformed, underdeveloped mentality. Instead it reflected an intense specialization derived from a particular form of physical and social activity. Study of the savage mind thus lent insight into the character of the modern mind. "If we search in any social group," he wrote, "for the special functions to which mind is thus relative, occupations at once suggest themselves. Occupations determine the fundamental modes of activity, and hence control the formation and use of habits." The particular mode of labor, with all its associated practices, was thus the crucial factor in the formation of social and ethical values. "Occupations," he continued, "integrate special elements into a functioning whole." Consequently, one could isolate a hunting mentality, a pastoral, military, trading, or manually productive mental type, that derived from different forms of social development. Like Veblen and other commentators, Dewey sketched a relationship between the predatory type of personality and modern business and sport.

The extraordinary character of the savage mind with its inability to grasp modern concepts, Dewey continued, had evolved from overspecialization. Hence the inability to understand "remote, generalized, objectified abstracted" ideas. Study of this limited ability offered insights into the perils of modern overspecialization, and also exhibited the process whereby limited social and ethical goals gained acceptance by a society. The function of psychology, he concluded, was to determine how the satisfaction of impulses could be turned to more general, socialized purposes.

Examination of education, it followed, was the study of the history of social institutions and the way in which they fulfilled the needs of the citizenry. In modern times, education should become the "adjustment of habits to ends, through the medium of a problematic, doubtful, precarious situation."[11] Education, thinking, and acting in a democratic and progressive society were synonymous to Dewey.

The practical application of this psychology of education meant nothing less than the transformation of the school into a miniature society. In this microscopic world the basic determinant of behavior was not an abstract moral order imposed by force from above, but the development of social and ethical order through the practice of the principal occupations of the society under ideal conditions. He wrote that, outside the school, the majority of a child's play was "miniature and haphazard attempts at reproducing social occupations." Therefore, the first principle of schooling ought to be instruction through work. In the practices of human labor the child could learn to integrate the diverse social functions that might otherwise confuse him.[12]

But what sort of work was this to be? Dewey did not propose specialized vocational training, and he lamented the growing division between physical labor and intellectual occupations. This division had been healthy, he remarked, during an earlier era when mental and moral training was "secured by our forefathers in the course of ordinary pursuits of life." This natural separation of activities did not lead to profound social division. In the industrial period, however, the continuation of traditional educational methods with their emphasis upon abstract learning intensified social divisions and the consolidation of elites.

The proper work of modern schooling must be, he concluded, some activity that would integrate all future citizens. It must recreate the conditions of labor so that the student could experience the broad ethical and social effects of the work ethic. But this could not be done by teaching specific modern skills, for, as he wrote, work was "no longer connected with a group of people all engaged in occupations, but [was] isolated, selfish, and individualistic." The child had, therefore, to experience work in an evolutionary mode, beginning with simple production (handicraft, weaving, spinning, candlemaking) where the effects of human labor were immediately apparent and where the cooperative function of people working in small groups would be obvious. Such primitive labor forms were a first step; when understood by the child, these occupations articulated "a vast variety of impulses otherwise separate and spasmodic, into a consistent skeleton with a firm backbone."[13]

Dewey's educational theory thus began with the direct experience of handicraft and social labor. However utopian or nostalgic this may seem, Dewey was not, like the theorists of the arts and crafts movement, attempting to challenge industrialism, nor was he wary of progress. Manual training and the teaching of handicraft were but the beginnings and foundations of an education whose purpose was to unite the diverse activities of modern society. With a firm "backbone" of practice in man's "fundamental relations to the world in which he lives," the child could then understand how such fundamental tasks had evolved into the current state. Interests, he wrote, "as they develop in the child not only recapitulate past important activities of the race, but reproduce those of the child's present environment." The function of education was, therefore, to provide the child with experience in labor that would allow him to extrapolate and to understand all forms of modern work. Education would guide the child through the evolution of society to the present. If faced with a life that had to be lived in spite of alienated labor, the child would at least have this knowledge and the ability to integrate his experience.[14]

Thus Dewey sought to instill an attitude toward work that was fundamentally at odds with the discipline and the compulsions of modern industrial labor. "The problem of general public-school education," he wrote, "is not to train workers for a trade, but to make use of the whole environment of the child in order to supply motive and meaning to the work." Education could overcome the industrial alienation that deprived industrial workers of any understanding of the function of their labor or the place of their isolated and repetitive tasks in the whole. Education could also end the isolation of the middle classes (as the advocates of sport had advised) from the experience of physical labor. This would instill in each student a knowledge of the "laws of natural and social science," for they too were now hidden by the complexities of modern industrial society.[15]

The classroom, organized by Dewey, would, he hoped, liberate human work from the obsession with financial gain. It would present human toil, not as a struggle against competitors or as a means to social mobility, but as the necessary and primary activity of all citizens. Work, once freed from the system of reward and remuneration, could become an experience that united school and society. The aim of work in the classroom was "not the economic value of the products, but the development of social power and insight. It is thus liberation from narrow utilities, this openness to the possibilities of the human spirit, that makes these practical activities in the school allies of art and centers of science and history."[16]

Practically, Dewey's educational system differed profoundly from contemporary vocational education schools, the Montessori schools, or even manual training. In vocational training students were prepared for specific jobs, the very opposite of the aim of Dewey's plan. Indeed, this training merely perpetuated a class system of instruction; he wrote: "Those who believe in the continued existence of what they are pleased to call the lower classes or the laboring classes, would naturally rejoice to have schools in which those classes would be segregated." All other citizens, he proclaimed, must unite against such proposals "to separate training of employees from training for citizenship, training of intelligence and character from training for narrow industrial efficiency."[17]

Montessori schools might, at first glance, appear to fit this educational formulation. Yet they taught children to work by themselves with self-correcting devices. Dewey felt that this could produce the wrong effects. Work was "essentially social in its character," he wrote, and it could not properly be separated from human needs and ends. In a school that provided the correct environment, work would at last become social and, therefore, truly individual. The dead hand of custom and class would be relaxed.[18]

The nostalgic, almost utopian, vision of the classroom as a miniature society engaged in reproducing the social and ethical values applicable to modern life recalls an extreme feature of the modern educational reform theory—the almost mystical faith in the capacity of the child and the limitless possibilities of education. But Dewey's theory had another characteristic of modern educational theory. It was firmly based in a biologically and materially oriented psychology. While Dewey cherished the open, democratic community, which was based upon handicraft and cooperative labor, he grounded his theory of instruction on a psychology that was implicitly environmentalist if not behavioral.

In Dewey's formula, the selective and determining features of the environment could be the source of constant enrichment. Once begun, the process of selection, reintegration, and education would never cease. For most other theorists and for the administrators and school officials who read and acknowledged him, Dewey's emphasis upon the selective aspects of schooling worked out to be something rather different. Education, redefined by them, meant selecting the proper person for a specific task. If this aim could be accomplished then an enormous problem of modern industrial life could be solved. Furthermore, if, as some claimed, industrial malaise and unhappiness did not necessarily occur in the factory, then alienation might be simply due to placing the wrong person in the wrong job.

The priorities of modern instruction were clear in this argument. School was to be a vast placement service. Unfortunately for Dewey, elements of this position, although they were caricatures of his ideas, were similar enough to his thoughts to lead to a confusion of the meaning of progressive education. Dewey's definition of human personality was drawn in materialist terms, but he was neither a hereditarian nor a behavioral determinist. His educational philosophy was part of a general movement toward redefinition of human personality in functional terms. But he refused to join in the mechanization of social ethics, and therein lay his genius.

10

The Child as Laborer:
Vocational Education

A major preoccupation of educational and sociological thinkers during the bewildering and restless period of the turn of the century was to find a systematic method of student placement. By most measures the older, informal selective agencies of family, community, hard work, and good fortune no longer (if they ever did) operated in a society that was now marked by vagabondage, drift, and social unrest. These older forms of restraint and direction only operated upon the inner motivation of the individual; they did not meet the explicit requirements of the new society.

Writing for the American Economic Association in 1899, sociologist Charles H. Cooley defined the function of education as reinforcing the major social and economic institutions of society. By this he meant that education should underscore and facilitate personal competition, the purpose of which was "to assign to each individual his place in the system." Quoting Emerson, he argued that education should select the "inherent bias" of each person and allow it to develop until it dominated the personality.

The selective process should begin very early, he continued, "in an intelligent and truly free system of education, opening to every child opportunity and incitement to find out and pursue that career for which he is naturally best suited." In this way the masses of Americans would receive a more individual education consisting of specialized instruction for each person. This new program of work would allow the student "to make the most of himself, for manual training and trade schools accessible to all, is a demand for a more rational and open competition."[1]

Although Cooley recognized some limitations to competition, he blamed the contemporary American "social crisis" upon the frustration of individuals who were trapped in inappropriate jobs and social positions. A competent, scientific education would, it was hoped, remedy this situation. But the schools could only prepare, they could not place students in jobs. Other institutions had to guide the student from his place of education to the work bench. Here too, the failure of the work ethic to integrate the individual with his labor and calling made it necessary for a social agency to intervene. Thus the experts who devised the new field of vocational training were most interested in devising institutions that could eliminate the crisis of career. They wished to smooth the transition from school to job.

The theory and practice of vocational education and advising derived from many of the same sociopsychological premises that influenced progressive educators. One of these redefined human personality in mechanical or biological terms. It was a psychological model that facilitated quantifiable mental measurements. The assumed similarity between physical characteristics and mental "capacity" was by no means new in the 1900s. This position did not always imply that every resource of the mind could be measured precisely. But the general tendency to reductionism was a first principle of the practical theorists who devised the early vocational institutions.

Another assumption was that work in itself did not necessarily lead to general satisfaction or ethical fulfillment. Indeed, happiness was defined in terms of the most efficient use of energy and talent. Social and moral elements in the workplace were looked upon as means of stimulating greater productivity, as capital to be invested in hopes of greater output, rather than as rewards accruing to the worker.

Hugo Munsterberg, the German psychologist William James brought to Harvard, was one of the leading figures in the development of a practical, industrial psychology in America. Contemporaries who distrusted his dogmatic certainty rightfully suspected his claims for such gimmicks as an infallible test for selecting trolley drivers. But he was, nonetheless, an important pioneer in the development of vocational selection. Like Dewey he examined the public and social life of citizenship, but he did so with a different purpose. Munsterberg considered the vocational life to be "the real center of all endeavors toward happiness." The highest social ideal was, therefore, to fit the individual to a proper job. Although he quoted Carlyle and spoke of individualism, it is clear that he rejected the romantic emphasis upon the inner capacities of the individual. To him, the individual was defined by his potential efficiency.

As Munsterberg saw it the era of manual labor was in no sense superior to the present age of industrial capitalism. Alienation was not, he argued, an automatic by-product of work; it was simply a matter of bad practice. Fulfillment and happiness could be achieved by using a complex system of charts demonstrating an individual's rank in such categories as knowledge, ability, and interest. At every level corresponding to points on such graphs, there existed an appropriate vocation for each person. "There is no technical work," he wrote, that did not allow an individual to succeed or fail—no task that excluded "suggestive" thought. "Everything," he noted, "depends only upon finding the right kind of work for the right personality."

Since every position, no matter how menial or, conversely, intellectually demanding, had a corresponding personality type, the task for Munsterberg and the vocational psychologists who followed his lead was to match the person to the job. This was the precondition to individual happiness and social order. But, as Munsterberg recognized, matching people and jobs flew in the face of traditional American individualism. "For a long while," he wrote, "it has been a kind of dogma, widespread throughout the nation, that any man can do anything." Pioneer life and democratic politics strengthened this belief. But, the psychologist noted, a "serious reaction [had] set in throughout the country." Not everyone, he concluded, had the same talent.[2]

Munsterberg was unnecessarily blunt in his attack upon the traditional assumptions of the work ethic and American individualism, in part, no doubt, because his more conservative German perspective rendered American traditions strange to him. But the psychologist rightly recognized the undemocratic nature of this new definition of individualism. Individual differences in capacity and intelligence, he believed, should be translated into appropriate social and economic positions on a hierarchical scale. If Americans were forced to give up the illusion that citizens were interchangeable parts in a democratic and mobile society, so much the better. It was time for illusions to cede to science. It was also time to apply psychological testing to the whole nation, he concluded.

Munsterberg's definition of personality in measurable terms, preferences, and abilities was an open and extreme statement of a new concept of individuality. Since the word "individual" was used by practically every social commentator of the day, it is important to recognize some of its different nuances. It was, in effect, a word whose meaning was as confusing in 1900 as it was seventy years later. But Munsterberg used the term rather clearly in opposition to another term, "equality." Traditionally both concepts had been related, but the psychologist found an important, practical distinction between them. As for the work ethic, he simply devalued it, placing the demands of industry before the rewards of the laborer.

Charles W. Eliot, also a leading figure in the reform of American education, agreed at several points with Munsterberg's analysis. But instead of a psychological examination, he proposed a different route to career happiness. He made the free choice and inclination of the students—not tests administered by experts—the mechanism for fitting each individual to his proper vocation. In an address to the National Education Association in 1910, Eliot justified his theory of vocational education using the arguments of progressive educators. Traditional pedagogy, he noted, was inappropriate to the current day, for it depended upon false premises. It was an instruction better suited to a leisured class of gentlemen. Useless knowledge—that is, impractical or esoteric information—was the traditional subject matter of teaching. As the audience at the N.E.A. surely agreed, such principles were incongruous with any universal educational system responsive to the needs of an industrial order. The old education, Eliot stated, created listless, uninterested students who gained nothing practical from their schooling. The result was a desultory population, bored with work and lacking in social and ethical motivation.

This critical problem of motivation, so Eliot thought, could not be solved by scientific psychological examination; it was more properly a matter of liberating free choice. By allowing the student to follow his inclinations the schools could place young people on the proper track. Encouraging a "life-career motive" in the course of instruction would be the best means to sort and select among students and vocations and to keep students interested throughout the crucial high school years. As Eliot noted, the happiest, most hard-working student was the one who had "made a primary decision with regard to his life career; he has determined the first direction of his preparation." Such students could be observed in YMCA evening schools, in commercial high schools, or at Hampton Institute—where blacks and Indians learned specific trades to better themselves. In all work-oriented institutions, such as industrial and corporation schools, students showed a keen interest in what they were doing because they could observe the practical results of their activities. Problems caused by the end of apprenticeship training or older forms of family or craft industry could thus be solved, Eliot found, in the newer vocational institutions.

Eliot challenged the schools to adopt the same reasoning. He suggested that they provide a far wider range of practical instruction, particularly at the upper levels. The educational system should bring self-motivation back into operation by allowing each student a wide degree of choice through the elective subject system. By following his natural bent, the pupil would discover a suitable career. At the end of his education, he would find "that by selecting the most congenial studies he will have prepared himself for the congenial trade or calling, because the same natural tendencies which directed him to the selected studies will direct him safely to the ultimate calling." Eliot did not add, but also must have thought, that if a wrong choice were made, it would be the student's fault.

Eliot's plan to revive some elements of the work ethic by liberating choice echoed certain tendencies of Dewey's educational theories, although ultimately he rested his proposals upon a different psychology. The major failing of modern education, he suggested, was that it did not reflect the realities and needs of industrialism. Education could function properly if it encouraged each person to choose a vocation appropriate to his or her inborn capacities.

No school could operate such a program unless it treated each individual separately, in terms of specific professional goals. Dewey might have agreed up to a point, but he was less willing to make efficient participation in the industrial system the primary goal of the school. His students, he hoped, would adjust to the industrial world, but he expected them to have the force and intelligence to change it. Despite Eliot's emphasis upon freedom of choice, the products of his system would, he hoped, happily perform the tasks to which each was called. This industrial priority in his thinking suggests the reasons he proposed the intensification of training, lengthening the school day, and summer sessions to combat "the evils of the long vacation."[3] The inside of Eliot's educational system, whatever one's measure of free choice, was a world of industrial "things in the saddle."

Vocational theories also developed outside the schools. Social reformers, particularly urban activists, diagnosed the drift of workers from one occupation to another as a major cause of contemporary vagabondage and social unrest. Probably the most important of the early advocates of practical vocational counseling at the turn of the century was urban reformer Frank Parsons of Boston. In Boston, where such public advising first appeared, Parsons's early work in the field made him an important national figure.

The Boston YMCA had founded a successful employment service as early as 1888, but it was Parsons, Meyer Bloomfield, and several others who helped transform the limited private efforts of settlement houses and groups such as the YMCA into sustained public efforts. The Vocational Bureau of Boston, which these figures founded in 1908, became a model institution that was copied throughout the United States.

Parsons justified the use of an elaborate formal and scientific vocational testing and placement system on his belief that the work ethic no longer functioned properly. The inner motivation of Americans, he remarked, had become corrupted or inoperative. The terrible pressure to succeed had separated economic reward from ethical and mental satisfaction. Thus dangerous and ambitious men like John D. Rockefeller rose to frightening heights of wealth and power on the "unstable bases of fraud and wrong." At other levels of society this malfunctioning work ethic placed individuals in the wrong employment.

Even the schools had neglected their role; the time of searching for work had become a period of uneasy drift between high school (or grade school) and vocation. The function of the vocational bureau was to fill the critical gap between education and work and ease the individual burden of choosing a life career. It could do so by instituting scientific matchmaking between ability and profession. Thus the vocational bureau could compensate for weaknesses in individual motivation. It would place persons, not where their ambition or ideology drove them, but where their innate capacities called them.

In his proposals for vocational guidance Parsons revealed a profound sense that the old order of American society was disintegrating. A new, conscious force had to be substituted for the old, automatic mechanisms that had once placed individuals in their proper stations. Science was to be that force. Parsons imagined the ideal division of society in a daydream interview with extraordinary implications: "If all the boys in Boston were gathered here together," he asked an imaginary applicant, "and a naturalist were classifying them as he would classify plants and animals, in what division would you belong?" Would the scientist place a candidate "in the mechanical group or the professional group, the executive group or the laboring group?"

The science that Parsons conjured up here was psychological testing to measure innate mental abilities and observation of physical traits that would reveal moral capacities. Discussing this latter category, he revealed how traditional his aims were and how class-biased the ideal society that he imagined was. Noting the health, education, and experience of a candidate, he also sketched his impressions of "the shape of his head, the relative development above, before, and behind his ears, his features and expression, color, vivacity, voice, manner, pose, general air of vitality, enthusiasm, etc." No doubt Parsons hoped to correct glaring faults of manners that might lose the applicant a desirable place. But certainly the elaboration of these categories also represented an effort to find visible, scientific criteria for the division of society into classes.

This aim was underscored in his discussion "The Would-Be Doctor." In this short sketch he described an interview with a candidate whose ambition it was to become a physician. Unfortunately the interviewee possessed a sickly physique, used poor language and had moist hands and little sense of acceptable manners. He had "no enthusiasms, interests, or ambitions except the one consuming ambition to be something people would respect, and he thought he could accomplish that purpose by becoming a physician more easily than in any other way." Parsons advised him to take up farming, carpentry, shoemaking, or clerking. In other words, he directed him away from a middle-class position toward a form of manual or unskilled labor.[4]

Certainly the whole of Parsons's reasoning is not revealed in this parable. But he chose to tell the reader that vocational advice could accomplish what the undirected drift into work could not. Vocational advice could establish the link that industrialism had disrupted between calling and ability, between inner mental and moral qualities and physical appearance. It might also tame the ambitions that had driven John D. Rockefeller to the destructive heights of his career.

Within the different emphases and institutional biases of Eliot, Munsterberg, and Parsons, there were important similarities. All three acknowledged that the older work ethic that presumably brought inner peace and social order no longer thrived under modern industrial conditions. Instead of trying to revive this ethic, they proposed to set up public institutions whose function it was to create the same effects achieved once by family, church, and apprenticeship. Rather than concentrate upon moral education or uplift, they wanted to treat only the phenomenon of behavior. They accepted the reality of alienation; thousands of Americans were rudderless and caught in eddies of inappropriate ambition. Thus the primary goal of vocational guidance was to devise a proper science of placement in order to eliminate the symptoms of alienation. Unlike those who sought to reinvigorate the traditional work ethic, theorists of vocational education and placement hoped to develop a new science of personality that would enable them to define each individual in terms of observable, physical characteristics and mental reactions.

The attention of vocational education and guidance advocates was almost exclusively directed toward children of lower-class background, toward industrial workers and immigrants, and toward any other population that required special training to fit the demands of the modern industrial system. In this category were black and Indian children to whom the movement devoted a good deal of attention. A further category of children and adults for whom vocational training was often advised were vagabonds and inmates of correctional and mental institutions. This concentration on marginal populations that were, in the eyes of many observers, the dangerous or potentially revolutionary elements of the nation suggests a conservative orientation of the early movement. But this political and social bias existed alongside a good deal of sympathy felt for such populations because they most obviously suffered from the inequities of modern industrialism.[5]

The industrial demand for menial and unrewarding labor was accepted as normal and permanent by the vocational movement; only people's attitudes toward it were wrong. Therefore the problem of modern social unrest seemed to reside with the inability of large numbers of workers to adjust themselves. As C. A. Prosser, secretary of the National Society for the Promotion of Industrial Education, wrote in 1913, the great dilemma of modern society was the existence of untrained, early school leavers. Condemned to rest at the bottom of the working class, "their menial, monotonous, more or less automatic work not only gives no skill which will be useful to them in after years but also arrests rather than develops intelligence and ambition." From this group came the "ne'er-do-wells, the loafers, the tramps, gamblers, prostitutes, and criminals" who burdened the state far more than might any efficient vocational program. If each child were given proper training "a better adjustment of every worker to the calling in which he can work most successfully" would result. Every worker would achieve happiness and a sense of accomplishment. The promise of the work ethic would be restored.[6]

Herman Schneider stated that the piecemeal nature of modern industry and the minute subdivision of labor had created ennervating work. "The spirit of unrest" evidenced by strikes of "automatic workers" and the questioning of the industrial system by university faculty members were testimony to a deep problem requiring solution.[7] This was precisely the problem that vocational guidance set out to solve.

Although vocationalism was related to manual training, the differences between the two movements may be illustrated in reference to the Hampton idea of Indian and black education, which Booker T. Washington was instrumental in popularizing. As the biographer of Washington has written, "the advocates of industrial education intended that the learning of a trade would be one outcome of their program." The Hampton idea did not result, however, in polytechnic training but, rather, in the "inculcation of Yankee virtues of industriousness and thrift, which [had] come to be called the Puritan work ethic."[8] Oscar Lovell Triggs, writing for the *Craftsman* in 1903, identified this element in the Hampton method: "The finest, soundest, and most effective educational methods in use in the United States are to be found in certain schools for negroes and Indians and in others for young criminals in reformatory prisons."[9]

Although this particular emphasis upon ethical, industrial, and citizenship training (Eliot cited Hampton and Washington's Tuskegee as two of the outstanding educational institutions of the day) was popular, the vocational movement was ultimately more interested in practical results for the majority of citizens. Blacks, Indians, and criminals were peripheral to the immediate problem of adjusting the masses of urban workers to the industrial system. And, even if a student could learn the ethic of work, there was still the problem of placement.

The major segment of the vocational movement moved, along with the common drift among educators, away from uniform education and toward differential instruction and categorization of students. In practice, this often meant the use of new standards of achievement in the classroom. The new individualism of productive norms and working to one's fullest capacity began to replace the older version of personality, which depended upon more intangible concepts like stewardship, social service, and inner contentment. These changes in the purposes and tools of education were reflected in an intensified division of labor among teachers themselves. Some were vocational experts; some taught academic subjects; and some instructed in manual skills.

Thus the vocational movement was partly a cause of and partly an expression of profound administrative changes in the education profession. These changes undoubtedly extended broader opportunities to people wishing to enter the teaching profession, but the pressures placed upon education, together with the commitment to universal training, also made pedagogy susceptible to the demands of political and industrial leaders. Whatever the plans of reformers, they would have to take into account the real needs of the industrial system, in which the success of vocational guidance and preparation could be measured statistically.

The first issues of the *American Teacher*, published in 1912 and 1913, reflected the tensions that buffeted the profession during these years. Keenly interested in the issues of vocational guidance and the role of the teacher in placing each student in a proper training course, editors of the journal were just as aware of the problems that beset the education profession itself. Struggling to succeed, working to establish the "dignity and influence of a profession," the pedagogic profession was in no position to resist the encroachments of pseudoscientific norms of success.[10] Thus, as the tasks of educators became greater, their dependence upon experts such as the vocationalists increased.

In the United States the vocational profession and a number of significant public bureaus were established by 1920. Moreover, the technical schools developed by major American corporations also acted to select and train workers for specific positions. This enormous diversity and success of an idea makes it fruitless to pursue the history of the whole movement. But by looking to the Boston Vocational Bureau and its operations it is possible to see how the concepts of Parsons, Eliot,

Munsterberg, and other pioneers came together in an institution that was widely copied throughout the United States.

The Boston bureau developed because of work by Frank Parsons, Meyer Bloomfield, and educational reformers from Harvard such as Eliot, as well as through the work of urban philanthropists. Before the turn of the century there had been scattered efforts in Massachusetts to provide specialized industrial training and vocational counseling. After the Civil War, for example, high schools began to offer commercial courses. But not until 1902 did vocational training on a large scale appear, and then it was largely in Wisconsin and Massachusetts.

By the end of the 1890s the lack of formal vocational instruction had become a national issue. Beginning in February 1898, *Cosmopolitan* magazine began an extensive campaign to arouse interest in guidance and specialized education. Two years later the magazine was still searching for some means to initiate such a movement. However, important steps had already been taken. In 1899 Harvard began a career-counseling service. With the help of private philanthropy Mrs. Quincy Adams Shaw and Frank Parsons organized Civic Service House, a settlement in Boston's North End. Here Parsons developed several vocational projects that he later put together in the vocational information Bureau, founded in 1908.[11]

The Vocational bureau worked with two major groups in Boston. One was the Employment Manager Association, created by several of the largest business firms of the city. Their joint efforts helped to create a new profession of specialists who worked inside large businesses and corporations to find proper occupations for employees. By 1911 the profession of vocational counselor was given additional prestige when Harvard University Summer School offered a course in guidance taught by the Vocational bureau.

The Vocational bureau also worked with the Boston School Committee, which, in 1909, asked the bureau to draw up plans for city-wide vocational guidance. Ongoing guidance institutions such as the YMCA also cooperated with the bureau. By 1910 the vocational movement had proliferated sufficiently to warrant a national meeting, the First National Conference on Vocational Guidance, held in conjunction with a meeting of the National Society for the Promotion of Industrial Education.

Meyer Bloomfield, who took over the leadership of the bureau that year (after the death of Parsons), hoped to make social reform the predominant aim of the organization. The movement, he wrote, was part of a national effort to make the school into an effective instrument in shaping a pupil's career. Its existence suggested the frank and active commitment of society to training and placing youth in appropriate careers. Bloomfield's own words recall some of John Dewey's writings. While enabling the student to understand the spiritual and political problems of the day, this new form of education would "render him responsive to our economic resources and problems, and in particular it shall bring home to him the importance and dignity of *work* of all kinds as the foundation of all individual and social welfare."[12]

Bloomfield concentrated most upon the difficult transition of young people from school to job. As he wrote in a short historical sketch of the vocational movement, "There is a blind drift of boys and girls from school to job, and from job to job." This aimless trek "through school, through work, and through life" could not, he continued, be redirected by exhortations to be more loyal, efficient, or interested. Such problems could only be solved if young people were able to discover their life's occupation. The bureau was to undertake the "thoughtful study of the problems of life-work and its choice"; through "creative sympathy real help [would] be given, where help [was] wanting, to thousands of perplexed youths groping through the complex conditions and demands of the twentieth century." The vocational bureau would adjust pupils or graduates to the demands of modern industrial life while preserving some similitude of the older relationship between the individual and his labor.[13]

Bloomfield's concern for the happiness and personal rewards of work was an important ingredient in the theory of vocational guidance. But the more practical pressures upon the movement diluted this reform element. For example, part of the impetus behind guidance and industrial education was the widespread pressure of reformers to end child labor. By keeping children in school, either in academic or industrial studies, they would eliminate the opportunity for young people to enter the labor market. Counseling would also direct students away from debilitating work that had no possibility for advancement or instruction.

On the other hand, a strong impetus for industrial training and guidance came from conservative groups who wished to reinforce a class system through differential education. While this latter effort largely evaporated after 1917, when the Smith-Hughes Act of Congress confined industrial training to the high school years (and not the grade schools as some educators had proposed), the conservative impulse within the movement remained strong.

As a result of conflicting purposes the industrial education and guidance movement took several different directions after 1910. The Boston vocational movement did not, as Bloomfield had hoped, become the leader of a reform movement. Instead, even in Boston, city educational administrators began to focus their attention on educational testing, and, in 1913, the Department of Educational Investigation and Measurement was established. The city refused to adopt the broad program of guidance and instruction that Bloomfield suggested.

On a national scale vocationalism merged with another new profession, personnel management. During the second decade of the twentieth century American corporations promoted their own versions of vocational training and guidance through such organizations as the National Association of Corporation Schools (later the American Management Association).

Perhaps the most lasting and original aspect of the guidance movement was its encouragement and adoption of new standards and methods of placement and testing. This had been a major factor in the thinking of Eliot, Parsons and Munsterberg. The desire for scientific intelligence and aptitude tests was an implicit recognition of the failure of the work ethic. It implied a new definition of personality based upon the phenomena of behavior. As Henrietta Rodman wrote in the *American Teacher* in 1912, the vocational movement was not based upon a series of esoteric guesses; it was firmly grounded in science. "Professor Thorndike's classification of types of mind as thing-thinkers and idea-thinkers, corresponds in the main with our classification of occupations. Those requiring thing-thinking are the arts and industries; idea-thinking is required in commerce and the professions."[14] She might have added that this mental division of labor was accompanied by a difference in wages and social position.

The development of testing and selection methods reflected the social and political biases of their originators; indeed, much of the early work in this field was based upon a racial or class bias. This conservative tendency was recognized at the time by such figures as the American sociologist Lester Frank Ward, who was able to demonstrate a number of errors in the early scientific theories of intelligence developed by the English anthropologist Sir Francis Galton. But the significance of the fact that intelligence and personality testing were adopted by the vocational movement is not the errors or distortions of such methods, but, rather, the theory that personality could be measured by an administered test.

Vocational advocates, unlike the supporters of manual training, were ambiguous about the effectiveness of the older notion of work. They rejected the notion that handicraft society was a utopia. Vocationalism represented a commitment to selectivity, and, as such, it joined the wing of educational reformers who proposed what they called the individualization of instruction.

Some of these reformers and even vocational experts continued to speak in the language of the work ethic and traditional individualism, but they had begun to place their hopes in a new science of personality and individuality that would be appropriate to the world of industrial labor. Under such circumstances, all that remained of the traditional work ethic was the admonition to work hard and live a respectable life. The rewards of labor would come, not from the accomplishment of creative tasks, but from society, in the form of wages and a better standard of living. The work ethic was crumbling before a new definition of labor as compulsion. The older definition of personality had been drawn in moral terms; the new individuality was sketched in terms of productivity.

11

Work
and the Asylum

Manual training, the vocational movement, and progressive
education sought to make industrial labor more attractive and
rewarding. The impulse behind homeopathic cures, self-help,
and the justification of sport aimed at the same problem of alienated
experience. They, too, sought to adjust the individual to the competitive and often inhospitable society of modern industrial America. But
for severe cases of maladjustment, which showed up in rising crime
and suicide statistics and in psychological disorders, a more immediate treatment was required.

Most of the victims who suffered from neurasthenia were assumed
to come from the middle classes. Their treatment was a form of individual regeneration, a priming of the will through physical and mental
therapy. For the vast majority of the obvious victims of modern industrialism, however, neurasthenia was an inappropriate description of
the causes of their maladjustment. It was difficult in 1900 to believe
that large elements of the population had medical or psychological
problems when they seemed so clearly to be suffering from moral or
physical degeneracy. Criminals, vagabonds, and even the feeble-
minded posed a frightening problem, one that could not be treated by
training and guidance. This part of the population seemed to represent a group that either refused to or could not cope with the rapid
changes of modern life.

The modern prison, reform school, Indian reservation, and mental
institution were given the task of forcing "abnormal" populations to
adjust to modern industrial life. These populations, whether marked
by severe cultural divergencies, extreme poverty, vicious habits, or
signs of mental disturbance, were apparently unable to answer the
demands of contemporary existence. In a period that devoted much
time to reexamining the definitions of human individuality, these inca-

pacitated groups seemed most urgently in need of treatment. Yet the practices of incarceration, treatment, and even diagnosis of the causes of maladjustment were all subject to intense argument and broad experimentation during the period. Were vagabonds and criminals the victims or the causes of social decay and political crisis? Were they the product of some fatal hereditarian flaw or the symptom of an unjust and destructive social arrangement? Were they mentally unstable, physically deformed, or morally stunted? What caused their sudden proliferation? Was there any hope for a cure?

The crisis of the work ethic had a special importance in the answers given to these questions. The indigent or incapable were identified by their inability to work. Thus cure often meant nothing more than an ability to return to the job. Under such circumstances successful treatment of these populations depended upon their ability to learn some form of work compulsion. But the traditional work ethic and individuality clearly did not apply to the problems of these sufferers. A new and surer definition of individuality was required. Scientific and quantifiable methods of selecting and measuring elements of personality seemed more desirable than the older informal tests of moral behavior. Prisons, reformatories, and mental institutions became increasingly dependent, in this period, upon the development of an exact science of mental and moral qualities that would enable them to proceed with reform and selection.

Modern society developed incarceration for those who were unable or unwilling to work. As the 1917 *Field Work Manual* of the New York State Board of Charities noted, "The ideal of the scientist in social economics is to have every citizen earn by daily toil at least the value of that which he eats and enjoys, and the eugenist can add to this the desire and expectation that every member of the race shall be fit mentally and physically to do his bit of the world's work." The decision of whether to eliminate the feeble-minded, the manual continued, depended upon their "productive power."[1]

By the turn of the century governmental agencies in the United States had become more actively engaged in the isolation of social undesirables than they had been in the heyday of early incarceration, the 1830s. This modern movement to separate and divide was more than matched by the appearance of large numbers of individuals who committed crimes against property or who refused to labor. To be an outlaw in modern society might be attractive or romantic, but it was also dangerous. As reformer Francis G. Peabody wrote in 1900 for the Massachusetts Association of Relief Officers, there was something attractive "about a man who in the midst of a world of work can be perfectly free from the trammels of industry, and live—like a professor—by his wits."[2]

The dual demands—study and reform of social misfits (the "floating population")—upon the asylum, reformatory, and prison in the United States made them, like the schools, susceptible to various and sometimes contradictory purposes and intellectual currents. Existing at a time of enormous innovation in psychological theory (which itself suggested different sorts of remedial treatment), awash with theories of hereditarian and environmental determinism, and beset by conflicting demands for punishment and social rehabilitation, such institutions naturally reflected the profound changes and growing indecision in American thinking about the nature of human personality and the relationship between individuals and work.

Advocates of prison reform, penologists, psychologists, and social reformers were apt to disagree on the nature of social maladjustment. One large group, for example, blamed alcoholism for practically every form of modern antisocial behavior. There were others who subscribed to a disease theory of crime and mental disturbance, which, they argued, could be treated and cured by restoring the function of the "organs of character." Others suggested adopting scientific standards of observation so that, by classifying physical and mental types, particularly among school children, society could discover which individuals had a tendency to criminal behavior.

For the practical problem of dealing with a population of tramps and ne'er-do-wells, many relief officers promoted a system of forced labor in work camps. For others the answer lay in education, beginning in kindergarten classes, where responsible behavior could be inculcated before the temptations of sloth and misbehavior were experienced. For criminologist Arthur MacDonald the purpose of incarceration was to reestablish the equilibrium between character and ability: "The prison should be a reformatory," he wrote, "and the reformatory a school."[3] Finally, there were those who argued that the function of asylums and prisons was to practice social eugenics and prevent the reintegration of criminals and the feeble-minded into society where they might reproduce themselves.

Many of these assumptions in the discussion of incarceration derived from traditions in American penology and social psychology that had been established as early as the 1830s. The principal changes in these institutions and in penological theory from 1890 to the First World War did not, therefore, relate just to the quality of treatment or even to the priorities dictated by society. More important was the development and application of a new theory of individual motivation and, consequently, the acceptance of the inevitable alienation of some elements of the population from the rigors of modern industrial life.

Prison officials most desired a useful guide to predicting human behavior. Some laws for this had already been suggested, in Quetelet's general rule of suicide, which predicted the inevitability of self-destruction in a given population, or in the mental tests of Alfred Binet and Hugo Munsterberg, or in the classification of mental and physical characteristics that marked modern physical anthropology. But each of these suggested the need for a new, general theory of the origins of human action that would also justify the modification of behavior.[4]

Before the Civil War the "moral treatment" of inmates was developed to regenerate prisoners. This was an effort to change behavior by providing an atmosphere conducive to cure that would not be viewed by the inmate as a punishment. Although the moral treatment of inmates was a predominant penological and psychological theory, many institutions during the nineteenth century, unfortunately, operated simply as custodians for social misfits. Even during the most optimistic years of prison reform many institutions were administered by medical officers, philanthropists, and public health officials who felt that the criminal and the insane were incurable. The proper treatment was isolation of these elements from the rest of society. Between the Civil War and 1900 there were many institutions in which nothing more than this was done.[5]

The guiding principle of those institutions which sought to reform inmates during the nineteenth century had been the imposition of discipline. The two most famous early prison systems, the Pennsylvania system and the Auburn Plan, while distinct from each other, provided discipline and order in an environment that stressed the individual's need to internalize the habits of obedience and good behavior. The Pennsylvania system with its total isolation of the inmate and its stress upon Bible study presented an unrelieved environment for introspection. This emphasis upon individual regeneration through self-contemplation was, no doubt, a reflection of the extreme individualism predominant in American culture during the 1830s. But it was also a judgment leveled against a society that did not always provide a congenial atmosphere to the development of self-reliance.

The Auburn, New York, plan was based upon similar psychological assumptions, but it was less extreme. It proposed to instill an individual ethic, but it also allowed inmates to have common meals and labor together, although, in principle, inmates were prevented from conversing. Of particular importance in the Auburn system was work. Productive labor was encouraged in the prison and, by the 1830s, the institution had become a source of profit for the state.

Despite wide divergences in theory and practice among penologists, several generalizations can be made about nineteenth-century asylums. There was an overriding hope that inmates could be cured. Moreover, the principles of separation and classification of populations and be-havior patterns were well established. The causes of serious social misbehavior, moreover, were thought to reside in society as well as in the individual. Thus the reforming institution hoped to compensate for the breakdown of order and discipline and for a lack of education.

Behind these theories of incarceration lay a traditional, Protestant view of personality and individual responsibility. Although this view was complimented by scientific theories, the assumptions about the process of cure closely resembled the process of Christian nurture or the acceptance of grace, for cure and grace both depended upon the same sort of individual conversion.

Whatever the treatment in prisons—extreme isolation, military dis-cipline, medicinal baths, or work—it was all designed to bring an internal change in the personality of patient or prisoner. The human personality, because it was primarily rational, was capable of respond-ing to such direct stimuli.[6] In this view science and morality coincided; reason, armed by the will, was the first principle of human conscious-ness.

The rationalistic assumptions and the evangelical overtones of Amer-ican incarceration persisted in the twentieth century, but there were some profound changes in psychological and medical theory, and optimism about the possibilities of cure was generally declining. Urbanization and industrialism rendered the criminal and incapable populations more obvious, and, apparently, more dangerous. The fear of vagabondage at the turn of the century and the belief that crime was increasing underscored the problems that penology was required to solve. By 1900 the population that refused to work seemed in spe-cial need of treatment. The movement to imprison tramps was a sym-bolic step in this direction; by 1910 it had achieved some success in such states as New York.

One of the most interesting experiments in rehabilitation was per-formed upon American Indians, who were treated as an incarcerated population in this period. Efforts to inculcate the work ethic took a new guise, that of the means of "civilizing" a population that was unfa-miliar with with industrial society. The St. Louis exhibition of indus-trial education among Indians in 1904 demonstrated the result of years of agitation by eastern reformers. Important in securing gov-ernment support for special Indian education was the Lake Mohawk Conference of reformers. Its leaders, including Merrill Gates and Lyman Abbott, were committed to integrating the Indian into Ameri-can society. Their program, which was a form of secular evangelism, resembled early prison reform. They hoped to convert Indians to Protestantism, to the work ethic, and to the virtues of modern capitalist industrialism. The method proposed by the conference (which was under the leadership of Gates after 1888) combined a mixture of actions designed to break up the tribal notion of communal property and provisions for industrial training and instruction in the virtues of frugality and industry.[7]

The vocational ideal expressed in Indian reform education was echoed in the goals of the George Junior Republic, a school for delinquent boys founded in upstate New York in the late nineteenth century. "Daddy" George, the leader of the reformatory, developed a program of treatment that was a perfect combination of progressive educational methods and industrial training, as well as a caricature of both.

George's "City Republic" began as a rural settlement for immigrant children, became a vocational school for the poor, and, finally, was transformed into a private reform school. George's methods of self-government and his industrial program were not entirely new. In the early nineteenth century the Boston House of Reformation had practiced a form of vocational training and self-government by inmates, and the Berkshire Industrial Farm had exhibited several aspects of self-discipline and government in the 1880s that George adopted somewhat later.

George's cure for misguided youth included an inculcation of the traditional American work ethic. To create a self-governing society for young workers, he designed an institution that paralleled certain elements of the experimental schools of Gary, Indiana, where the principles of democracy and labor were taught in programs demanding wide participation in the running of the institution. George's condemnation of idleness and his belief in the restorative function of labor placed him on the side of traditional penologists in a period when the principles of criminal reform were rapidly changing. Although his simple-minded emphasis upon the work ethic would probably have doomed his experiment in the long run, George's personal eccentricity and extravagant claims made his work more controversial than it needed to be. In spite of their reservations, several leading reformers approved his efforts. Theodore Roosevelt, in particular, was intrigued by the Junior Republic motto—"Nothing Without Labor."[8] John R. Commons, Jacob Riis, and others supported George's program, but it was ultimately rejected by most professional penologists, whose ideas he failed to accomodate. The public attention he received indicates the continued popularity of reform programs that emphasied the traditional work ethic.

The work colony idea was applied to vagrants as well as to Indians and delinquents. In the *Craftsman*, commentator Florence Finch Kelly outlined the various sorts of programs that existed in 1906 for putting indigent populations to work. There were several forms of work camps, she noted, ranging from the Detroit plan for allowing the unemployed and vagrant populations to cultivate vacant land within the city, to the more formal, rural work camps organized by the Salvation Army, located in Fort Romie, California, and Fort Amity, Colorado.[9]

The most elaborate plan was that designed for New York State. After several years of pressure from private citizens, philanthropic groups, and professional reformers such as the State Conference of Charities and Corrections, New York passed legislation creating a farm penal colony in 1911. The purpose of this farm was, according to one of its major advocates, socialist Edmund Kelly, to rehabilitate vagrants and tramps. The law was stated thus: "A state industrial farm colony is hereby established for the detention, humane discipline, instruction and reformation of male adults committed thereto as tramps or vagrants."[10] Local New York authorities were granted the option of sending any male adult deemed a tramp to the colony. Normal sentences were two years, unless the inmate had previously been convicted of a crime.

Behind the creation of such institutions as the New York farm colony lay considerable efforts to discover some sort of forced labor system for reforming vagrants. By removing them from society (and temptation) and exposing them to hard work, reformers hoped to revive a flagging work motivation. Although the general secretary of the American Prison Association, Orlando Lewis, proposed a national system of labor camps in 1907, this movement ultimately had limited success. Like the Indian industrial schools and the George Junior Republic, the farm colony was a utopian community designed to inculcate the traditional work ethic during a period when the principles and practices of incarceration were rapidly changing.[11]

More typically, prison institutions combined the older notions of reform based upon the work ethic with newer forms of treatment that related to behavioral or biological theories of personality. The most impressive of these institutions was the state prison at Elmira, New York. Elmira officials accepted traditional notions of work and reformation, but they also experimented with new penological tools such as anthropometric measurements and personality tests.

This reformatory, founded in the 1870s, was a much-discussed model during the next twenty years. The opening of Elmira coincided with another important event in the history of penology—the publication in 1877 of Richard L. Dugdale's study of the Jukes family. The Jukes study (which examined heredity, retardation, and criminality within a specific genetic and social group) and Elmira represented different emphases in criminology. The former was a popular, scientific, statistical, and hereditarian study of crime and feeble-mindedness. Elmira, by contrast, was largely devoted to rehabilitation through moral and industrial training.

Elmira began as a prison based upon inculcating citizenship and the work ethic. As Z. R. Brockway, head of the prison, wrote, the purpose of the reformatory was to change individuals so that they might take their appropriate place in modern industrial society. To achieve this goal, he argued, a prison must provide a comprehensive environment of discipline and education without the distractions and temptations of civilian life. Every prisoner was made aware of the complex system and social order of which he was a part.

Brockway, in his autobiography, spoke of himself as the "chief provider and *entrepreneur*" of Elmira. This was a reference to an early function of prison superintendants who, until 1888, were allowed to organize prison labor into competitive economic units. When New York State removed this privilege Brockway still thought of himself as a captain of industry, and he ran his reformatory on the principles of business efficiency. Prisoners were referred to as "wage earners" and their place or status in the system related to their work performance and behavior.

The prison was organized according to a military model, with training in discipline and a complex ranking system through which the inmate was supposed to pass. Activities of prisoners included physical exercise, baths and massages, manual and industrial training, and exposure to a complete educational system. Theoretically the inmate could receive instruction at any level from grade school to academic training. Religious and moral instruction were, of course, important aspects of the prisoner's day. For all of these characteristics, Brockway proudly referred to Elmira as the "college on the hill."[12]

In a description of Elmira, William D. P. Bliss noted two advances from earlier penological institutions. The first was Elmira's social arrangement, in which inmates were given more physical freedom and social freedom than could be found in either the Auburn or Pennsylvania systems. Second, the "college on the hill" provided work and industrial training. In order to comply with laws that prohibited competitive, productive labor in prisons, inmates were taught tasks that stressed development of manual dexterity and specific skills.[13]

In 1898, in a report for the *American Journal of Sociology*, R. C. Bates summarized and explained the theory of penology at Elmira. The author acknowledged the moral instruction and training in the work ethic that lay behind the activities of the prison. He also recognized that modern educational and psychological theories were changing traditional penology. Manual training, he noted, arrived at Elmira in 1895. It was founded, he suggested, upon modern pragmatic psychology as well as upon traditional wisdom about the work ethic. To deal with the problem of men who came from generations "with a total abhorrence of honest labor," Brockway and his associates had developed a program of instruction to incite a better attitude toward labor. As Bates remarked, "It was early discovered that deep physical and moral causes were fundamental, and that the restoring means must operate directly upon the sensory organs, and that the man must be additionally influenced by developing activities."

Bates also noted that the educational theories of Froebel and Pestalozzi underscored the possibility of acquiring virtue through the internalization of "virtuous habits." The manual training system, he continued, worked because of the physiological fact "that for every important part of the body, of those which are under control of the will, there is a region of the brain by which it is controlled, and these are what are known as 'centers.' " By setting these centers into motion special sorts of training could make virtuous action become habitual. Tangible experience was the best instructor; the way to morality was through practice.[14]

Manual instruction merged well with the disciplined life to which the Elmira inmate was exposed. The division of each day was marked by military maneuvers and formations. The prison population was divided into squads that were commanded by inmate officers. Each inmate officer, in turn, was responsible to a higher official. With promotion within the ranks possible for good behavior, inmates could achieve certain concessions of power over other prisoners or privileges such as better food. Simultaneously, promotion and advancement within the educational system were possible.

The umbrella of rigorous discipline, elaborate hierarchy, and manual instruction was designed to achieve the permanent reform of inmates. Given the indeterminate sentence, this program could be applied for as little or as long as prison officials deemed necessary. Clearly, what the prison offered was an intense environment of work and discipline designed as a cure for the confusion and disorientation that the new industrial world had caused. Following this reasoning, crime was thought to result from the breakdown of old ethical inhibitions; therefore, the criminal should be, not punished, but reborn. As Enoch Cobb Wines wrote in 1880, Elmira ought to be thought of as a home, for it affected the prisoner as much as a family did. The purpose of such institutions was to inculcate those traditional virtues once thought of as belonging in the family. Elmira was a school whose graduates should become model citizens of the new industrial world.[15]

The models of the ideal work society and capitalist enterprise were important in prison thinking in the 1890s, but they were not the only ones. The results of the Jukes study in 1877 and the impetus toward scientific criminology begun by the publication of Cesare Lombroso's *The Criminal* in 1876 offered a different interpretation and cure for crime and mental incapacity. The "scientific" study of crime and mental disease up to 1900 received its major stimulus from European theories of heredity and criminal and mental typology, although there was some pioneering work done by Americans. Development of mental and physical tests, again, largely in Europe, de-emphasized ethical attitudes and the reformation of inmates, and substituted a more behavioral approach, often called the "individualization" of treatment.

This individualizing trend in penology paralleled similar developments in educational attitudes and vocational training, which prescribed separated, special treatment for each case. This new attitude was a divergence from the disciplined but traditional order of Elmira. It suggested that prisons become individualized laboratories of behavior modification. By the end of this period institutions such as Elmira had attempted to accommodate the scientific theories of personality. And by the First World War the new theories of personality and character had made broad inroads into the theory and practice of incarceration.

Study of criminal typology had been conducted as early as 1888 at Elmira. In 1886 prison officials began to include in their annual reports what they called "anthropological photos" of inmates. These photos purportedly demonstrated oddities of physique and countenance, which, in turn, suggested criminal weakness. Hamilton Wey reported that efforts to define criminal characteristics led to some conclusive results. Minutely detailed prison statistics revealed the typical criminal to be underweight, with "repulsive features," "an asymmetrical head," and "heavy in his movements." "His mind," Wey continued, "while not diseased, is underdeveloped, or it may be abnormally developed in certain directions."[16]

The problem of such study was to suggest the permanence of physically induced social maladjustments, which no amount of retraining could suppress. In the end Brockway proved himself a believer in both traditional discipline and criminal anthropology. Under his leadership both systems were made to work together. "Scientific" diagnosis went hand in hand with moral treatment. But, after Brockway resigned in 1896, the system he had built quickly disintegrated. Manual training, ethical instruction, and other elements of his elaborate program were downgraded.[17]

The modern scientific theory of penology in the United States was more often enlisted in these years in finding the causes of crime than in rehabilitating criminals. Enormous pressure was placed upon mental and criminal asylums to identify physical and mental types and to categorize and choose among them. This enhanced the attractions of the sciences of selection and rehabilitation and eclipsed the older programs of self-discipline and work.

If the criminal, the vagabond, and the extreme neurasthenic all suffered from a collapse of will, this moral paralysis, observers concluded probably had physical or even hereditarian causes. By developing and applying a theory of normality and abnormality based upon physical and mental tests, experts could recognize criminal tendencies or mental weaknesses before they developed. Prior to any outbreak of antisocial behavior, potentially dependent populations could be discovered, isolated, and treated. The prison would thus become a scientific laboratory in which measurements, related statistically, could be compiled to sketch a criminal typology.

This new science of personality and character suggested two corollaries. One was the usefulness of installing paramedical and psychological facilities, designed to spot the first symptoms of aberration, in the schools and factories. Another and more Draconian possibility was eugenic control of populations. Criminals and the feeble-minded could, on the basis of certain tests, be selected and then retired from society. The more severe cases could be prevented from reproducing —it was hoped that their disease or crippling heredity would die with them.

Scientific tests for mental and moral weakness could, of course, be put to both purposes. For example, in an article written in 1911, Henry H. Goddard and Helen F. Hill recounted an experiment they had performed on reformatory girls. Using the Binet test for mental age, they discovered that all but four of the fifty-six girls examined were feeble-minded. The coincidence of crime, incarceration, and mental incapacity, they concluded, made it imperative that such populations be prevented from reproducing.[18] Using the same general Binet test for more positive purposes, American army psychologists during the First World War attempted to develop a positive selective device that would allow them to place recruits in positions of their greatest usefulness.

Perfection of a science for identifying criminal types through physical and mental testing was a priority often urged upon the American government during the first decade of the twentieth century, and it was probably only the efforts of Education Commissioner Harris that prevented the creation of an official study. Arthur MacDonald worked for a decade to secure passage of a bill that would have committed the government to the new science. Although he was never successful, his efforts attracted a good deal of support in Congress and in the medical profession.

MacDonald felt that the government should institute a laboratory to study criminal types. His own studies, he wrote, confirmed the modern theory that certain specified physical traits pointed to mental weakness and a propensity to crime. For example, he said, criminals (the same was true of the "laboring classes") were less sensitive to pain than were the wealthy. Criminals were more inclined to be left-handed. A "potentially vicious child" usually had some characteristic animality or an obvious physical defect such as a stutter.

MacDonald believed that strict discipline and moral instruction might return some of these individuals to the point where they could rejoin society as useful workers. He recognized, however, that there was a theoretical dilemma in his advice. If criminality, antisocial behavior, and insanity were based upon physical degeneracy, then how could vocational training, discipline, or a military regimen have any effect? MacDonald's answer, although inadequate, was very suggestive. The training of the "abnormal character does not differ," he wrote, "from the training that develops character and ability in the case of the normal individual." Abnormality was therefore a slight variation of normality; it did not indicate a completely new type of human.[19]

Such arguments shifted the issue of criminality away from a moral interpretation of behavior to a sociological or physical one. In the reasoning and practice of this science, abnormal traits were identified with the characteristics of populations at the bottom of the social and economic order. Slum children were more likely to become criminals; they also seemed to exhibit more physical signs of mental degeneracy. All behavior conformed to the same scientific laws. The criminal and the madman existed, not because they lacked an internalized morality, which was merely the result of their prior condition, but because they deviated, physically, from the normal. They could be cured because modern educational methods, as MacDonald sensed, were not based upon moral regeneration but upon soliciting proper behavior.

Charles North, writing for the new publication *The Delinquent*, in 1916, analyzed the criminal's mind in much the same way. Mental development in deviants, he said, remained snagged at a childlike or savage stage. Thus criminals, children, and savages all betrayed the same characteristics: moral insensibility, egotism, lack of remorse, low reasoning power, and habitual use of slang, which he called the language of degenerates. North's penological theory followed the lines set out by Arthur MacDonald, August Drähms, and Cesare Lombroso. He suggested that mental and moral characteristics were revealed by physical marks. Crime was not, he concluded, a matter of individual responsibility. It could best be explained by social and physical phenomena.[20]

The shift to physical and environmental explanations of behavior entailed what Roscoe Pound of the Harvard Law School called "a *system* of individualization." This new system required careful study of each case and the application of unique treatments to fit the criminal's special requirements. By de-emphasizing moral responsibility and treating crime as a disease, penologists were implicitly recognizing that human freedom was not an absolute. Punishment should not fit the crime, it should fit the individual. "Punishment" should be transformed into a period of incarceration used to rehabilitate the criminal.[21]

By the second decade of the twentieth century, in criminal theory as in education, the traditional emphasis upon internalizing Protestant morality through the inculcation of the work ethic had begun to cede to newer, scientific and behavioral models of social order that stressed individual responsibility less, but individualization of education and formation more. Confusing as this distinction was—and is—it represented a profound change in attitudes. The older theory that an individual acted according to an inner calling gave way before a theory that stressed the mechanical and behavioral elements of character. The word "individual" remained in constant usage, but its meaning changed. In the hands of the new social scientists, educationists, penologists, and psychologists, it was detached from the concepts of freedom and responsibility.

III

*A New Definition of Work
and Human Personality*

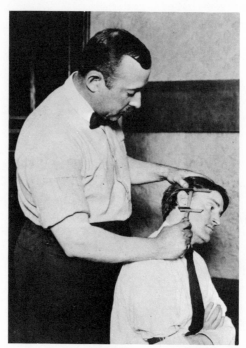

Taking Bertillon measurements, New York Police Headquarters, c. 1910.

Reformatory inmates from auditorium stage, Elmira, New York, c. 1910.

12

Discovering Virtue and Vice:
Physical Stigmata

In 1897 French sociologist Emile Durkheim devoted a major study to discovering the causes of suicide, one of the most disturbing social phenomena of his day. He suggested that mental disease, crime, and other problems—as well as suicide—were normal by-products of social progress. In this perception he did not differ from most observers. But he went further, by denying the underpinning of traditional wisdom about work and social ethics: "Perhaps what is abnormal for individuals," he wrote, "is normal for society."[1] In this disturbing formulation he upset the balance and harmony between individual behavior and society. He rejected the classical assumption that lay behind the work ethic, which decreed that society was the sum of its parts. Society was now conceived to be something more and the individual less.

The impact of this sort of thinking was intensified at the turn of the century in America because of the failure of those advocating a return to the old principles of work to discover and apply a program to reform and regenerate the whole society. Their ineffectiveness was compounded by a profound shift in psychology and philosophy that began to crumble the foundations of the work ethic itself and the assumptions about personality and individualism that had buttressed it. The deepening crisis of work was not solved by appeals to the past or by any of the various reforms invoked in the name of tradition. The stage was, therefore, set for a thorough reexamination of work and human personality with modern behavioral psychology and philosophic pragmatism as the principal actors.

The most important thinker to examine these deeper questions was William James, although, of course, others, including John Dewey and Edward Thorndike, thought through the implications of the new attitudes toward work, personality, and human psychology. But from the fertile imagination of James came the key ideas used to develop a new social and individual psychology and, ironically, the philosophic doubts that indicted them.

As a focal point for understanding how a new psychology of work and personality was developed, James the psychologist can be seen as a dominant figure. James is also crucial as the philosopher who doubted both the older traditional of idealism upon which the work ethic was based and the newer materialism upon which the behavioral model was erected. James's ambiguities and contradictions were the profoundest ambiguities of his age. In every sense—personally and intellectually—he participated in the crisis of work. He contributed a deep awareness of the dilemma his own theories helped to create and a body of philosophical works that sounded the depths of aliena-tion in his society. And, by his reluctance to enunciate a social ethics, he demonstrated the difficulty—if not the impossibility—of adhering to the values of individualism in modern industrial society.

The key psychologcal assumption James provided for his age was his theory that the human mind is entirely organic in nature. His argument was certainly familiar to many psychologists, but he pre-sented this dictum with such force and elegance in his *Principles of Psychology* (published in 1890) that he persuaded a generation of its validity. Moreover, his psychology was extended and popularized by his students. Intellectually, then, James stands at the source of a school of psychology, developed and elaborated toward the end of the nine-teenth century, that defined the human mind in functional terms, and human behavior as activity solicited by an environment.

If mind were described as organic and functional in nature, then, modern psychologists asked, what were the laws of its development? Was heredity or environment the key element in its formation? By what means could the functions of mind be measured? Once such con-troversies were settled, social problems that accompanied progress could conceivably be solved through social engineering. The crisis of work, some enthusiasts proclaimed, could be ended by altering false expectations about the relationship of citizens to their society.

The materialist basis of this new orientation in philosophy and psy-chology was acceptable to many commentators, but its practical ram-ifications were not always popular. Trying to develop a new science of social and psychological selection to substitute for the old work ethic touched off sharp debate. In this age of practicality even the defenders of the work ethic could point to some tangible, visible proofs of their philosophy. They claimed that joy, community, success, hap-piness, and social harmony—all highly visible qualities—marked the society arranged and ordered by the traditional dictates of the work ethic and old fashioned morality. The new sociopsychologists sought the same goals, but they invented new measures of men and women.

No one in 1900 suggested giving up hard work as the duty of each citizen; individualistic ethics still reigned in popular culture. But the reality shifted and buckled under the foundations of these terms. Confusion and accomodation were simultaneously characteristic of this period of American thought. But, as James argued, the scientific model of ethics, human behavior, and intelligence was a new and radical departure.

If, in 1800, it was incumbent upon a citizen to know who he was and where he might find an appropriate place in the social hierarchy, it was increasingly the case, after 1900, that society assumed this burden of placement. Arthur MacDonald wrote in 1914 that it was necessary for society to study all forms of behavior and all types of individuals, including the insane, the genius, the criminal, or the congressman. One simple scale of measurement was required for all citizens: "There must be a general criterion or measuring rod for estimating and understanding physical and mental superiority and distinguishing them from the average and the mediocre."[2]

Before any such measure could be discovered the principles of selection had to be established. As psychologist Lewis Terman wrote, "Just as many a man has been hanged on the evidence of his finger prints, so many an individual might safely be committed to an institution for the feeble-minded on the evidence of ten or a dozen intelligence tests which have been standardized according to age norms." Even for less drastic decisions Terman argued that mental testing could direct individuals into general social and economic positions. "Such data would suggest," he continued, "that the IQ of 75 or below belongs ordinarily in the unskilled class, that 75 to 85 is preeminently the range for semi-skilled labor, and 80 to 85 is ample for success in some kinds of skilled labor."[3]

The behavior model in social and psychological theory aimed to solicit desired action rather than instill Christian virtue, although in practice it was hoped that the two would coincide. Separation of motivation from action was a key element in the thinking behind this orientation. The resulting definition of human psychology emphasized the mechanical and the unconscious. It de-emphasized language, ethics, and conscious aspiration. While few thinkers of this age went as far as the behaviorist John Watson in separating intention from action in psychology, the tendency to do so was characteristic of a whole school of social theorists.

This definition accepted a picture of mankind as inherently alienated; it described behavior as unconscious and unreasoning. This reduction of ethics to language or biology made a virtue of what others in this era held to be the greatest problem of modern society. Pushed further, the definition suggested that man was not divided or alienated, but his understanding and expectations were false. All human history up to the modern era had, therefore, been needlessly confused by the belief in reason, by dreams of liberty and freedom of the will. The pressing problem of modern society was not to end what some defined as a state of alienation, but to use it creatively.

Therefore, the perfection of a science of selection promised to control crime, vice, and degeneracy. As Hugo Münsterberg wrote of his experiments with mental reaction time, "That is just the wonderful power of the psychological experiment, that it can analyze the largest social movements in the smallest and most schematic miniature copies of the mental forces involved, and from the subtle analysis is only one step to the elimination of dangers."[4]

The effect of this thinking was reductive, for language, events, and behavior could all be translated into experiments reproduced in the laboratory. It was impossible to believe in a reasonable universe that behaved according to scientific propositions and still hold that man's intelligence was defined by spiritual or unknowable forces. Thus Münsterberg was only being consistent when he wrote, "As the organs of man are merely combinations of cells and tissues, so his mental personality is a complex combination of elementary states."[5] Precise testing and selective judgments were dependent upon the possibility that complex mental states could be reduced to simple operations.

The general philosophic tendency of the behavior model was, therefore, to reduce questions of mind and ethics to manageable proportions. It promised no internal moral regeneration but, rather, the possibility of improved action. It accepted the effects of alienation as the reality of modern life. By definition man was alienated because his own expectations and dreams were illogical and preposterous. His aspirations to dignity and mental power contradicted the facts of life. The new economic reality revealed the essential nature of the human spirit. The function of will in psychology was demoted; scientific description replaced moral exhortation. By definition man was a machine or an animal whose essential character was not mystery or intelligence, but complexity.

The measure of moral and intellectual qualities by physical signs was, in 1900, both the oldest and newest of sciences. Striking physical traits had always been taken as symbols; birthmarks, deformities, or other such features were interpreted variously before this time as witches' marks, signs of God's wrath, or external excrescences of internal immorality. The mutual association of madness, divinity, intelligence, and clairvoyance was an ancient and respected tradition in Western culture.

The new science of physical stigmata, which was begun, principally, by Sir Francis Galton and developed by such psychologists and criminologists as Bertillon in France and Lombroso in Italy, no doubt owed some of its popularity and acceptance (and, perhaps, even its origins) to its unconscious association with what must be called an undercurrent of black magic and submerged fear of physical deformity. In this sense the new science was as old as popular wisdom and prejudice. But it became an integral part of modern biopsychology. It was supported by statistical measurement and a more efficient and precise analysis of mental and physical reaction times, made possible in the laboratory.

Anthropometric systems of identification (the generic term for this science) offered an apparently sure and practical way to distinguish human typologies on the basis of deviations from the norm. The development of delicate scales and measures, it was hoped, would make it possible to describe genius, normality, and criminality as slight variations or different combinations of the same elemental characteristics. Assuming that moral and intellectual qualities had physical and even visual character, practical psychologists, criminologists, and sociologists extended the materialist attack upon traditional, rational theories of individualism and behavior to the very citadel of their existence. They tried to prove that there was no need to believe in the existence of innate mentality or a separate spirit since all thought and behavior could be reduced to a physical process.

To an age that worried desperately that the old social order and its familiar signs of stations, quality, and hierarchy were disappearing, anthropometrics, the identification of syndromes of physical and mental characteristics, was enormously welcome. The possibility of reclassifying a citizenry on the basis of physical qualities offered scientific confirmation of what many people assumed to be true. The criminal had a low and vulgar aspect; the lower classes were weaker and smaller physically than the upper classes; blacks and immigrants were racially, intellectually, and morally inferior to native whites; genius was a variety of mental disease just as epilepsy was a physical disease.

Like any science oriented toward solving social problems, this theory of anthropometric systems reflected the biases and interests of contemporary society. Many of the early leading figures, such as Galton and Lombroso, were not disinterested laboratory technicians; they were men of broad interest and commitment to the principles of biological and hereditarian determinism, and to particular social arrangements.

The development of anthropometrics appeared to provide a scientific explanation for the increased incidence in 1900 of divorce, crime, vagabondage, and social disorder. Those who developed this science of physical and mental measurements, unlike the enthusiasts of moral regeneration or the advocates of such programs as manual training, did not worry about the fall from a state of perfect labor and community. Their assessment was realistic, empirical, and, often, pessimistic, because the deterministic laws of human behavior that they invented seemed to suggest another, more pressing, problem—declining physical and mental national stock.

For some of these theorists, particularly Americans, the delineation of an exact science of physical types offered the possibility of a eugenics program that could improve the racial stock or, if not that, at least the probability that social control could become more effective. They spoke to a nation that was racked by racial fears and suspicions of immigrants. They embellished the theories of scientific racism that had begun to emerge in the United States after the Civil War.

The most important early works in anthropometrics were by Francis Galton. Galton's best known book derived from his work in statistical theory and evolution. Using the *British Dictionary of National Biography* he compiled figures on the incidence of success and hereditarian background in a work, *Hereditary Genius: An Inquiry into Its Laws and Consequences*, which he published in 1869. This and other works were widely discussed for the next thirty years in the United States, and became the bases for the American eugenics movement.

Galton's theory had two principal premises. He assumed that mental and moral characteristics were organically determined, and he believed that these factors were passed from generation to generation by means of physical inheritance. "I propose to show in this book," he announced, "that a man's natural abilities are derived by inheritance, under exactly the same limitations as are the form and physical features of the whole organic world." Just as one might breed fine horses for their qualities of speed or durability, he continued, "so it would be quite practicable to produce a highly gifted race of men by judicious marriages during several consecutive generations."[6]

By using the names in the *National Dictionary,* Galton automatically incorporated the biases of that work and the special selectivity of the British class system into his science, and perhaps this was his purpose. But he defended his work by dismissing, with a few exceptions, the possibility that culture, misfortune, or the social system could prevent the discovery and expression of talent. Quite naturally, he held high hopes for the science of eugenics and the positive selection of human characteristics.

British and American psychologists and sociologists closely examined the theory of Galton. Genius was, for them, a test case. Despite one modern tendency to identify outstanding mental capacity with neurosis, epilepsy, or degeneration, various lists of eminent men seemed to illustrate the laws of physical evolution and the inheritance of talent. Havelock Ellis's A Study of British Genius (published first in the United States in 1900 by Popular Science Monthly) was a work that updated Galton's ideas and assessed a large new English and American literature on inherited genius.

Ellis had done his own original work on classifications of race, class, regional origin, heritage, and intelligence. He found, like Galton, that genius, with the single exception of painters, derived from Anglo-Norman upper-class stock. The English psychologist could not resist the implications of his correlations. There was no reason to believe, he concluded, "that the education of the proletariat will lead to a new development of eminent men; so far as the data before us show, it has not exhibited any tendency to a higher yield of genius, and what production it is accountable for remains rural rather than urban."[7]

Inevitably, statistical evidence of this sort invited comparisons between physical appearance and genius. Galton himself was deeply interested in such possibilities, and published a work in 1892 on the results of his comparison between types of fingerprints and identifiable qualities of race and temperament. Unfortunately, he concluded, the system of classifying fingerprints developed in France by Bertillon was only useful in identifying individuals. There was no pattern to their appearance among geniuses or criminals. Fingerprint shapes were entirely random in the human species.[8]

Galton emphasized class and birth in his works on inheritance, but Cesare Lombroso developed the link between physical and mental qualities in another direction. Also basing his work on statistics, Lombroso sought to prove that genius, as well as insanity and criminality, had common and obvious physical markings. His theories were both popular and controversial in the United States, and widely discussed in penological and sociological literature.

Lombroso assumed that genius was a form of mental disorder or neurosis, a concept that the German Max Nordau had developed more extensively in his work Degeneration. He also suggested that there was such a thing as the criminal type and that this type represented a racial atavism. (Certain other forms of antisocial behavior, such as anarchism, also seemed to fit the pattern.) Thus abnormality in one form was genius; in another guise, it could result in crime, poverty, and mental degeneration.

The signs of abnormality were visible, he wrote. The protruding jaw signaled a criminal tendency; the small cranium indicated the possibility of potential political activism. Creative inspiration, on the other hand, resembled epileptic phenomena. As Lombroso concluded, if a study of the great morbid minds of history were made, "as well as the men who have passed through the glorious parabola of genius without demonstrable mental taint," both would be found "distinguishable by many traits from ordinary men."[9]

Other writers besides Lombroso made such points, but he and Galton were both widely remarked upon and discussed in America. Each represented a different tendency in the emerging science of physically determined mental and moral qualities. If American thinkers did not adopt such theories *in toto*, they were, nonetheless, intrigued with the potential usefulness of such ideas.

Of the American criminologists who followed most closely in the steps of Lombroso, Arthur MacDonald and August Drähms were probably the two most important. Drähms, the chaplain at San Quentin prison, published the results of his anthropometric studies on 2,000 prisoners in the first decade of the twentieth century. In an introduction to this book, Lombroso described the author as one who "thoroughly understands my ideas." But Drähms did not necessarily agree at every point with the Italian criminologist. The causes of crime, he wrote, did not suggest an airtight typology. Criminal behavior derived from individual—personal and physical—causes, external causes, and biological causes. Thus there were moral criminals as well as physical degenerates. Discovery of the general causes of crime could lead to the treatment that would rectify the particular criminal's disabilities.

Drähms referred to MacDonald as the most eminent criminological expert in this country. From his position with the United States Bureau of Education as specialist in the "Education of Abnormal and Weakling Classes," MacDonald agitated before Congress for the establishment of a laboratory to study "the Criminal, Pauper, and Defective Classes." Like many other American students of psychology in his era, he studied in Europe: medicine at the University of Berlin and psychology at Leipzig, after preparation at Harvard and Johns Hopkins. In 1901 he was elected honorary president of the Third International Congress of Criminal Anthropology.[10]

Although MacDonald generally agreed with Lombroso's theory of a physical-mental syndrome of traits that would betray the criminal, he tempered Lombroso's pessimism and determinism. Implicit in the Italian's notion of the criminal type was a physical determinism that was unacceptable. Because he believed in the possibility of a cure, MacDonald argued that the environment could be of some significance, either in strengthening or repressing physical tendencies toward wrongdoing. Therefore the highest social priority ought to be the scientific study and classification of criminals. Development of such an exact science would hasten the day when the nation compiled a record of every individual's strengths and weaknesses—fashioned after the Bertillon fingerprint file. This scientific data would be welcomed, he concluded, by all honest and worthy citizens who had "not the least fear of a law compelling an adequate record for the identity of all persons. If one be conscious of some weakness," he continued, "this part of his identity being known would have a good effect and might keep one from falling."[11]

When society undertook the study and classification of abnormality, MacDonald already had extensive results of his own research to contribute. Along with Lombroso, he believed that all human typologies should be considered on the same scale; genius was an exaggeration in one direction and criminality in another. As he put it, "Abnormal man may be abnormal in the right direction, as genius man, talented man or statesman; or in the wrong direction, as criminal, pauper, defective, or mattoid man."[12]

His study of criminals convinced him that antisocial persons could be identified by two tests. The first was physical appearance. Criminals generally had diminished skull size, a protruding jaw, or other such obvious deformities. They also exhibited mental characteristics that could be detected by physical tests. Among these were tendencies to blush, a high pain threshold (criminals were, supposedly insensitive to pain), interest or lack of interest in the Bible, and the use of slang instead of proper language. This latter trait linked criminals to primitive peoples, who also had the habit of "indicating the objects by one of their attributes."[13]

Because these traits of abnormality and criminality were obvious and measurable, MacDonald felt that moral sensibilities could be discovered by means of a lie detector test, using the plethysmograph to measure slight reactions. Even if the individual tried to disguise his feelings, even if he willed a temporary change in personality, science would trap him.[14] Here was an ostensibly objective and entirely external science of measurement that offered to treat social problems as physical abnormalities. The potential for social control and selection by institutions using such guides was immense, because nowhere in this new science were there the obstacles of individual regeneration— no revolution of the will was necessary. MacDonald's science offered the possibility of cure without reform, of behavior modification without moral regeneration.

Similar sorts of hypotheses about the physical nature of moral and social problems were pursued in America during the first two decades of the twentieth century. In developing scientific social selectivity and infallible standards for placing citizens in various economic positions (or, in extreme cases, in asylums), early physical and social anthropology promised to fill the vacuum left by the rapidly evaporating effectiveness of traditional individualism and the work ethic. The terms of such a science were naturally controversial, because they dealt with sensitive questions of race and intelligence. In such journals as *Popular Science Monthly* during these years, there were frequent debates over statistics concerning criminal skull sizes, eye colors, jaw formations, heights, and other characteristics, and their relationship to psychological and social development.[15]

When this new science of anthropometrics approached popular wisdom, its uses became explicitly and primarily the confirmation of social prejudice. One writer, J. Abbott Cantrell, announced in 1913 that it was possible to judge an individual's moral and social condition by his facial expressions. After extensive research, he concluded that social class was apparent in the physiognomy of every person. If the face was responsive, a high position was indicated. If not, the individual, no doubt, would be condemned to a lower social position. Intelligence, he concluded, was quite literally stamped upon the countenance.[16]

The mixture of science and popular prejudice was also important in the amateur science of personality assessment. One of the most important works in this field was Katherine Blackford's and Arthur Newcomb's *Analyzing Character*, which appeared in 1916. Blackford's purpose was to offer a new science of social placement and vocational selection. The great social cry of her age, she argued, was for a sure method of placing a person in the right position, "the problem of fitting the man to his work," as she put it.[17] Confronting the problem of industrial alienation, she admonished modern Americans to overcome their fear of machines. With her method of self-analysis (a form of classifying physiognomies and other physical traits) individuals might be able to discover what position in society they should occupy —where they belonged in the complex and confusing new social order.

The sorriest expression of continuity between physical and moral characteristics was scientific racism. Theoretically it might be possible to believe in a link between mental and moral qualities and physical traits and still not descend into racial stereotypes, but in the period under consideration, such restraint was practically impossible. The new science of anthropometric systems was generally linked with racial stereotypes or eugenic conclusions. Animated by the fear of rapid change and immigration, convinced that the census showed declining morality, and confused by the enormous pressures of success and mobility, many American psychologists and sociologists could not resist using the new science to proclaim the superiority of the Anglo-Saxon race and English culture.

Classification of human types by visible traits was not invented in the late nineteenth century, even if psychologists, anthropologists, and penologists believed that their sciences of selection were completely original. Nor was racism, as an intensely felt but abstract scientific generality, anything new in the United States. Early-nineteenth-century phrenology (the study of skull configurations and their link to mental and moral traits) suggested a popular and abiding belief in the link between visual and spiritual qualities.

Numerous studies and classifications of human species by type and visual distinction existed before the publication of Darwin's *Origin of Species* in 1859. But Darwinism gave enormous energy and respectability to such studies in the United States and Europe. During the Civil War, for example, the United States Sanitary Commission undertook the examination and classification of union soldiers by race, nationality, brain weight, and skull size, thus analyzing questions of race with the new science of statistics.[18]

In the period between the Civil War and the turn of the century, study and classification of racial types proliferated. John Fiske in the United States, Herbert Spencer in England, and Darwin himself classified certain physical stereotypes as inherent parts of racial heritage. The linking of evolution, racial distinction, heredity, and criminal syndromes quickly followed. Most observers refused to believe that criminals were a separate race; nonetheless, many believed that they exhibited physical and mental marks of a more primitive being that, unfortunately, lurked in the human heritage. Given this argument, the practice of sterilization of "degenerate" types, widely discussed in the United States and England at the turn of the century, seemed an inevitable and progressive step.

From another vantage point, linking physical and mental traits amounted to a profound attack on what remained of nineteenth-century individualism and the democracy of innate rationality. The description of physical traits that presumably overpowered individual desires or assertions implied a predominance of the physical over the mental that proved to be a demolishing argument, one that rationalists were hard pressed to answer. The rediscovery of Mendelian genetics at the end of the century provided eugenists and the proponents of anthropometric systems with another key argument—a missing scientific link, as it were—precisely at a time when their rationalist opponents were already on the defensive.

Indeed, so powerful was the materialist explanation of human behavior that the internal dispute among scientists over the mechanics of transferring physical and mental traits completely overshadowed the initial question of whether mental and moral traits could actually be identified by physical examination. The squabble between environmentalists and hereditarians over the details of perpetuating syndromes of behavior disguised the fact that the old rationalist argument, which postulated free will and the necessity of individual responsibility, had lost enormous ground. Whether formed by an inherited cast of characteristics or developed by the pull of the environment, the personality in the new vision had little resemblance to traditional American individualism and little relationship to the work ethic.

From the 1880s until 1920 the dispute over heredity versus environment in determining individual traits was confused and controversial. The complexities of this argument and its uncertainties resulted, in part, from the inconclusive experimentation in genetics during this period, and also from the rather simple-minded transfer of physical traits into the social and psychological realms. The disagreement between Darwinians and Neo-Lamarkians, between those who believed in the integral, unalterable unfolding of racial history, and those who suggested that acquired characteristics could be transmitted to the next generation, was translated to the heart of sociological theory.[19]

During the first decades of the twentieth century the nature-nurture controversy was complicated still further by the effects of professionalization in the sciences, anthropology, and psychology, and by the elaboration of the laws of genetic heredity discovered by Mendel. One result was an attack by sociologists and anthropologists upon the rigid hereditarian theories that lay behind scientific racism and eugenics. Books such as William Healy's *An Individual Delinquent,* published in 1915, did much to demolish the simpler anthropometric arguments.[20] Discovery of mutation and compound heredity, as well as the demonstration of environmental effects upon development, weakened the hold of hereditarian theory upon social-psychological sciences.

There were a number of observers who believed that the avenues to the inner personality were not necessarily physical or, more accurately, a matter of visual classifications. Such trait-tracing seemed to be primarily the province of criminologists, who used physical characteristics as a negative measure of selection. Moreover, the advocates of anthropometrics often proved, like MacDonald, to be more controversial than profound. In 1902, when MacDonald was fired from the Bureau of Education, the attempt to make anthropometry the official policy of the federal government suffered a permanent setback although racial stereotypes continued to influence immigration theory.

To many psychologists the results of measuring physical traits and matching them to spiritual qualities were inconclusive at best. While such critics rarely denied the physical origins of human behavior, they rejected visual evidence as simple-minded. Thus, Hugo Münsterberg wrote, the tests and classifications made by Lombroso, as well as the theory that such traits could be transmitted directly through heredity, were fascinating but not convincing. "It was," he wrote, "of the highest value to study the bodily and mental characteristics of the inmates of our prisons, to gather anthropological and sociological data of their misshapen ears or palates, of their tatooing and their slang, and finally to make psychological experiments as to their sensitiveness and their emotions. But no result justifies the claim that criminals are born as such." The only sure thing to be said, he concluded, was that criminals were recruited "especially from the mentally inferior."[21]

On this point, the psychologist was prepared to assume leadership of the quest for a surer science of behavior. With his lie detectors and associational and skill tests, he claimed to have the means to classify levels of mental development for the whole population. Society might use such information as it wished—to prevent access of abnormal individuals to a harmful environment or to place specific mental levels in certain vocations. In any case, this mental testing seemed a surer, less controversial form of selection, not encumbered by obvious race or class prejudice. It was a more scientific, more exact tool of measurement and placement, a science that acknowledged the predominance of mental traits in human development, but still had a materialist base. Mental testing did not halt the reduction of psychological factors to a physical, quantifiable basis; it shifted the ground of this process. Man was, admittedly, a determined creature; the secrets of his nature were, however, mental.

13

Discovering Virtue and Vice:
Mental Stigmata

The mental and intelligence testing movement was a profound
legacy of the pragmatic description of mind as a functional
tool. Whereas anthropometrics degenerated into racial prejudice and outlandish claims, mental testing developed a more acceptable definition of personality. Beginning with the assumption that
human intelligence was specifically related to the evolution of instincts
and psychic potential, this new mental science also employed statistics,
norms, and comparisons to develop means for selecting and choosing
between individuals. But it did so in a more positive sense, thereby
skirting the pessimism and overt determinism of anthropometrics.

William James's psychology had a particular and direct pertinance
to this movement. Several of his students, including Edward Thorndike, were instrumental in creating the psychological premises of mental behavioral psychology. More important, his psychology lent itself
to the new mental science. James's place in the history of modern
reductive psychologies such as behaviorism was as a founder. An
experimental psychologist, he opened one of the first—if not the first—
psychological laboratories in the United States. He encouraged his
students to develop theories of animal psychology; the results of such
studies helped lay the ground work for behaviorist psychologies. They
extended his argument that the subjective and objective aspects of
experience are entirely intertwined in the human consciousness. Cog-
nition or thought, he argued, was not abstract; it was an integral part
of stimulous and response. The implications of this principle were
enormous.

What philosophers had heretofore called "mind," he suggested, was
neither innate ideas inherited from God, nor a separate stuff of spirit.
Nor was consciousness, on the other hand, a mere sum of matter in
motion or the circulation of bodily juices. Rather, the intelligence

could be defined best according to its operation; reason, he proclaimed, was productive. Pursuit of purpose was the mark of thinking.

A further refinement of this view opened the behavioral door. James argued that mental states were either active or habitual, and that active thought, if it satisfied the aims of the individual, could become habitual. The process he described was one in which conscious activity passed into habitual, unconscious reaction. This, precisely, was the process assumed by the traditional work ethic, provided that the activity take place in a specific sort of physical and cultural environment. James, however, suggested that the physical environment could be extended; almost any learning situation could lead to the internalization of desired behavior. It was a short but enormously important step from this point to the assumptions of social engineering proposed by the new sciences of mental selection and placement.

In a Columbia doctoral dissertation written in 1901 under the supervision of James McKeen Cattell, anthropologist Clark Wissler recounted his extensive experimentation with correlations between physical traits and mental capacity. The results were clear and distressing for those who advocated anthropometric systematization and physical testing. There was no demonstrable tie, he concluded, between statistical norms in Galton's or Lombroso's physical measurements and mental ability. Physical evidences such as eye color, manual dexterity, sloping heads, brain sizes, and pain thresholds had only an arbitrary relationship, if any at all, to intelligence indicators such as rank in university class. Furthermore, no physical test for mental qualities such as reaction times had any use in testing intelligence. There was no link between physical appearance and mental ability.[1]

Wissler was not chagrined by the results of his work, nor did he revive idealist assumptions about the nature of human individuality. Instead, he was delighted to clear the route to what he felt would be a more accurate assessment of mental capacity. With simple-minded theories out of the way, it might be possible to develop a useful mental test for intelligence. Thus the materialist (or physical science) assumptions of the mental testing, plus the influence of Jamesian functionalism, kept the movement out of the rationalist camp. Leading American practitioners and theorists, such as Edward Thorndike and Lewis Terman, did not give up the beliefs that mental activity was physical in nature and origin and that skills could be measured in terms of quantity.

Another assumption operated in this science, as it did in most of the literature about the crisis of career and status at the end of the century: The inequalities or individual distinctions between persons should be the basis of differing social rank and economic reward. Thus psychologist Robert Yerkes reported in 1920 to the surgeon general of the American army that the purpose of the alpha beta intelligence examination of recruits for the selective service was to place them in positions they deserved to occupy, and where they might operate most efficiently.[2]

The mental testing movement represents an evolution of some of the assumptions of anthropometrics. It shared in common with that orientation and modern behavioral psychology a modern approach to individuality based upon a mechanical definition of human nature. It brought to the crisis of the work ethic a new science of character before which any effort to rejuvenate the inner strengths of the individual seemed spurious. Any effort to change the conditions of work seemed a mismanagement of resources.

The materialist description of mental capacity was, in general, also an attack upon romantic individualism. Although it represented only one phase of the movement away from idealism and rationalism, this philosophic position was crucial because it dealt directly and experimentally with the most profound psychological assumptions of romanticism. The materialist definition of consciousness and its description of mental process as being socially or genetically determined undercut the basis of traditional individualism.

The importance of this new persuasion to the crisis of the work ethic is obvious, for it reversed cause and effect. The new philosophy tended to locate the problem of alienation in the ethos of individualism; that is, in the belief that one individual was equal to another in the economic and social spheres. Social unrest occurred, not because the system did not operate properly, but because uncontrolled mobility conspired to place a person in the wrong vocation. A properly organized society in which each member was placed in the position of highest operating capacity would eliminate the causes of social unrest and reverse the rising curves of immorality.

Sociologist Luther Lee Bernard singled out "hedonistic individualists" like Dewey as the chief opponents to an effective social control. Their opposition, he wrote, "comes from the old subjectivistic, individualistic, and hedonistic dogma of *personal liberty* and the co-ordinate term *self-realization* which are mainly pleas for personal license in more attractive forms." Bernard was perceptive to divide contemporary social philosophy into two schools, one functionalist (including Durkheim, Spencer, and Lester Frank Ward) and one hedonist, in which he placed European socialists such as Fourier and Morris together with the American pragmatists. But Bernard was not interested in arguments over individualism as much as he was in sharpening the tools of social control.

In no small measure, his desire was answered by the appearance of new mental tests and behavioral definitions of personality. The day was imminent, he wrote, when social control—not immediate, total control, but the gradual application of discoveries—would be a reality. "When a social fact is established," he declared, "it should become as obligatory as the laws of astronomy or physics."[3]

The modern positivist philosopher Frederic Harrison juxtaposed the ideal of a scientifically run society to one immersed in traditional individualism. Positivism, he noted, "eliminates individual activity altogether, proving that an individual is an abstraction. There is no such thing in reality. A dangerous and criminal lunatic is the nearest approach in Europe to an individual (and of course his whole life is dependent on society and he is only an individual subjectively)."[4]

But even the asylum could try to regulate individual caprice. As Professor C. E. Seashore wrote for the *Popular Science Monthly,* "Adjustment transforms an institution of detention into a house of happiness and usefulness, and, instead of being expensive, it makes the institution more nearly self-supporting, for every individual is assigned to the place of his greatest efficiency." This miracle of order could be accomplished, he argued, by applying the Binet test for mental age to the inmates. This new "mental economy" was akin to the scientific management of a modern corporation: "The principle is the same, and the one measure is as tangible as the other."[5]

In such places objective mental measurements and selecting devices were intended to supplant the old moral psychology. A good index to the extent of this transformation may be seen in the decline in "mental science" traditionally taught in American schools. Mental science as a subject disappeared almost entirely from the curriculum by 1900. Historian of American textbooks Charles Carpenter has written of this phenomenon, "Under its present status it has passed entirely beyond the reach of common school students."[6] The reason for the sudden "difficulty" of mental science is not hard to imagine. Mental science was, at the turn of the century, transformed from moral exhortation based upon a faculty psychology to a teaching tool, an instructor's aid in manipulating and testing the educational environment. In the shift from individual to environmental emphasis, the student was no longer the subject—he was now the object of psychology.

The social and institutional context surrounding the development of the science of mental behavior helped determine its direction. Theories promising selection, adjustment, and management, devised by such figures as Elton Mayo of Harvard Business School, found immediate use by clients such as the Western Electric Company of Chicago.[7] This working relationship between theory and practice was also characteristic of the schools. The result was a close dependence of experimentation upon the specific practical problems of industrial and educational institutions.

Thorstein Veblen emphasized this in his examination of higher learning in America: "The habits of thought induced by workday life impose themselves as ruling principles that govern the question of knowledge; it will therefore be the habits of thought enforced by the current technological scheme that will have most (or most immediately) to say in the current systematization of facts."[8] Veblen also noticed that the university as a whole absorbed the ethics and priorities of modern industry. The major American contributions to mental testing were made in these corporations of higher learning (as Veblen called them).

Mental testing, like all of modern psychology, had an international parentage. Much of the early work was done in Germany, England, and, particularly, France and the United States. The developers of mental testing were found generally in universities or as psychologists attached to mental asylums. In France Alfred Binet, who perfected the mental achievement test, worked at Salpetrière Mental Institution in Paris. Similarly Henry Goddard of Vineland New Jersey Institute did early practical testing in the United States. The psychological laboratory was also an important location for developing mental tests. By the First World War laboratory work and functional psychology, and mental testing in particular, had become practically synonymous.

The most original and important early expert in mental testing (as well as in anthropometrics) was Francis Galton. His work contained two assumptions that were developed in mental testing. The first emphasized statistics and the possibility that comparing large samples could create a definition of "normal." The second was that reactions associated with vision and speech could reveal mental ability. Begun by Galton, motor testing was developed particularly in Germany, where many American students of psychology received their professional training in the nineteenth century.

Probably the most influential of the experimental German psychologists was Wilhelm Wundt; his psychological laboratory acquired international fame. Wundt's influence in sensory testing was profound, but he lacked interest in the social or clinical application of his results. Some of his students, however (James McKeen Cattell, who made the psychological laboratory at Columbia University into a center of mental testing in the United States, for example), attempted to use Wundt's subtle measurements to develop intelligence tests. Cattell developed a series of tests in 1890 based upon sensory reaction time and a primitive measure of conceptualization. The psychologist examined eyesight, hearing, reaction time, sensitivity to pain, color preference, and physical features. But he also recorded artistic tastes, dreams, preferences in games, and future plans.[9]

Other scientists, including Hugo Münsterberg and Franz Boas, developed variations of such tests almost simultaneously. In 1893 Joseph Jastrow organized a demonstration of sensory mental testing for the Columbian Exposition in Chicago. By 1896 both the American Psychological Association and the American Association for the Advancement of Science had set up special committees to sift the results of psychological testing.[10]

But while Cattell and his students—Boas, Wissler, and Thorndike (who also studied with James)—had established the importance of the gathering of data and the measurement of individual deviations from an established behavioral norm, there was growing doubt, by 1900, even at Columbia, about mental tests that relied exclusively on the measure of sensory skills.

In France Alfred Binet, who considered the results of American and German sensory testing to be inadequate, redirected mental examination toward differences in the higher mental abilities. In 1904 Binet was given the task of developing a means to segregate "children in the public schools for more effective pedagogical purposes."[11] Binet began where Galton had, in establishing a norm of intelligence against which to measure the individual. But Binet made the mental skills of an age group his norm, thus stressing the idea of intellectual development. To measure this he tested attention, comprehension, aesthetic appreciation, will, and other mental qualities. While sensory discrimination was important in such examinations, the major emphasis was upon efficiency of conceptual, mathematical, and literary skills.

At first the Binet tests were scarcely noticed in the United States, perhaps because in France they were employed primarily to distinguish types and categories of mental retardation. Their early adoption in America was also associated with the examination of the feebleminded. After Goddard published the results of his use of the Binet scale in evaluating the intelligence of Vineland school students, much more serious attention was paid to this new testing form. In 1909, for example, a committee of the National Education Association drew up a report on tests of "exceptional and mentally deficient children," based, in part, upon Goddard's work. By 1915 Lewis Terman, G. Stanley Hall's student, had transformed the Binet scale into what he called the Stanford test for the intelligence quotient.[12] In so doing he changed the emphasis and use of the Binet tests, employing them as general tools for social and educational selection.

Reinforcing the popularity of mental measurement in the United

States were convincing new materialist descriptions of the human personality. Edward L. Thorndike, who, like Terman, was an important innovator in practical mental testing during the second decade of the twentieth century, built his theories on the groundwork laid by James. Thorndike provided a crucial step in the materialist reduction of mind to mechanical functions by comparing animal and human intelligence.

Binet had demonstrated that feeble-minded and genius were different points of deviation on the scale of normality. Thorndike likewise argued that animal and human intelligence represented different poles of complexity on the same scale. When Thorndike went to Harvard, James was still teaching psychology and running the psychological laboratory, and he, no doubt, gained from James's last active years in the laboratory a taste for laboratory work and some guidance toward his later study of animals. But when James gave up experimental work Thorndike went on to Columbia, where he finished his thesis on animal intelligence under the supervision of Cattell.

Thorndike embroidered upon James's functionalism, which defined the mind by the tasks it accomplished and the operations it performed. But he altered James's proposition that mind was activity by arguing that mind should be seen as behavior. This subtle shift in terminology represented a profound redirection in psychology. Thorndike added to this a more genetic orientation and a strong dash of evolutionism. This enabled him to make two theoretical advances toward a purely materialist definition of mind. He assumed that all mental processes, since they were grounded in quantitative physical factors, were consequently either simple or complex, without true qualitative differences. He argued that the place of each species and individual on the simplicity-complexity scale was, secondly, determined by evolution and perpetuated by genetic heritage.

These conclusions were very similar to those put forth by the anthropometrists, but Thorndike's attitude toward identifying mental traits put him squarely in the camp of Binet and Terman. He merged the selective purposes of the older testing school with sophisticated mental measurements devised by conceptualists such as Binet. To demystify the notion of human intelligence, he redefined it as behavior appropriate to the situation.

Unlike James, Thorndike believed that the closer one pursued the "psycho-genesis" of mental attributes, the more clearly one could see how mental processes operated. In other words, mental processes could be divided into smaller components and investigated. On the basis of this analytic approach, Thorndike wrote several seminal articles for the *Popular Science Monthly* in 1901. In "The Intelligence of

Monkeys," he concluded that monkeys—and animals in general—were unable to learn by imitation. The example of other creatures had little effect upon them. Instead, the monkey learned because of the interaction of impulse and environment; that is, he learned because a particular response of his was appropriate to a given situation. Man's closest evolutionary relation could learn, but he could not think in any accepted meaning of that term. What might appear to the layman as imitation or thought was actually, he argued, the result of stimulous and response. The actions of young children illustrated, Thorndike suggested, that the monkey might be considered the prototype of human behavior.[13]

In a more general article, "The Evolution of Human Intelligence," Thorndike extended the startling conclusions of his animal experiments. The difference between intelligence in humans and animals, he wrote, was a question of minor variation. Human intelligence was generically the same as animal intelligence, although it was certainly more complex. But even the most complex processes of reason and self-consciousness, he suspected, were only secondary effects that had emerged in the course of biological differentiation.

"Amongst the minds of animals," he wrote, "that of man leads, not as a demigod from another planet, but as a king from the same race."[14] Animals and man behaved—that is, thought—in much the same way. Acquired behavior, or learning, amounted in both cases to the selection of an appropriate response in a given situation. Man and the animals were alike enough to justify transferring the results of laboratory study of animals to human psychology.

Another continuity between animals and man that Thorndike discovered was a historical-biological one. Evolution was both ancient and modern. It had occurred in a historical sense, and it was reproduced in each individual. Each person advanced through the stages of infancy (animal intelligence) to adulthood (human intelligence). "If we could prove," he wrote, "that what we call ideational life and reasoning were not new and unexplainable species of intellectual life but only the natural consequences of an increase in the number, delicacy and complexity of associations of the general animal sort, we should have made out an evolution of mind comparable to the evolution of living forms."[15] This is precisely what Thorndike felt he had done.

Thorndike's position was an extreme version of the functionalist idea. Whereas James's description of the mind in terms of action and activity raised dilemmas over which he puzzled for many years, Thorndike almost immediately accepted a reductionist definition of mental activity. For him, consciousness and reason were secondary effects to impulse. For those who went beyond Thorndike, any traditional description of thinking could be dismissed as what behaviorists called "verbal behavior."

In his *The Psychology of Learning* (which was dedicated to James), Thorndike expanded his conclusions, promulgating what he called the "law of exercise." Simply put, this law defined learning as a process of repetition. Biological in nature, complex, and constantly evolving, human intelligence seen this way could be measured in quantifiable terms. The most creative thought might thus be defined as efficient behavior in a given situation. Variations in intelligences were, therefore, relatively minor and difficult to distinguish, except in scientific terms.

Thorndike felt it was now possible to understand extremes of intelligences in terms of the same scientific norm. Traditionally, he noted, "we shift our basis of judgment as the limit is approached and misinterpret moderate intrinsic differences as very great ones because they occur seldom, become famous, and are given large financial rewards."[16] Properly understood, such deviations as genius were only slight variations in a scale of human response.

In practice, Thorndike's materialism was a telling argument against the old enemies of modern pedagogy, traditional faculty psychology, and mental discipline. Thus he joined the progressive educators' campaign for an educational revolution. Where older methods of instruction sought to stimulate mental functions in hopes of developing an abstract discipline that could be applied to different situations, Thorndike defined learning as precisely the opposite. Acquisition of skills in a specific situation, he wrote, made learning possible in a related field only if a similarity between the two could be demonstrated. Thus education, like psychology, must proceed from the simple and measurable to the complex and less familiar.

This psychology was enormously appealing in an age when traditional forms of selection and social control seemed indecisive or useless. In 1912, as the result of his work, Thorndike developed an interest test that was somewhat like an earlier handwriting scale he had invented to measure abilities. This test for interests, like the Binet-Stanford test, was designed to aid the field of practice with respect to early diagnosis, vocational guidance, and other work in directing young people toward appropriate economic pursuits.

With the dream of a conservative, hierarchical society (which he shared with traditionalists), Thorndike reversed the means for attaining this utopia. Work, moral imperative, and individual regeneration belonged, with faculty psychology, to the history of human thought. These ideas could not alter society. Instead of relying upon moral exhortation and individual decisions, he advised society to make the social survey and the expert the means of effecting change. In this vein, Thorndike called for a "national mental census of children." By classifying the youthful population, it would be possible to determine who should continue toward higher studies and who might benefit society in other occupations.[17]

Basic to this proposal for a mental census was an abstract definition of human individuality characterized as talent and productivity. Psychologists such as Thorndike rarely had only such narrow purposes in mind, however, and there is little justice in calling them the servants of industrial capitalism. Nonetheless, the general drift of their approach was to answer problems unique to the new industrial society. To treat child psychology as a stage in evolution from animal behavior to human intelligence was not merely a suggestion to improve the approach to infant study. It had immediate applications in the world that industrialism had created. Whatever the purposes of the new psychology, the functionalist assumptions about human personality made their way quickly to the heart of contemporary social and psychological thinking, and the efforts of a few thinkers like Dewey, Veblen, and James to raise questions about alienation, for example, were either overlooked, or their insights were distorted and used in industrial and educational management.

The new functional mental science was, above all, a social psychology that concentrated upon typologies, not individuals. For all the discussion of individual variations in talent and interest, the purpose of understanding distinctions between individuals was to place each in an appropriate social position. The new individualism rested, therefore, upon the proposition that a person should develop to the highest point of his efficiency, whatever else his consciousness, moral position, or ambition might incline him to do.

An example of the desire to fit mental processes to the categories and language of mechanics—the reduction of thinking to efficient behavior—was the investigation into what was called mental fatigue. Once again Francis Galton was an innovator in what became an important later aspect of modern psychology. His investigations into overwork among school children became widely known at the turn of the century. The effects of repetitious mental labor were subsequently examined by James, MacDonald, Thorndike, and a number of other modern psychologists.

The results of these investigations further discredited mental faculty psychology. But more significantly, psychologists probably became interested in investigating this problem because, after 1880, repetitive physical and mental labor were becoming much more familiar, indeed, characteristic, of modern labor. It was important to know if repetition increased or decreased efficiency. This was the purpose of Thorndike's article "The Influence of Improvement in One Mental Function upon the Efficiency of Other Functions." The psychologist felt that he had conclusive evidence that mental ability was not transferable from one type of activity to another. Related work by Thorndike, Elton Mayo, and others centered on fatigue in modern industry, the reveries of workers, and methods of lessening boredom in modern labor.[18]

Functional psychology and mental testing thus breached the gap opened by the proponents of anthropometrics. The new psychology reduced mental states, reason, effort, and consciousness, not to a syndrome of physical traits, but to a subtle code of mental symbols that could be measured and quantified. The new science borrowed the metaphors of mechanics and the laws of motion and energy to describe human intelligence. Laboratory proof of a material basis for mental process was added through observing animal behavior. Using the new system of mental categorization, practical social psychologists such as Edward Thorndike and Lewis Terman developed a productive definition of individuality. Before this the traditional work ethic had defined the individual in terms of productive labor. But by 1900 the marketplace had changed, and the mode of labor to which most psychologists attended was industrial. Ability to adjust to this system represented the ideal; therefore, any measure of that ability was highly desirable.

In 1893 W. Townsend Porter, writing for the American Statistical Association, called for a standard scale of mental and physical growth against which to measure the development of school children. "The skillful breeder of cattle," he wrote, "depends on systematic weighing to inform him whether his efforts to secure well-developed animals are meeting with success, but children are left to grow at haphazard."[19] Twenty years later Lewis Terman perfected such a scale and showed how it might be applied in a program of conscious social planning. On the basis of this accomplishment he became one of the leading figures in the American mental testing movement.

Although Terman worked with Binet's methods as early as 1911, he did not publish his revised scale in 1916. Prior to his work with Binet's results, Terman had formulated his own basic approach to mental testing, which tells a good deal about his general purposes. In an article, "Genius and Stupidity: A Study of Some of the Intellectual Processes of Seven 'Bright' and Seven 'Stupid' Boys," published in 1903, he rejected the results of anthropometrics.[20] Physical characteristics did not, he wrote, indicate a child's potential for achievement in school. On the other hand, he argued, conceptual skills, linguistic abilities, and mathematical understanding generally proved to be good indicators of intellectual capacity. By measuring these skills, psychology might aid in the identification and education of future leaders. He wrote in an article one year later that mental capacity generally coincided with social class: "The pupils who were leaders in the tests are larger, better dressed, of more prominent parentage, better looking, greater readers, and less selfish than the automatons."[21] Terman's social conservatism, embellished by technological language, helped make a convincing case for the practicality of his mental testing program, for it discovered results that coincided with popular prejudice.

When he employed the revised Binet scale, Terman assumed he was on even surer ground. The results of tests seemed to confirm hereditary determinism. He wrote in 1919 that any layman or teacher would be surprised that a simple ten-minute vocabulary test could have any decisive meaning, but it was true. "One might very well suppose that the child's vocabulary would depend upon home environment and formal instruction, that it would be an index of special rather than general ability, and that anyway it could not be accurately enough measured by a list of 100 words selected at random from the dictionary. As we have shown elsewhere, all of these theoretical objections are contradicted by the facts."[22] Environment counted, he wrote, for almost nothing in the formation of intelligence. The revised Binet scale could, therefore, accurately measure the internal, permanent, and inherited capacity of an individual. It was with such certainty that Terman suggested several practical steps. Using tests, school children could be safely streamed into professional or vocational courses. Criminals and delinquents could be identified, potential leaders might be chosen, and specific vocational intelligence quotients established.

Terman had an opportunity to demonstrate all of these promises when he and a corps of psychologists, including Thorndike and Robert Yerkes, undertook the testing of recruits in the American army during the First World War. The famous alpha, beta tests, devised by Terman and others, set a standard scale for examining literate and nonliterate draftees. To find the standard norm, preliminary tests were given to inmates in reformatories, prisons, and asylums. The results of these first tests, as Robert Yerkes wrote, revealed some significant tendencies in the mental constitution of the American population. There was, for example, a high correlation between intelligence and education. Those with middle-class jobs in civilian life tended to make higher scores. Furthermore, when applied to recruits, Terman and Yerkes found that high military rank generally coincided with superior scores on the examination. And, finally, the scores of American blacks and foreign-born immigrants were generally lower than those of native, white Americans.[23]

The functional psychology begun by James in the 1890s was taken one final step before the First World War, in the behavioral movement led by John Watson of the Johns Hopkins University. Watson built upon the animal comparison studies of Thorndike, combining them with ideas he gleaned from the works of Ivan Pavlov. Unlike Thorndike, however, Watson discarded hereditarianism, and wrote of intellectual development almost entirely in terms of environment. For the Hopkins psychologist, human psychology was a matter of behavior. Consciousness and reason were verbal equivalents of physical activity. The mind was, he concluded, entirely synonymous with the physical and organic functions of the brain.

The reflex arc, or the theory of stimulous and response that Thorndike had developed and used in his definition of mind, was transformed by Watson into a complex description of how the environment increased the probability of a specific response from a given organism. Concepts of consciousness, will, and spirit were consigned by Watson to the history of philosophy and to philology. Psychologists had need to concern themselves only with the process whereby behavior was solicited from the individual. As Watson put it, the reflexes or reactions of all organisms were the building blocks of behavior. All habits, learned or instinctual, could be reduced to the simple reflex. All behavior, he continued, was either habit or habit in the making, and, therefore, was also based upon the reflex. Like Thorndike, Watson believed that objective study of human and animal psychology would reveal a close relationship between the "thinking" of all species.[24] For whatever species, "thought" could be described only in the passive voice.

The fruits of Jamesian functionalism thus grew upon two branches of laboratory psychology, one predominantly hereditarian, and the other, environmental. Whatever the remarkable differences between them, however, there were several common characteristics. Both stressed material causes for mental phenomenon. Traditional assumptions about the consciousness shrank until words like "will" disappeared from technical descriptions of behavior. With this evolution the psychological justification of traditional individualism evaporated.

Further doubts about the validity of traditional individualism came from the early proponents of mass psychology. Gustave LeBon's work *The Crowd: A Study of the Popular Mind* was just that. Published in 1895 this book, together with such works as Georg Simmel's *Soziologie* (which appeared in 1906), received wide attention from American scholars.[25]

LeBon's work proposed a simple but devastating equation that challenged the foundations of democratic thought. The crowd or mass, as he wrote, was not the sum of its parts; rather, it represented a different social unit governed by distinct behavioral laws. The modern period, he continued, was characterized by the increased prominence of crowds, and, hence, by unfamiliar forms of behavior. Individual psychology was of little use in considering these crowd actions, for mass activity was determined by unconscious influence. "The substitution of the unconscious action of crowds," he wrote, "for the conscious activity of individuals is one of the principle characteristics of the present age."[26] This meant, he noted, that there was a special mental unit called "crowd" whose behavior was guided by identifiable, non-rational desires. A crowd acted as a unit because it was guided by the images and symbols of those desires. Its activities, through ritual, released primitive instincts.

LeBon's theory was an impressive contribution to the general development of a psychology of behavior stressing unconscious or irrational causes. As an attack upon individualism and traditional definitions of consciousness, it demonstrated a fundamental weakness of accepted theories, which presumed that citizens acted according to rational principles. LeBon summarized the intellectual climate of his day thus: "At the present day, the great fundamental ideas which were a mainstay of our fathers are tottering more and more. They have lost all solidity, and at the same time the institutions resting upon them are severely shaken."[27]

The theory of crowd behavior, like functional psychology in its practical applications, dismissed human consciousness in favor of a theory of behavior that only the expert or the observer could understand. Individual reformation (once the mainstay of rationalist social theory) looked, in this glaring new light, suspiciously like irrationality and religious enthusiasm, or a romantic return to primitive, instinctive behavior.

In developing the various materialist or functional generalizations of modern practical psychology, men such as Terman, Yerkes, Thorndike, Watson, and LeBon pursued the same goals as those who sought to revive the traditional work ethic: the restoration of social order and control. But the new psychology accepted and built upon the alienation others feared, turning the separation of the individual's traditional concept of himself from a problem to an advantage. The failure of inner control was the measure of need for outside social control, and the new psychology provided access to individual behavior. In this fashion the crisis of modern work might be ended, if only the new psychology and sociology could be applied with diligence and skill.

14

William James
and the Crisis of Work

The various participants in efforts to revive the traditional
work psychology and the new advocates of social control
acknowledged that America had reached a turning point in its
social, economic, and cultural development. But they rarely understood the deeper meanings of this change, nor did they articulate, in
general terms, the implications of their own theories. Few were interested in asking questions about the ultimate nature of society or human existence; few examined the philosophic implications of their
ideas. The most notable exception to this was William James, who
armed both camps with insights in the intellectual struggle, and who,
ultimately, laid siege to both.

James, whose insights helped launch functional psychology, found
the results of this broad movement unacceptable. The scientific philosophy that emerged was, as he described it, a denial of individuality,
variety, and pluralism. On the other hand, James was particularly
sympathetic to the cultural aims of the traditional work society—he
cherished individualism—but was severe in rejecting the philosophic
grounds of traditionalism.

This dual role of participant-critic, of disapproving father of modern experimental psychology and son who was rebellious against tradition, led James to the philosophic center of the crisis of work. From
this perspective he demonstrated the depths of social and cultural
change that beset his age. Committed to science and experimentation
as well as to traditional individualism, he managed an uneasy philosophic synthesis, which showed, if nothing else, that the society of his
day could not sustain its older ideas unless it discarded the culture of
science.

James lived these two lives: scientist and experimental psychologist,
and sufferer from the problems of work and career. Because of this

180

his biography is of enormous intellectual importance, but it is also a study in the crisis of the calling. In James the traditional, work oriented, secular Protestant ethic clashed repeatedly with the behavioral commitments of modern social science. The result was a brilliant critique of the philosophic ideas of the day that had disjointed his life.

That which was only suggested and implied in the practical discussions of work and personality became, for James, the plummet of ethics and metaphysics. In his life and thought, elements of the crisis of work and individualism are everywhere apparent. But, unlike more practically oriented psychologists, economists, or social theorists, James responded to such influences as if they were all parts of the larger puzzle of human perception and existence. This added dimension was almost uniquely his, for few other American thinkers felt this crisis so personally or were willing to examine its philosophic ramifications with such persistence. James, like a mirror of his age, reflected images of conflict, doubt, and reevaluation. The profounder element of his thought went to the heart of the intellectual revolution that stirred America at the turn of the century. The resulting philosophical literature posed the problem of individualism in the context of modern industrialism with a clarity and depth unexcelled in his age. His answers to these problems flashed back over tradition, reflected upon new theories, and highlighted the nature of the whole dilemma.

In his search for a calling James shared the severest vocational anguish of his age. Striken by what he diagnosed as neurasthenia, he sought spiritual relief by medically accepted means as well as through sessions with a mind curist. When he did settle upon a profession (that of professor), he continued to despair the reduction of its status and the compromises that the university made to the demands of practicality. For James the question of genius was emblematic of deeper problems. He did not agree that high intelligence and creativity were neurotic or attached to brain lesions or epilepsy, as some psychologists had written. Nor, he said, was it due to a more fortunate wrinkle in brain cells.

James, like his acquaintance Brook Adams, was sympathetic to the need to express fundamental and even violent human instincts. In his *Moral Equivalent of War* he demonstrated the degree to which the issue of physical regeneration; sport, vitality, and self-help held sway in his mind. His reflex was to disparage the clinical utopias of the single taxers and other reformers of his day, who, he felt, had lost sight of the most vital ingredients of the human psyche. Like that most feared symbol of his day, the vagabond, James was an intellectual wanderer—restless, dissatisfied, and easily exasperated by routine and the orderly minds of American university administrators.

Genius and vagabond, James was thus a symbol of the crisis of calling, for he was the sort of person whose very existence was being challenged by the transformation of the priorities of American society.
James's relation to the crisis of individualism was far more than that
of an interested spectator. He was also a cause, for his psychological
laboratory at Harvard and his seminal work *Principles of Psychology*
had a profound impact upon the development of functional psychology
in America. James's philosophic orientation shook the premises of
idealist philosophy and British empiricism, which, in America, had
been the major pillars of traditional concepts of individuality. In
developing his variety of pragmatism, James let loose a functional definition of intelligence that the developers of behaviorism were quick
to change into an attack on the concept of mind itself.

Nonetheless James's position was not the same as that of the mater-
ialists who claimed his heritage, for he wedded his pragmatic method
to an abiding search for religious significance. He did not hesitate to
explore the mystical and secret realms of human experience. Thus
James helped to weaken traditional philosophic individualism at the
same time that he attempted to reconstruct it upon the base of a
firmer, modern psychology. His method focused upon the tender spot
of all philosophies of individualism, the function of human will. Here
he located the creative energy that was the basis of all meaningful
human assertion.

For no other American philosopher have the problems of the self
and its independence so completely captured the field of philosophic
play. Few others allowed such an explicit intrusion of biography into
philosophic thought. For James impersonality and abstraction were
the symbols of lifelessness. Thus the essence of his thought was its
clamor for a life worth living, based upon the rude assertion that the
self could will values into existence. But, at the same time, there was
a deep and melancholic James, a James whose very acts of assertion
were retreats from suicidal depression.

James was also a traditional philosopher. Throughout his later years,
in retirement from Harvard, he often spoke of synthesizing his views
into a major philosophic work, free, as he insisted it must be, from
the literary style that had accounted for the popular success of his
books and lectures, and also for their philosophic inconclusiveness.
Although he did leave the sketch of such a manuscript at his death
(subsequently published as *Some Problems of Philosophy*), many of
his technical philosophic insights were left hanging in essays and
letters.

James's failure to produce such a work was not entirely accidental
or temperamental. His ethical bias directed him toward a field of

experience that could best be related by metaphor. Because part of his philosophic position came to rest upon the quicksand of mysticism and psychic phenomenon, he had few real followers aside from those who elaborated upon one or another of the technical elements of his psychology or metaphysics. Such a mixed system of science and mysticism, investigation and faith, could only be sustained because James confronted head-on the contradictory philosophic impulses that stemmed from the intellectual crisis of his day, and because he felt them personally.

As it was for his brother Henry, language, to William, was the painter's brush he used to color the shapes and shades of his thought. At crucial turning points in his work he called upon memorable metaphors to carry the weight of his argument. Such terms as the "cash value of ideas," the "will to believe," and the "sticky edges" (of concepts) mark his prose. They make his work enticing and, yet, confusing, for, as his critics were well aware, such notions could not be translated into academic philosophy.

This refusal to play the game of reduction was a reflection of James's desire to turn brittle concepts and equations into the poetry of individualism. He wished to flesh out philosophy into a pluralism that would sustain his free-ranging spirit. As he wrote for the Oxford Gifford Lectures, "Religion is the very inner citadel of human life, and the pretension to translate adequately into spread-out conceptual terms a kind of experience in which intellect, feeling and will, all our consciousness and all our subconsciousness together melt in a kind of chemical fusion, would be particularly abhorrent."[1]

James's family vociferously clung to the twin ideals of practicality and spiritualism. The peripatetic education, the unremitting philosophic and ethical quest of Henry James, Sr., the brilliance of siblings Alice and Henry and of acquaintances like Emerson, made the James family flash with ideas. This atmosphere induced in its members an exquisite moral and aesthetic sensibility, and, also, a tendency toward morbidity and desperation. Four of the Jameses—Henry, Sr., Alice, William, and Henry, Jr.—were writers whose works moved about the same philosophic and aesthetic problems, like shadows playing about an open hearth.

The source of that family fire and William's inspiration for what he called "warm ideas" was, of course, Henry, Sr. The elder James wavered between intellectual inquiry and fits of depression and doubt. He was born into a wealthy New York family, rich also in intellectual ties. At the age of thirteen, Henry suffered an agonizing accident that cost him a leg. After a slow convalescence he regained physical health and spirits, but his later life was marred by depression. With an income sufficient to make business unnecessary, James turned to intellectual matters, which he made into his life's work. A writer, a prophet, a seer, and a romantic, his published works puzzled rather than influenced his contemporaries.

The James family became both a miniature educational utopia and philosophic community, the perfect society of intellectual labor. The stern but kindly guidance of Henry, Sr., indelibly marked each child, and, if each did not reproduce his particular philosophic orientation, nonetheless, the question of calling and the sense of personal inadequacy before the ideals of the father sometimes surfaced in William, Henry, Jr., and Alice. This search for the ideal profession was something of a *Pilgrim's Progress*, for, as Henry James, Jr., wrote, the question of career was, in the family, also a question of character.[2]

The general orientation of William James's philosophy shows repeated traces of his father's mind. As Henry, Jr., wrote of the family. "Variety, variety—that sweet ideal, *that* straight contradiction of any dialectic, hummed for me all the while as a direct, if perverse concentration, with some of its consequent, though heedless, dissociations."[3]

Something of the manner in which these ideals may have been transmitted is suggested in an unfinished dialogue, "On Creation, between a Father and Son," written by Henry, Sr. The structure of the dialogue is Socratic, with the father turning the half-thought responses of the son into long philosophic disquisitions. While the father expounds, the son replies, "I dimly perceive that I have been in error."[4]

If such a relationship was, to the father's mind, the ideal, it was not for William. He accepted the family intellectual heritage, but he invested it in his own fashion. The elder James was, like his friend Emerson, intrigued by the reform ideas of Fourier, whose combination of community and variety, self-expression and self-denial, fit the paradoxical bent of his mind as well as the social and political dreams of a nascent industrial society. James's and Fourier's tolerance for all types of personalities and experiences echoed in William's pluralistic philosophy.

Henry, Sr., was, more than his son, a religious seeker. For him, religious experience and individualism were interwined into a complex philosophy for which he found confirmation in the works of the Swedish philosopher Swedenborg. In Swedenborg Henry, Sr., detected the articulation of some of his profoundest feelings. Following a severe depression, which he experienced in 1844, he had what Swedenborg called a "vastation," or the feeling of a collapse prefiguring a later integration of the personality.

The elder James introduced his family to several of Swedenborg's principle ideas. One was the philosopher's claims to clairvoyant and mystical experience. Another was his stress (common also in American puritanism) upon the meanings of human freedom and choice. For Swedenborg freedom was the precondition of individuality; it entitled a person to choose love and eternal life. A further influence was methodological. To Swedenborg happiness meant service to others: individualism meant the unfolding of talent and genius. Or, as he expressed it, "All man's knowing, and all his understanding and being wise, and therefore all his willing, ought to have use for their end."[5] While this is certainly not identical with William James's pragmatic dictum, it prefigured the application of the pragmatic method to ethical behavior for which the younger James is justly known.

Henry James, Sr., employed the Swedenborgian definition of freedom and individuality in his notion of socialism or "the redeemed form of man." In a paper entitled "The European and American Order of Manhood," the elder James contrasted two forms of individuality: the prevailing legal individualism of England to the inner, spiritual, self-regulated and spontaneously good individualism of America. This distinction between external and internal, legal and ethical, reflected a separation between freedom of the flesh and that of the spirit. As he put it, individualism meant the fulfillment of the calling: "What our rulers officially avouch on their side is, that every man alike in whose brain or hand any productive or administrative skill resides, is divinely entitled to aspire to the lead of human society, and to reap its highest honors."[6] Unencumbered by institutions, the American, unlike the Englishman, stood before God alone, to be judged by what he made of himself and by what choices he followed. In its purist, clearest form, the work ethic was the ethic of the elder James.

Henry James, Sr., was also deeply suspicious of religious dogma and social systematization, as well as of the claims of scientific absolutism. He was sympathetic to obscure and unpopular ideas of his age (for example, the possible validity of extrasensory experience). This extravagant tolerance blossomed in the literary energy and openness that marked his works with a confusing but elegant metaphoric style, which was highly unsuited to the tasks of technical philosophy.[7]

William James also inherited his family's melancholic disposition. In 1893 in a letter to F. W. H. Myers, a fellow philosopher and investigator of psychic phenomenon, he spoke of his recent low spirits: "My state of mind is also revolutionized since that time. I had a pretty bad spell, and know now a new kind of melancholy. It is barely possible that the recovery may be due to a mind-curer with whom I tried eighteen sittings." Myers had, perhaps, elicited this comment by a remark that went straight to the problem: "Your mental and physical disorganization is never by any chance perceptible to *anyone* but yourself."[8]

Experiences of depression and temporary cure alternated throughout

James's life. Like his father, brother Henry, and sister Alice, he pursued self-analysis through long marches of despair and moments of lucid optimism. In later life these depressions became more benign. But they were strong and serious in the long, terrible melancholy that James suffered in the winter of 1869–1870 in Germany. The uneasy cure he achieved gave him a lifelong sympathy and insight into the problems of calling and individuality that came to befuddle his age.

James's breakdown took a psychic form, but, as he realized, it had an important and lasting intellectual impact. The experience was, in some sense, a model one, for it recurred during later life and he resolved it by the sort of assertion of will that he doggedly pursued in early 1870. Surrounding this experience and growing out of it was James's investigation of experiences that altered normal vision, perception, and understanding. In diary entries shortly before his crisis, he noted two books rather extensively, one on the effects of chloroform and the second, J. Moreau's *Hashish and Mental Illness*, on the effects of drugs upon consciousness.[9]

James crisis was the experience that probably made his decision to become a philosopher inevitable. It transformed his doubts into a basis for continuous validation of the ethical principles that germinated in his decision to explore the mind, rather than abandon himself in suicide. What James felt in the winter of 1869–1870 was a very severe variety of the career dilemmas faced by others of his generation. It is not difficult to imagine that, at a different time or in another society, James would have been untroubled in his search for a calling. He might, for example, have become a minister, except that his father's generation had already made that position untenable. He might have become a gentleman scholar, but, again, the threshold between gentleman and professional had been crossed in the generation before him by such notable men as Charles Darwin and Louis Agassiz. It was James's fate to live in an era of great change during which it was still possible for some to pursue older sorts of callings—but not for him.

James's melancholy and indecision before the moral undertaking of a calling was, no doubt, exacerbated by a family environment that crackled with religious tension. Henry James, Jr., chose an electrical metaphor to describe the presence of religious sentiment. Established religion, the father dismissed as a kind of "higher prudence," and so he refused to instill in his children the ordinary rituals, fears, and consolations of Protestantism. But the home was alive with religiosity: "I was troubled," wrote Henry, Jr., "all along just by this particular crookedness of our being so extremely religious without having, as it were, anything in the least classified or striking to show for it."

Together with the "sweet ideal" of variety and tolerance, this religious impulse focused upon career itself, transforming the search for a calling into an act of ultimate significance.

No doubt this family sensitivity sharpened William James's perception of the social, psychological, and philosophical problems raised by an era that had begun to doubt the traditional mysteries of work and individuality, but that still clung desperately to the larger outlines of a secular, Protestant commonwealth. In a letter to his brother, Henry seemed to be aware that William's philosophy was a response to this dilemma. After reading *Pragmatism* he commented, "As an artist and a 'creator' I can catch on, hold on, to pragmatism and can work in the light of it and apply it; finding in comparison, everything else (so far as I know the same!) utterly irrelevant and useless—vainly and coldly parallel!" In his brother Henry saw a philosopher for whom the act of creativity was the key interest.[10]

William James's philosophy begins and ends with the problem of individuality. While institutions, dogmatism, and the new industrial culture threatened traditional concepts, this emphasis upon distinctions, creativity, and individualism made James particularly aware of the intellectual consequences of the crisis of work. To him the encompassing or total institution was especially threatening. His most noted political position was opposition to the imperialist designs of American policy in the Spanish-American War. As he wrote to the psychologist Carl Stumpf in 1901, "Do you feel as sad as I do, at the savagery of 'empire' that is pouring itself over the world?" On a smaller scale, James was distressed by the state regulation of mediums and clairvoyants, and he opposed such laws when they were debated in Massachusetts. This seemed to him an example of the accumulating "bigness" of American society, which he disliked; as he put it, "the mania for more laws."[11]

James was generally uncomfortable in the political world and rarely crossed over its frontiers. But he was aware of institutions close to him that intersected his own career. On the subject of the university, James poured out his scorn for the transformation of education and the degradation of knowledge. As he lamented to the Swiss philosopher Theodore Flournoy in 1892, "Love is dead, or at any rate seems weak and shallow wherever science has taken possession. . . . What an awful trade that of professor is—paid to talk, talk, talk! I have seen artists growing pale and sick whilst I talked to them without being able to stop."[12]

James's comments on the changes in Harvard recall the analysis of higher education made by Veblen. Harvard, from being an intellectual center, was becoming a professional school. From a place that encouraged variety, it was, as he wrote, becoming a Ph.D. mill. The predominant metaphor, or, better, the invidious comparison James used in discussing the faults of the university was, like Veblen's, industrial and commercial. He contrasted the imperialist, aggrandizing impulse to the pursuit of variety and rationality. The accumulation of riches and commercial success accentuated the dangers of absolutism and routine.

In his well-known *Talks to Teachers on Psychology; And to Students on Some of Life's Ideals,* published in 1899, James characterized much of contemporary scholarly work as a gratification of "the accumulating and collecting instinct." "A man wishes a complete collection of information, wishes to know more about a subject than anybody else, much as another may wish to own more dollars or more early editions or more engravings before the letter than anybody else."[13] This was not necessarily wrong; indeed, such an impulse lay behind the proof of evolutionary theory. But the business-university rapport could be destructive. In a letter to Flournoy, James spoke of the narrow-minded acquisitive Protestantism of John D. Rockefeller, "a devout Christian of the narrowest sectarian type, not an interest in any subject except *business,* and the endowment of universities which he has taken up as a fad or hobby in middle life. He has created Chicago University, which is now a really magnificent institution. God helps us when men of such power have such narrow ideals."[14]

Part of James's malaise in the university resulted from his own uncertain health, which ill-prepared him for the rigors of laboratory work. Part, no doubt, stemmed also from his own eminent position in philosophy in the American university. The pioneering standards he set for himself were often either impossible or unattractive to others.

Like many men of his day—Charles Darwin, for example—James felt the debilitating effects of intellectual specialization and routine. Because it was defined by special training, professorship was an uncomfortable calling for him. As he wrote to F.C.S. Schiller in 1907, for thirty-five years he suffered from the demands of this profession, the demands of "meeting the mental needs and difficulties of other persons, needs that I couldn't possibly imagine and difficulties that I couldn't possibly understand; and now that I have shuffled off the professional coil, the sense of freedom that comes to me is as surprising as it is exquisite."[15]

The growth and changes in the university threatened to divorce the cultural meaning of education from instruction of techniques and sciences. Toward the end of his life James posed this problem in the following fashion: A technical school might turn out a first-rate specialist who would lack a liberal culture, and "he may remain a cad, and not a gentleman, intellectually pinned down to his one narrow subject, literal, unable to suppose anything different from what he has seen, without imagination, atmosphere, or mental perspective." As James stated the problem in an earlier essay, an education should *"enable us to know a good man when we see him."* There could be no more perfect statement of the educational dilemma as seen at the end of the nineteenth century.[16]

Presumably, this is also what Charles W. Eliot had in mind as he worked to transform his university from what philosopher George Santayana called a "local puritan college' into a cosmopolitan institution. Eliot also argued that the university should avoid overspecialization, and he invoked Emerson's words on the value of manual labor to attack the "bookworm, the monk, the isolated student." But Eliot's athletic conception of the gentleman was quite distinct from James's liberally educated man, however much the two shared the same social perspective. Eliot wished to educate men who were gentlemen, but for different purposes. As he wrote in an address of 1903, the "Service of Universities to a Democracy," the function of higher education was to provide distinguished instruction for businessmen.[17]

James's position (Santayana noted that Harvard philosophers were like "clergymen without a church") resisted this invasion of business ideals. Harvard was, he warned, being transformed into just the scientific, bureaucratic, and business-oriented institution that Eliot desired. The university accounted success in terms of degrees, which he felt, was a "grotesque tendency." James could accept neither this behavioral evaluation of training, nor the emphasis upon efficiency.

No doubt James's persistent and ineffective efforts to find a university position for fellow philosopher Charles Peirce helped convince him that the university was becoming a "tyrannical machine." This chilling metaphor was an appropriate description of the efforts of educators and psychologists to reduce the intellect to quotients or degrees. It was high time, he concluded, "to cast a critical eye" upon such tendencies.

While James lamented the size of institutions, the incursion of business culture, and the regime of practicality—that is, the intellectual division of labor in the university—he also criticized the underlying assumptions and philosophic premises of which these transformations were symbolic. He opposed all large organizations as such, especially national ones; he was against "all big successes and big results; and in favor of the eternal forces of truth which always work in the individual and immediately unsuccessful way."[18] But the deeper issue remained. Could variety and individuality exist in the shadows of a forest of absolutisms?

Thus James saw absolutism as emerging from trivialization and specialization. The development of manipulative generalizations derived from the growth of division. What James had uncovered was a terrifying implication of modern alienation: Absolutism and totalitarianism thrived upon the constant division and redivision of the intellectual and physical tasks of modern society.

Idealism and materialism were the two philosophic forms of absolutism that James opposed, although he could never quite decide which he liked the least. At different times in his life he attacked both. At first he seemed most disturbed by the followers of Hegelian idealism. Toward the end of his life the claims of science seemed more distressing. As he wrote to L. T. Hobhouse in 1904 on the importance of the creative intellect as he had portrayed it in *The Will to Believe*, "In my essay the evil shape was a vision of 'Science' in the form of obstruction, priggishness and sawdust, lording it over all."[19]

James was fond of saying that dogmatism was desiccating; it was cousin to habit and routine. Against this bleak description he contrasted intellectual creativity and variety. Along the edges of the fault of this profound dichotomy James lined the opposing intellectual and cultural forces of his day. With some adjustments and transformations, this separation between the false security of dogma and the creative insecurity of variety and doubt can be found at all of the principal points in James's philosophy. Against the abstract definition he placed the reality of activity, which defied established categories of thought. An individual was either what he made of himself or he was condemned to be defined by exterior and abstract standards. In this opposition the philosopher captured the essential philosophic issues at stake in the discussion of work, self-regeneration, and personality formation that intrigued his age.

The transformation of reason, science, and work into an obsessive pursuit of financial success represented to James a fundamental cause of American nervousness and unrest. In this insight he echoed what other observers had said about the degeneration of the work ethic. Undoubtedly he also had in mind something like Beard's definition of neurasthenia. Referring to the psychological problems of his day, he wrote, "I suspect that neither the nature nor the amount of our work is accountable for the frequency and severity of our breakdowns, but that their cause lies rather in those absurd feelings of tension and having no time, in that breathlessness and tension, that anxiety of feature and that solicitude for results, that lack of inner harmony and ease."[20] "Our ceaseless scheming for the future," he lamented, "has undermined for us all sense of reality in the present."[21] Americans, he noted, suffered visibly from overexertion and excitement. The faces of such victims expressed a "subdued agony or anxiety, or else a smile so intense as to squeeze all further possibilities out of the countenance."[22]

James's sympathy for the neurasthenic was personal and philosophical, and a part of his love of variety. Nowhere is this bias clearer than in his discussion of genius. He rejected the notion that genius was a form of neurosis or madness, and he would not accept Spencer's bleak and mechanistic notion of special evolution. Determinism was beside the point, he wrote, for genius was a mysterious quality whose origins were "inaccessible to the social philosopher." A genius was, therefore, defined by what he created, not by his origins. A genius was a person who rearranged existing knowledge or social relations; he changed society. The man of brilliance (like Charles Peirce) could flourish only in an atmosphere of variety, plurality, and tolerance—the very atmosphere that was being destroyed by theorists who denigrated the originality and importance of intellect.[23]

James quite rightly saw the slogan "survival of the fittest," advanced by Social Darwinists to be a harsh, natural determinism that granted no place for variety and plurality—or even for individualism as he understood it. Those who explained differences in human behavior by reference to such highly charged concepts as neurosis or madness missed the lessons of social and intellectual progress. Those who proclaimed that individual distinctions derived from the energies of the social group were also wrong, because, James argued, institutions were a constant source of corruption. On the contrary, the individual was self-created and a product of his own labor.[24]

James viewed the decline of variety and genteel individualism from the perspective of the international intellectual elite to which he belonged. Precisely because of this internationalism, he could refuse to bury his interests in a single institution such as Harvard. He solved his own crisis of career by refusing to alight, for too long, on one small branch. He remained a traveler, an intellectual vagabond, open to new currents of thought, and always selecting and choosing and changing. His friends and correspondents included many of the most important philosophers and writers of his day; H. G. Wells, Rudyard Kipling, Josiah Royce, Charles Peirce, George Santayana, Oliver Wendell Holmes, Jr., and Henri Bergson. This network often placed him at odds with the transformations of intellectual life in the United States.

Most American students educated abroad in the late nineteenth century did not assimilate, as James did, an international culture; they borrowed specific facets of learning that would serve the demands of American society. Professionalization and adaption went together in their plans for revamping American higher education. Even James participated in the professionalization of psychology and philosophy, but he remained beyond total absorption with such narrow tasks because he found them onerous.

James, the solitary genius, was conscious of novelty. The ease with which he encountered new situations and ideas set him apart from others. To him, the ability to innovate, to alter life and thought, was to be encouraged by the university. As he wrote in his essay on the social value of the "college-bred," "In our democracy, where everything else is so shifting, we alumni and alumnae of the colleges are the only permanent presence that corresponds to the aristocracy in older countries." We have, he contended, a continuous tradition: "our motto, too, is *noblesse oblige;* and, unlike them, we stand for ideal interests solely, for we have no corporate selfishness and wield no powers of corruption. We ought to have our own class consciousness."[25]

James's "class consciousness," as he called it, consisted of aesthetic, social, and, above all, philosophic evaluations of the transformations of American life. Although he left no consistent or focused social commentary, his thinking was clear and concise. The ideal world, to him, was plural, competing, and filled with variety; the worst was mediocre and dogmatic. James personally resisted both routine and mediocrity, but, more generally, he condemned them as threats to individualism. As he admitted in *Pragmatism: A New Name for Some Old Ways of Thinking,* such practical interests lay behind his philosophic discussion: "Accordingly, in every genuine metaphysical debate some practical issue, however conjectural and remote, is involved." The remote and conjectural in James's case was his refusal to give himself over to the intellectual and professional imperatives of industrial civilization.[26]

In the essay "Moral Equivalent of War," he paraphrased the militarist's creed as only an observer of his day could have—that is, before the First World War demonstrated the deadly triviality of warfare. War's " 'horrors,' " he wrote in the book of his that comes closest to social commentary, "are a cheap price to pay for rescue from the only alternative supposed, of a world of clerks and teachers, of co-education and zoophily, of 'consumers leagues' and 'associated charities,' of industrialism unlimited, and a feminism unabashed. No scorn, no hardness, no valor any more! Fie upon such a cattleyard of a planet."[27]

This was no warrior's lament. Rather, James used this extended metaphor as a picture to expose the social values of his day. He contrasted warfare (traditionally assumed to be the forge of individuality) to the soft and mediocre institutions of modern life, not because he loved war, but because it symbolized the most dramatic situation in which human personality was formed by choice, perseverance, and heroism.

In another passage James recounted his impressions of a week's trip to Chatauqua Lake, where he discovered a modern utopia without disease, poverty, or crime, but, also, a community without interest, and with an overbearing middle-class aspect. "An irremediable flatness is coming over the world," he wrote, "Bourgeoisie and mediocrity, church sociables and teachers' conventions, are taking the place of the old heights and depths and romantic chiaroscuro. And, to get human life in its wild intensity, we must in the future turn more and more away from the act, and forget it, if we can, in the romancer's or the poet's page." Thus James did battle with a new world that threatened to disarm the imagination.[28]

To James, his philosopher friend Thomas Davidson represented a valiant warrior against both "rapacious individual competition" and fainthearted socialism. Both were symbols of modern civilization "with its herding and branding, licensing and degree-giving." Society did not recognize men such as Davidson, for it no longer rewarded independence and creativity. "Messrs. Rockefeller and Carnegie," were its new heroes, not because of their personal excellence, but because social ethics in modern society were uprooted and contradictory. There was still heroism in such men as Davidson, in young warriors, in sports, in struggle, "in the daily lives of the laboring classes," but not in the leather-lined bureaus of modern business magnates.[29]

James himself was partly responsible for what he deemed to be the growth of intellectual justifications for mediocrity. Although he refused to agree with some of his followers, he had helped provide the modern functional psychology that others transformed into the dogmas of behaviorism, mental testing, and materialist definitions of mind. James's contribution to modern psychological theory had, in part, been in definition only, for he described aspects of thought in terms of their operations and not, as many philosophers and psychologists before him had done, in terms of their origins. While he freed psychology from the engulfing shadows of traditional metaphysics, he did not eliminate the problems of God, soul, and free will, and immortality from his consideration; he merely postponed them.

Other psychologists, such as Thorndike and Watson, were more hardy soldiers of materialism. Their understanding of the measure and meaning of mind was factual and quantitative. For them, language became a form of behavior and adjustment and never, as it was for James, a deep well from which to draw the poetry of self-expression. Friendly and supportive as he was toward the efforts of functionalist psychologists, he could not accept a reduction of individual distinctions to quantifiable terminology. On no issue was he clearer: "And I for my part," he wrote in The Will to Believe, "cannot but consider the talk of the contemporary school about averages and general laws and predetermined tendencies, with its obligatory undervaluing of the importance of individuals, as the most pernicious and immoral of fatalisms."[30]

James also answered the determinists who fleshed out their definition of intelligence with quantitative comparisons to animals. Man was different from brutes, he wrote, in "the exuberant excess of his subjective propensities" and in the "unnecessary" character of man's moral, intellectual, and aesthetic desires. The difference between animal and man was a question of quality. In the "mind" of an animal, he wrote, there existed nothing but the swamp of immediate experience, condemning it to a lifetime of enslavement to specific, irresistable instincts and to a world of inevitable routine. In mankind the mind was willful; that is, man defined his own reality by choice, by perception, by substituting a part for the whole, and by capturing a distinction in a continuum, according to "our purpose, interest, or point of view at the time."[31] Man was unique because he created his own reality; he made things happen. Mankind seized experience; an animal was determined by it.

James added two judgments. The primitive mind of man was entirely bound by concrete images. Primitive man could understand only by analogy to real experience. At the other extreme was the genius, who either felt or perceived a new identity between diverse forms of experience. The genius created relationships where others saw none. Thus the human mind ranged from the primitive, whose qualities of will and association were limited, to the genius, whose thoughts leaped toward innovation.

As James saw it the modern social and intellectual crisis threatened the genius and the individual by emphasizing the routine and habitual—the savage—in the process of thinking. Moreover, modern industrial ethics as he understood them snuffed out the effects of individual effort. As he wrote to H. G. Wells, he felt that a terrible moral flabbiness had stricken the United States because of the American pursuit of success: "That—with the squalid cash interpretation put on the word success—is our national disease."[32] Contemporary philosophy, rather than offering insight or consolation, contributed to the problem. Arguments snarled between the "stagnant dogmatism of orthodoxy" and the "no less insolent barbarism of science." Neither side had much to offer him, even though he had a certain friendliness toward both.

Positivism, or the explanation of the world by scientific propositions, represented a profound and shrewd attack upon philosophies of innate ideas or God-given reason, because it reduced propositions of idealism to assertions of faith. As James so aptly saw it, positivism also made philosophy a science of averages and logic. Its widespread acceptance, he felt, marked a new phase in the history of philosophy. "Up to about 1850," he wrote, "almost everyone believed that science expressed truths that were exact copies of a definite code of non-human realities."[33] Now science and such extraperceptual concepts were at loggerheads.

James proposed a very different definition of science, one that allowed him to keep hold of the "non-human realities." He wrote: "If we think clearly and consistently in theology or philosophy we are good men of science too. If we think logically in science we are good theologians and philosophers." Unlike the positivists, he suggested that clear, scientific thinking could be used to validate any human activity. On the other hand, dedication to accuracy, experiment, and inductive reason did not automatically ensure that human experience would always be understandable.[34]

Striking out in another direction, James found that idealism made equally extravagant and reductive claims because it defined experience in terms of unseen structures of mind implanted by God. Belief in this unseen rational order was distressing to James, partly because there was no way to prove its validity, and partly because it suggested that some aspects of experience, especially those relating to perception, were meaningless. When James called modern idealists "bureaucratic and professional," his choice of terms indicated that he opposed, not just their ideas, but also the social implications of their theories.

In James's eyes, when idealism did battle with materialism, it did not do so to defend individualism. On the contrary, only by making individual experience the center of philosophy, as he did, could one defend uniqueness and creativity. No experience, he suggested, ought to be reduced to its constituent parts, for this was tantamount to the substitution of a general rule for a unique moment. Believing that all experience should be examined, he focused on the fringes of consciousness that other philosophers and psychologists overlooked. A mind on the verge of a sudden transforming insight was a mind that was creating and acting. Novelty was real and immediate; habit was only personal history. Absolutism in any form was merely the measure of the automatic, unthinking behavior of mankind.

James called his psychology and philosophy "pluralism." While the technical content of this and other terms he employed was of great importance to him and often occupied his attention, its bearing upon his definition of individualism is of greatest interest here. Rarely did he write what might be considered technical philosophy that was not strewn with tangible examples of experience and vivid metaphors. Because he saw his task as that of validating individual experience, he wrote as if this took priority over more general forms of knowledge.

Thus the personal, literary qualities of his work reinforced a philosophic bias in favor of singular testimony. He could not resist a metaphor because it was part of *his* perception of a question.

Language was, for James, the means to change the focus of communication and transmit the overtones of ideas and experience, and to lay their unique validity before the world. As he wrote, "There is very little difference between one man and another, but what little there is, is very important."[35] This might also be said of human experience; differences animated life and intelligence.

In some respects this orientation placed James close to the British empirical school and, particularly, near the tradition stretching back to John Locke. But James did not base his theory of individuality upon social guarantees of property or assumptions such as natural rights. The variety and pluralism he described were more mystical and private. Time and again James returned to the theme of individual perception and its validity. It was, in some respects, another way of approaching the problem of his chosen calling. Moreover, the international elite to which James belonged was buffeted by attacks upon the independence of reason in the name of institutionalized intelligence that could be harmonized, measured, and used by advancing industrial nation states. As one who resisted this tide, James anchored his social theories upon the independence of heroic man, and his philosophy upon the validity of self-created truth of the sort that existed only because someone lived it.

James did not oppose science. His own technical experiments in psychology and his ability to synthesize the scientific works of others were of great importance and influence in his age. But he employed science in a unique way, for he insisted upon examining all experience: religious, mystical, and poetic. He suspected all scientists or philosophers who used the inductive method of reducing the play of human intelligence and of eliminating from experience what he knew only too well was of immense importance for the way people lived their lives. Instead of opposing science, James transformed it into his theory of pragmatism, which became the means for examining the practical effects of belief. He thus took the philosophic components of the work ethic, of self-creativity and individualism, and made them the focus of philosophy.

15

Pragmatism
and the Work Ethic

The deepest structure of James's thought expressed the opposition between inertia and novelty, between the whole and a puzzle piece that would not fit, between the individual and the race, and between the reality that might be and the reality that was. Pragmatism was a way to resolve such paradoxes. It appealed to neither scientific law nor a priori assumptions; it was a way of integrating the effects of an experience with the continuum of individual and human history.

In psychology, James also perceived a division between habitual action and the response to novelty. In his commentary on social ethics, the same opposition appeared. Life was a struggle to assert the self against history and social reality; it was a search for individuality in a world of determined causes and effects. Where a new reality might be advanced by an act of will, James centered his attention.

James's philosophic method and his tastes were thus preoccupied with the doubtful but vivid moments of religious and ethical experience. This placed him in a highly ambiguous position. His scientific interests aligned him with one camp, and his openness to religion and mystical thought placed him in another. Trying to straddle this division of modern philosophy and human experience, he was forced to clarify the deeper issues at stake in the dispute over individuality.

The crisis of individualism and the crisis of alienation from modern industrial culture strongly impinged upon the way William James perceived the philosophic problems of his day. A simple way of stating what was a complex development is this: the late-nineteenth-century crisis was one of fragmentation, one in which the unity of personality, of experience, of individual and social life, of labor and work, flew apart. The much-vaunted individualism of that period, associated with raucous capitalist development, contributed little to solving this prob-

lem, for it did not unite men to each other or to historical values, traditional wisdom, or assumptions about career and calling. It was a
caricature of the work ethic.

James wandered from the narrow compound of modern American
university life with its growing intellectual division of labor to European friends, mediums, and mystics. His restlessness, his congenital
dissatisfaction, rescued him from the easy acceptance of some tendencies in his own thought. The place he reserved in his philosophy
for individual experience drove him to the limits of mental phenomena.
Following the uncertain overtones of experience, he revitalized traditional ethical concerns like gentility, aristocratic stewardship, and
of the Protestant sense of calling, in a world that was quickly extin-
guishing such values. James insisted upon the reality of experience.
It was the basis of his philosophic system. He fervently believed in
individualism, but not in the way it appeared in modern economic
man, who pushed and shoved his way through crowds of competitors.

For James, truth and validity were, in the last analysis, noninstitu-
tional. They rested upon the experience most foreign to modern
thought—the relationship of the individual to the continuous mental
self that experienced the world of spirits, of God, of becoming, and
of possibility. Thus James stretched the boundaries of mental experience at a time when the thrust of psychology and philosophy was
toward limitation.

James's affirmation of individualism rested upon the possible reality
of mystical, psychic, religious, and ethical experience. An individual,
by an act of will, he felt, could both create beliefs and test their reality
in action. He thus returned to consider a problem posed by his
father, whose mystical experiences had led him to Swedenborgianism.

James's interest in psychic research, in the experience (not the
dogmas) of religion, and in the meaning of insanity was integral to
his philosophic position. They were the testing grounds, as it were,
for his belief in the irreducibility of each human life. His first writing
on psychic phenomenon came very early, in 1869, in the notice of a
book on planchette writing. In the 1880s this interest became more
serious, for he then met the English psychic researchers Frederick W.
Myers, Edmund Gurney, and S. H. Hodgson. From that point until
the end of his life James passed through periods of intense interest in
mediums, haunted houses, and other psychic happenings.

Psychic research was, in James's mind, tied to other unexplainable
mental phenomena, as well as to his deep concern for traditional
philosophic questions about the existence and nature of God, universal
order, the possibility of immortality, and the freedom of the will. As
James wrote to J. H. Hyslop, an English psychic researcher, in 1903,

he favored the endowment of research "into mediumship, alternative personality, subconscious states in general, and the borderland between abnormal (or supernormal) and normal psychology." He added that the best work that might be done would record the experience of "certain rare personalities"[1]—for example, the psychologist Pierre Janet's cases of multiple personality, Flournoy's medium, and, of course, Mrs. Piper, whom James himself studied frequently.

He expressed much the same idea to Frederick Myers slightly earlier. It was important, he stressed, to make psychic research a branch of legitimate science. Any attempt to foreclose upon the results of such a science would be deeply discouraging. In the 1880s he admitted to G. C. Robertson in London, "Words cannot express my contempt for much of the medical legislation that is current." What he referred to was legislation limiting the practice of medicine to licensed degree holders.[2]

Psychic research represented an ingress into a world of experience that James clamored to enter. If validated, it could enormously enrich the impoverished contemporary scientific explanation of mental phenomena. It was, quite possibly, a window to the vast, unseen world anticipated by James's pluralism.

In the 1870s in England, a number of intellectuals at Cambridge University had begun to investigate mediums. Together with several eminent men of letters and politicians, they founded the London Society for Psychical Research in 1882. In part, James's interest was awakened by the activities and publications of this group. But his most unflagging attention was paid to the case of Mrs. William J. Piper, whom he met through his Mother-in-law, Mrs. Gibbens, and his wife, Alice. Both had visited Mrs. Piper and easily persuaded James to attend a sitting.

The philosopher was intrigued by his visit and returned several times, during 1886, to attend seances, which he carefully observed and studied. He also arranged sittings for several of his friends, and recommended Mrs. Piper to the London Society for Psychical Research. One result of his activities was that, working with G. Stanley Hall and Josiah Royce, he founded the American Society for Psychical Research in late 1884. The American group kept close ties to its English counterpart and, in 1889, it was amalgamated with the British society. In 1893 James reluctantly accepted the presidency of the London organization, which was, except for a required presidential address, largely a nominal position.[3]

Although he never quite accepted a literal interpretation of the testimony he studied, the task of explaining the psychic powers of Mrs. Piper continuously intrigued him. To James and his English cohorts, Mrs. Piper demonstrated an uncanny knowledge about the subjects who attended her sittings. In her trances a "control" (that is, a person from the world of departed spirits) relayed messages through her to those who attended the seances. James concluded, after many observations, "My own white crow is Mrs. Piper. In the trances of this medium, I cannot resist the conviction that knowledge appears which she has never gained by the ordinary waking use of her eyes and ears and wits."[4]

James's analysis of the Piper testimony went straight to the heart of the then current philosophic debate. Hers was an experience impossible to explain—if one accepted her words literally—in modern scientific or rationalist terms. Neither mechanical rationalism, as James called it, or practical science, as understood by most philosophers and psychologists, could accept the implications of what Mrs. Piper reported. As he wrote in his presidential address to the London society, "Science has come to be identified with a certain fixed general belief, the belief that the deeper order of Nature is mechanical exclusively, and that non-mechanical categories are irrational ways of conceiving and explaining even such a thing as human life."[5]

This incisive picture revealed two dimensions of James's thought. Psychic phenomenon seemed, in his mind, much the same as religious, ethical, and aesthetic experience. Clairvoyance and being a medium indicated a "moreness" or pregnancy of individual thought. James also assumed that such mental phenomena manifested themselves in specially gifted individuals, and that this experience was not reducible to scientific laws. It could not be described as irrational behavior or neurosis. The interested interpreter must take seriously, and perhaps even accept as valid, exactly what the medium or religious mystic reported to him. Thus the integrity of individual experience, even in such outlandish forms, was the touchstone of philosophic inquiry.

James's approach required a willing suspension of disbelief, but he also felt that there was a truly scientific explanation of psychic experience that suggested the possibility of continuity between matter and form; he speculated that there was a subliminal world that opened out upon a universe of spirit. Quite conceivably hypnosis, telepathy, psychic phenomena, dreams, drug-induced states, split personalities, and other forms of mental disorder opened into the same submerged world. Thus psychic experience was a legitimate field of psychological study—the sort of subject that James had declined to discuss in his *Principles of Psychology.*

Like Freud, James used dreams and mystic experience as evidence of an unconscious world, but his understanding of such a world was different from Freud's. He credited his friend Frederick Myers with the discovery of a substratum of mind whose existence was detected by hypnosis and psychic experience. Myers had also developed a theory of mental telepathy. This examination was enriched and reordered by the French psychologists Janet and Binet, who worked on the origins of the split personality and who proposed the existence of a "hypnotic realm."

In 1890 James summarized and interpreted these works on the unconscious. Diagnosis of the split personality offered the possibility for curing serious mental disease, that "direst of human afflictions." Insanity might be defined, he proposed, as a "fragment of consciousness nourishing its narrow memory of delusion."[6] But to James the secondary self was not necessarily or merely pathological. Possibly it was also attuned to deeper realities of the universe. The secondary self could know things that the conscious self might never realize. As he put it in A *Pluralistic Universe and Essays in Radical Empiricism,* "I find in some of these abnormal or supernormal facts the strongest suggestions in favor of a superior co-consciousness being possible."[7]

One can understand why James experimented with drugs like hashish. He was, undoubtedly, provoked both by a scientific interest and an ethical, moral and religious yearning to see for himself that other world reported by mystics and clairvoyants; to know, for sure, in other words, that his own dreams, depressions, and melancholia were not madness or neurasthenic symptoms, but a form of consciousness breaking in upon his own. The results of such mental processes, he wrote, were "new ranges of life succeeding on our most despairing moments,"—to use Swedenborg's term, these experiences were like "vastations."

This understood, James's remarks on Freud become comprehensible: "I can make nothing in my own case with his dream theories, and obviously 'symbolism' is a most dangerous method." He rightly scored Freud on this point. Symbolism was dangerous because it was a reductive translation of evidence from one sort of language to another, from metaphors and poetry to categories. In this transformation the ethical and supernatural resonances were lost. For Freud psychic phenomena were an indication of neurosis or mental distress. For James it presented evidence from another world of experience.[8]

Despite James's extravagant credulism, he maintained strict standards about evidence from his witnesses and associates in psychic research. This care indicates the personal importance of his search. Two sorts of people figured in James's essays on psychic research: experts like himself and his English counterparts, and mediums. Among the latter group, Mrs. Piper was the most important, but there were others, and they, too, tended to be middle-class women from whom extraordinary intelligence, perception, and intuition were unexpected. As he told the Massachusetts legislature during hearings on the bill to outlaw mind curists, this phenomenon occurred among "respectable" people.[9] Describing the widespread appearance of performing mediums, he wrote, "We college-bred gentry, who follow the stream of cosmopolitan culture exclusively, not infrequently stumble upon some old-established journal, or some voluminous native author, whose names are never heard of in *our* circle, but who number their readers by the quarter-million."[10] On the other hand, James showed little interest in what he called "central African Mumbo-Jumboism," which, he noted, was excessive and wholly personal and romantic naturalism, unchecked by rationality. Thus he excluded from his purview a whole arena of psychic experience of the underworld of popular fortunetelling, voodoo, and mysticism. He was more interested in the experiences of "solid citizens."[11]

Almost instinctively, James was drawn to phenomena that seemed to reveal the hidden strengths of the personality. He was intrigued by evidences of multiple selves and by those who, perhaps like himself, experimented with social and intellectual roles, or who evidenced in their behavior the enormous flux and uncertainty that affected the American middle class in the late nineteenth century. This uncertainty seemed particularly characteristic of women. The complex conditions of civilization, he argued, strained individual resources, wreaking nervous and mental havoc. In the New York asylums, for example, 34 percent of the inmates were from the "brain-working classes," and of these, 73 percent were women. Evidently, under modern conditions of increased mental strain, the most intelligent and vulnerable citizens became victims of exhaustion.[12]

Whether James ever saw an explicit link between psychic phenomena, increasing mental strain, and uncertainty about personality formation in the late nineteenth century is difficult to say. But it was implied by his work and by his analysis of mental process. To him, the mind was susceptible to various sorts of understanding (scientific and experimental as well as spiritual), for, as he wrote, there were evidences of a "thin and half-transparent" place of the mind responsible for "religious thinking, ethical thinking, poetical thinking, teleological, emotional, sentimental thinking, what one might call the personal view of life."[13]

With James's description of various levels and kinds of valid experience, it is not surprising to discover in him the suggestion that some forms of mental derangement or mental disjunction might provide access to realms of experience unattainable through ordinary consciousness. As he noted in his Lowell Lectures, "If there are devils, if there are supernatural powers it is through the cracked self that they enter."[14]

To exaggerate this point and argue that James saw madness or insanity as a form of reasonable experience would do terrible violence to his theories and extend what was only an implicit suggestion into an overt thought that he would have rejected. Indeed, he continuously skirted the philosophic meaning of madness, and he was careful to distinguish between psychosis and hallucinations and psychic experience. Sometimes, however, the dividing line was frayed, as in his famous remark to students after a visit to two insane asylums: "President Eliot might not like to admit that there is no sharp line between himself and the men we have just seen, but it is true!"[15]

Philosophically, the term "madness" had a special function in James's vocabulary. It was a misleading, mistakened experience of otherness; it lay at the fringes of consciousness, alongside psychic phenomena and religious experience—except that it was destructive where the others were creative. As he wrote to colleague Boris Sidis in 1902, "I regard the Varieties of Religious Experience as in a sense a study of morbid psychology mediating and interpreting to the philistine much that he would otherwise despise and reject utterly."[16]

James's effort to mediate and interpret the experience of otherness reached remarkable intensity in The Varieties of Religious Experience: A Study in Human Nature. Perhaps nowhere else, other than in his correspondence, did he write as beautifully and metaphorically. Because religious sentiment lay beyond the cold categories of science, and because it was an irreducible experience, James considered it with great care. Religious experience was, like psychic phenomena, the exception that proved the rule that extraordinary individual perception was the hole in the veil between consciousness and the larger unseen world of spirit. As he noted in The Varieties, "I suppose that the chief promise for my hospitality toward the religious testimony of others is my conviction that 'normal' or 'sane' consciousness is so small a part of actual experience."[17]

James explored one other area in his examination of human experience. This was the brutal and real struggle for life, which he associated sometimes with the military instinct and sometimes with working-class life in America. Although mention of this latter example is rare, it is striking. In a passage in Pragmatism, for example, the notation that reality was strongest at the bottom of society exploded the intellectual categories he was discussing. In his analysis of the philosophic crisis caused by overbearing scientism and absolute idealism, he stopped to quote the anarchist writer Morrison I. Swift, as if to say, "here is the reality that absolutism in its various forms trys to disguise."[18]

He dipped for examples into the underworld of working men on other occasions; when he recounted his impressions after observing railroad workers, for example. They were, he wrote, the heroes of modern life—"These the very parents of our own life." When he caricatured the irrelevant and abstract life of his own social class, he wrote: "we of the highly educated classes (so called) have most of us got far, far away from Nature. We are trained to seek choice, the rare, the exquisite exclusively, and to overlook the common." Possibly only the tramp, the mystic, the dreamer or loafer could "hope to attain to any breadth of insight into the impersonal world of worth as such, to have any perception of life's meaning on a large, objective scale." This underworld, like the other realms in which intense experience prevailed, was, for James, exemplary of the most vivid moments and meanings in life, and unavailable to the laboratry scientist or the bookish rationalist.[19]

Thus James perceived the crisis of work and self-creativity to be a challenge to individuality, both in social and philosophic terms. He clung to the hope that, in those categories of intensely felt individual experience that he so admired, there might remain the possibilities for an ethical universe. Through self-assertion or will he hoped to reintegrate all forms of human experience into a philosophy and metaphysics of belief.

The one absolute necessity to this philosophy of individualism was variety and plurality of culture. Such institutions as Harvard, he wrote, ought to take the lead in encouraging such experience. Unfortunately, the translation of intelligence into money-making skills and the idealization of "swindling and adroitness, and the indulgence of swindling and adroitness, and cant, and sympathy with cant—natural fruits of that extraordinary idealization of 'success'" was a strong corrosive force in American culture, which prevented the realization of such ideals.

To combat this economic force and establish the reign of intelligence, the "true" Harvard should become a "nursery for independent and lonely thinkers." It should tolerate eccentricity. It should draw students who were attracted "because they have heard of her persistently atomistic constitution, of her tolerance of exceptionality and eccentricity, of her devotion to the principles of individual vocation and choice." This atmosphere, he hoped, would promote "genius," a term that meant, to James, the ability to wrest a new perception from ordinary experience. The delicate, peripheral vision that existed only in the few could never be discovered in the commercialized professional schools.[20]

James quite rightly contrasted the intellectual laissez faire in the university to social determinism on the one hand, and hereditarian determinism on the other. He took his stand alongside earlier, romantic theorists of the personality such as Emerson. He celebrated a life of heroism, of struggle, of sport and contact with nature.

The beginning and ending point of social existence was, thus, the individual, not the race, the nation, the class, or the average. As he told the audience at the Lowell Lectures of 1896, the "normal man" was a "nullity." Individuality was the phenomonology of truth and meaning. Only on the singular level did the experience of will and self-regulation have meaning. Only here could James's own precarious but creative integration of aesthetic, moral, and cultural ideals satisfy the intellectual and religious orientation of his upbringing and his culture. For him, the best commonwealth "will always be the one that most cherishes the men who represent the residual interests, the one that leaves the greatest scope to their peculiarities."[21]

This was striking advice from a man whose sympathies lay with the mystics of all ages, the mediums, the "loafers," and the underworld of common men engaged in a brutal struggle for life. Of all modern philosophers, of him, it is most appropriate to say: "A philosophy is the expression of a man's intimate character, and all definitions of the universe are but the deliberately adopted reactions of human character upon it." Or, to quote his definition of thought, "The intellectual life of man consists almost wholly in his substitution of a conceptual order for the perceptual order in which his experience originally comes."[22] Thought was the act of individual reconstruction of experience.

James's thought transformed the crisis of career and métier and enormous resulting social confusion—the rapid institutionalization and professionalization of intellect and work of the late nineteenth century —into a deeply personal philosophy whose meaning is impossible to separate from his own experience as a participant in that world of confusion and change.

James suspected that the validification of individualism and ethics lay in extraordinary moments of intuitional experience, in dreams, in drug-induced states, in mystical and religious experiences, in morbidity, and, possibly, even in madness. But the fundamental structures of his philosophy of individualism paralleled the traditional view that individual assertion and work were the physical forms of creativity. Placed in the industrial culture of the late nineteenth century and the context of technical philosophy, this orientation, this "will to believe," offered a striking, almost desperate, insight into the fundamental dilemma of the age.

How could mankind survive the determinisms of the world it was building? James's answer was literally a leap of faith. "We can and we may," he wrote, "jump with both feet off the ground into or toward a world of which we trust the other part to meet our jump—and *only* *so* can the making of a perfected world of the pluralistic pattern ever take place. Only through our precursive trust in it can it come into being."[23] Thus James's pragmatic will focused philosophic attention upon the essence of what had been the work ethic: the promise that effort and exertion could generate an ethical world.

He contrasted his world to contemporary philosophic systems. "The actual universe is a thing wide open," he wrote, but "systems must be closed." "Between the two extremes of crude naturalism on the one hand and transcendental absolutism on the other, you may find that what I take the liberty of calling the pragmatistic or melioristic type of theism is exactly what you require." An absolutist philosophy was, for him, a dreadful, almost immoral abstractness: "This is the famous way of quietism, or indifference. Its enemies compare it to a spiritual opium." On the contrary, James's philosophy encompassed that "zone of insecurity in human affairs in which all dramatic interest lies. The rest belongs to the dead machinery of the stage."[24] Modern determinisms had effectively solved (to their own satisfaction, anyway) the age-old problem of the relation of mind to body, spirit to matter, and thought to perception, but only at the cost of eliminating a whole range of experience that James cherished. Thus pragmatism was a plea to reopen the case for individuality.

As a scientist in his own right, James had no inclination to discard inductive inquiry; on the contrary, he brought scientific thinking into new realms. The literal testimony of individuals, kept in the context of its presentation, was subjected to scientific scrutiny. The reason for this was important: "To no one type of mind," he wrote, "is it given to discern the totality of truth. Something escapes the best of us—not accidentally, but systematically, and because we have a twist."[25]

The proposition that minds were different, each with its own twist, cast new light upon the psychology of the divided mind or split personality as analyzed by Janet, Binet, and Freud. But James was less interested in this phenomenon as a pathological symptom than as a particular form of vision. The relation of the unconscious to the conscious, and the relation of the self to the other and to the universe rendered each mind distinct. As he wrote to Peirce, this belief in the original validity of individual perception was worth the "risk."

There were thus gradations and levels of perception. James examined habitual, mundane mental activities, instinctual behavior, and creative insight in his works on psychology. In his philosophic writings he examined the sudden transforming insights of spirituality and ethics. Habitual activity and instinctive behavior, he noted, represented a limited form of thinking and were more characteristic of primitive men or animals. Apparently only civilized man could break the bonds of tradition. The opposition between habit and innovation, between inertia and action, was one of great importance. In isolating two such worlds of activity, he felt he had discovered a realm of *becoming true,* of emergence whereby history advanced and wherein moral and ethical truths became tangible.

The realm of habitual thinking was, therefore, the stuff of past history. For the behaviorists, however, this history was sufficient raw material for social control. For James it only represented the "stage of equilibrium in the mind's development." As he put this proposition in *Psychology: Briefer Course,* "Habit is thus the enormous fly-wheel of society, its most precious conservative agent. It alone is what keeps us all within the bounds of ordinance, and saves the children of fortune from the envious unrisings of the poor." James, ironically, conceded that such habits might be open to scrupulous scientific analysis, but felt they could not be considered the totality of mental activity.[26]

A rarer, higher form of intelligence perceived novelty—and disrupted social order. When confronted with a decisive question demanding action each human being, he wrote, must consider the potential effects of his behavior. The thoughts called forth in such situations organized new unities and new relationships. As he argued, "ideas (which themselves are but parts of our experience) become true just in so far as they help us to get into satisfactory relation with other parts of our experience, to summarize them and get about among them by conceptual shortcuts instead of following the interminable succession of particular phenomena."[27]

At every level of James's consideration of knowing, there is a dialectic between passive and active, the habitual and the novel. Of course, he was no dialectician, as his mocking attitude toward Hegel revealed. But the dynamic between the known and the unknown was the essence of his pluralism. Neither science nor rationalism by themselves could adequately explain human behavior, for both excluded the possibility of novelty. Each reduced mind to an abstraction based upon cause and effect. It remained for James's pragmatism to reverse this process, for, to him, effect was the author of cause.

Traditional questions about the existence of God, immortality, and free will could be answered only through experience. James suggested this when he complimented his friend Benjamin Blood, the "pluralistic mystic." "I feel now as if my own pluralism were not without the kind of support which mystical collaboration may confer."[28] There were, he concluded, a multitude of possibilities and truths in the universe, and only a pluralistic philosophy could enable mankind to understand them.

For James experience was whole and indivisible. The mind was not like a factory, assembling bits and pieces, colors, textures, sounds, space relations, and the like. Rather, the mind perceived these analytic bits as well as the relations between them. By choice, the mind could focus upon parts and relationships or objects and functions. It could also apprehend qualities and ethical implications.

James's argument that mind perceived relationships and differentiated sense stimuli allowed him to use the pragmatic test of validity against both sides of the raging dispute between rationalism and materialism. Whatever concept led to an enrichment of knowledge or a furtherance of man's ability to act was undoubtedly more valid than concepts that contradicted and divided experience. Quite simply, a scientific hypothesis was valid if, by acting upon its premises, one obtained the expected results. In the world of subconscious and religious experience, the pragmatic test also had validity. If, for example, belief in God resulted in a transformed life, if the expected effects flowed from a belief, then this, too, was a form of verification. As he wrote, "There are cases where a belief creates its own verification."[29]

This remarkable application of the inductive method to the unseen and unreproducible inner world of each individual was, for James, no mere search for traditional religious answers to the hackneyed propositions of theologians: "Not God, but life, more life, a larger, richer, more satisfying life, is, in the last analysis the end of religion."[30] He had no interest in logical proof of God's existence; he wished to measure the effects of belief in God. Whatever concept worked, that is, whatever act or thought created meaning, change, and adjustment to the novel; whatever unified memory, personality, and experience; that, which humans willed and acted upon, could be true. This was the meaning of his ironic and misunderstood declaration in favor of the "cash value" of ideas. James had only selected a metaphor that he thought everyone would understand.

James's optimism, good taste, and fundamental humanism lay behind and enriched his epistemology. The pragmatic test of truth and value depended, ultimately, upon a community of values and a culture that James never thought to question. But it was precisely this culture that rapid industrialization and modern social theories threatened; this was the culture in crisis.

His philosophic position was also highly individualistic; indeed, it is close to solipsism. From the point of view of modern technical philosophy, this is perhaps decisive and fatal. From the viewpoint of the cultural and intellectual crisis of the late nineteenth century, however, it reveals that James invested his whole self and his own desire to communicate what was deeply personal into a search for a valid individualism.

The deepest wellsprings of James's philosophy are personal and metaphoric. During a lecture in 1905 he proposed to unify all human experience through an extended analogy about variety. His belief in "radical empiricism" suggested "the social analogy: plurality of individuals, with relations partly external, partly intimate, like and un-like, different in origin, in aim, yet keeping house together, interfering, coalescing, compromising," and gradually coming together.[31] This unity in diversity was the secret nature of the universe.

Each human sentiment was rich and warm and overflowed the containers of memory beyond the brim of simple experience. Each individual received from the flow of his consciousness into the continuum of larger life nothing more or less than "affective" truth, or truth that changed life. The universe, he concluded, was a duality consisting of actuality and possibility, and the individual was simultaneously a personal history and a future.

This was James's response to the determined worlds of modern science and ancient idealisms. The individual was the beginning and end of philosophic consideration: "The spirit and principles of Science," he wrote, "are mere affairs of method; there is nothing in them that need hinder Science from dealing successfully with a world in which personal forces are the starting-point of new effects. The only form of things that we directly encounter, the only experience that we concretely have, is our own personal life."[32]

Conceiving, fixing, and holding fast to meanings had no significance, he wrote, "apart from the fact that the conceiver is a creature with partial purposes and private ends." In this sense James admitted to a form of alienation and isolation. But, he argued, individual perceptions could be transmitted to others. "*We believe our PERCEPTS are possessed by us in common,*" he declared in his book *The Meaning of Truth,* a sequel to "Pragmatism."[33]

Communication, ethical behavior, and growing understanding created a meaningful personal world in a pluralistic universe. "It means *individualism,*" he wrote, "personalism: that the prototype of reality is the *here and now;* that there is a genuine novelty; that order is being *won*—incidentally reaped; that the more universal is the more abstract; that the smaller and more intimate is the truer,—the man more than the home, the home more than the state or church. . . . It means tolerance and respect. It means democracy as against systems which crush the individual."[34]

James's philosophy of pragmatism and his psychology of will led him to assert the validity of the ethical and psychological context of the work ethic and individualism. He used pragmatism as an extraordinary tool to examine the philosophic premises that lay behind two enormous intellectual efforts of his day, one attempting to recreate the propositions of traditional rationalism, and one asserting a new scientific, behavioral position. He found that both—and science in particular—were proposing a sort of world that fragmented mankind from the fuller meanings of experience and alienated modern man from the fruits of his ethical labors (just as industrial culture destroyed the continuity between work and satisfaction). In his day there was no clearer or more profound understanding of the larger changes occurring in social and psychological theory, and no more direct critical commentary on new behavioral theories of the personality. In his writings the crisis of work and alienation appeared as a profound disruption of American individualism and religious faith.

This leads to a final point about James and his attempt to restore individuality and plurality to the center of philosophy. It leads back also to the James family and the close but seemingly contradictory paths traveled by novelist Henry and philosopher William. There was, in fact, no contradiction between these directions. The problem of wholeness, of the fragmented personality and culture, which William James faced, was not unique; it was and is a central problem of fiction.

William and Henry, each in his own way, resisted the destruction of a culture threatened by modern institutions. Each created a world in which those values could still work. The philosophic world of William James, like the novels of his brother, was a fictional creation. Perhaps this is what novelist Owen Wister intended when he wrote to James in 1908 congratulating him on the publication of *Pragmatism:* You have validated the world of fiction, wrote Wister. There was no further need for anyone to devise such a theory henceforth, "since all anybody has to do is to apply the doctrine of your book to the arts which I attempt to practice."[35]

The test of the self, of struggle and heroism, so highly praised by James, was a sort of heightened fictional reality. The vivid metaphor integrated his life and his philosophy into a celebration of individual worth that has probably never received so exquisite a statement. But because the world that James created bordered upon fiction—in fact because it had to remain on the edges of reality—it became part of what has become a regrettable development in modern social and philosophic criticism—the withdrawal of ethical judgments from the practical world. His universe of philosophy, like the imagined utopian worlds of craft and hand labor, operated as a myth in modern society. James ironically demonstrated that the individuality and variety he so cherished had little operational value in the advancing industrial culture of his time; these ideas could only be nurtured in romantic opposition to that society.

Conclusion

The philosophy in which William James assembled the facets of work, individualism, and effort was one of the last assertions of an ideal that had been the essence of American self-understanding during the nineteenth century. He examined the new theories of personality and individuality founded upon behaviorism and judged them to be illusionary. They were optical distortions of extraordinary brilliance based upon a blind faith in a dogmatic understanding of science. The old way was also elusive, but James trapped rationalism in its sleight of hand, as it portrayed innate ideas as mysteriously impinging upon and organizing the objective experience of every individual. James's critique of these two dogmas charged both with inattention to the details of life as it was lived. Both were comprehensive theories that withdrew the variety from experience.

James was friend to or sympathizer with most of the movements of his day that tried to reassert the old propositions about work, creativity, and self-assertion. He obviously felt the alienation that was epidemic in the society of modern intellectuals to which he belonged. His position, however, was far more complex than most, for he never gave up a fundamental scientific orientation that, in the hands of others, was proving to be a weapon to demolish old theories of personality and individual effort. James was, quite literally, caught between two broad conceptions of man's condition, each based upon different sets of intellectual priorities. His reaction was one of strategic retreat, which allowed him to resist the temptation to turn alienation into a tool of manipulation. He did this because he understood that individuality could only be preserved on the basis of the sorts of distinctions that were being extinguished by modern industrial society. His most telling criticism of behavioral theories and materialist dogma was that both rejected most of what people hoped, wished, or imagined. He understood that society was rushing to worship a new God whose touch turned every object into a saleable commodity.

By looking askance at society James caught the image of modern alienation. But the price of his intuitional restatement of the coherence of personality, individuality, and work was to be misunderstood.

His effort to salvage something from the wreck of ideas that had buoyed previous generations struck many as odd. Professional philosophers were sometimes put off by his language, and, disregarding most of his works, tried to fit him into the niche of one or another philosophic school. Those social thinkers who might most have benefited from the collectivity of his works on individualism and alienation seemed unaware of them, as well they may have been, because he never wrote a coherent social ethics.

In a different sense, however, James's reaction to the industrial culture of his day was typical. Like others who sought to compensate for lost individuality and community, he was attuned to the older assumptions that linked work, effort, and creativity to social order and aesthetics. He even encouraged schemes designed to test the importance of individual effort in human affairs. Perhaps more important, James possessed a healthy hostility to the manipulative social engineering proposed by men like his colleague Münsterberg. In this skepticism he proved to be correct, for, while the Watsons, MacDonalds, Frederick Taylors, and Münsterbergs of his day caught the ear of public worry and fear over industrialism and its consequences, they did not then, nor have they since, prevailed. Whether this good fortune has come from social inertia, opposition of political and economic forces, tradition, or a lack of sustained economic and social crisis, it is true that American society has neither overthrown the older work ethic nor entirely accepted the new compulsions of alienated labor. Thus, in the unresolved crisis of modern industrialism, critics such as Dewey, Veblen, and James, with one foot in tradition and the other advanced toward industrial behaviorism, strike us as fresher and more up-to-date than the apostles of a managed society.

The problems that the generation of the 1890s uncovered have neither gone away nor diminished. Practically every subsequent generation has rediscovered them, although not always with the same intelligence or sensitivity. Each American generation has continued to believe in work and individualism, and each has abruptly learned how small is the basis for either belief.

The same solutions to industrial alienation in a society that cannot recognize its "good men" have appeared. Mental testing, particularly after the alpha, beta tests were given to American army recruits in the First World War, seemed a perfect tool with which to reshape the too-fluid social structure of the nation. Similar scientific measures of selection have appeared since that time. There were those in 1920 (as there are, undoubtedly, in 1977) who believed, along with Henry H. Goddard, that the Stanford-Binet test could be used to examine the intelligence of human beings in order to place each in an appropriate social slot.

At the same time, there have always been advocates of the older, moral, work-oriented view. This was the theme, for example, of the Institute of Social and Religious Research, organized in 1921 to study the American character. Its analysis of religious motivation and morality led it to finance major projects on rural churches, American Indians, and what was perhaps the most important study of the American character of that decade, Robert and Helen Lynd's analysis of Muncie, Indiana, published as *Middletown* in 1929.

Behind this continuing debate the problem of alienation (the condition of modern industrial mankind) has deepened. In the 1950s this situation exploded with special force in the works of David Riesman and Paul Goodman. *The Lonely Crowd* was a sociological novella, half-history and half-fiction, that focused upon the 1890s as a time when the older forms of personality were altered by demands for a more marketable personality structure. Riesman, like the celebrants of the "American character," constructed a psychological typology to serve as the symbol for an age.

Riesman specifically defined his task as the delineation of two sorts of personality, the inner-directed man and the other-directed man. The first was associated with nineteenth-century nation-building, where each person required an internal gyroscope implanted through rigorous upbringing. This rendered one morally inflexible, but instilled great resources for activity. The modern personality, or other-directed man, was oriented toward society and even determined by the opinions of others. At his worst this new character suffered from "galloping anomie."

Riesman and his associates placed this character change into the context of alterations in the work situation. A person's real labor, where he would like to throw himself emotionally, "cannot now conceivably coincide, perhaps in a majority of cases, with what they get paid for doing," wrote the authors in 1950. Riesman looked back to more fortunate eras of unalienated labor, to the New Deal Civilian Conservation Corps camps, and, ideally, to Edward Bellamy's proposed industrial army, outlined in the author's utopian novel *Looking Backward*. His solution for the 1950s was for people to concentrate upon making leisure the source of character integration, performing the function that work had once done.

Social critic Paul Goodman asked much the same question of his alienated society in his book *Growing up Absurd*, published in 1960. For Goodman development, adulthood, and achievement in modern American society were literally absurd, for they demanded meaningless striving. One was forced to ask, "Is it possible *how* is it possible, to have more meaning and honor in work? to put wealth to some real use?" Goodman's arguments stretched back into the original debate over industrial alienation and repeat most of the ideas that had been stated fifty years before. "Vocation," he wrote, "*is* the way a man recognizes himself as belonging or appoints himself, in the community life and work." To give up the religious "community of work," he lamented, "is a great loss."[1]

This stinging indictment of alienated work and splintered community was prelude to Goodman's counterproposals for establishment of a work and leisure ethic that would reunite people to their ethical and aesthetic senses. His contemporaries, the beat poets, and even juvenile delinquents, he wrote, were acting out some of the implications of such an ethic. They followed their spiritual and emotional instincts and refused to conform to the divisive consumption and status-oriented ethics of their day. But Goodman (and the beats) moved very little beyond the insights of the intellectuals who, in the early twentieth century, had also yearned for a restoration of experience and life to the center of existence.

The problem of uniting personality development to work and to concepts of individuality has been restated in different forms for different times, but rarely, if ever, with the coherence and sympathy of such thinkers as William James, Thorstein Veblen, and John Dewey. Undoubtedly such restatements of the problems of alienation will continue as long as we still believe that ethics and culture flow from work. Or perhaps work will, at last, become the sort of coherent, integrative function it has long been supposed to be.

Notes

INTRODUCTION

1. Studs Terkel, *Working* (New York: Pantheon, 1972), p. xi. See also the important essay on work by Herbert Gutman, "Work, Culture, and Society in Industrializing America, 1815–1919," *American Historical Review* 78 (1973).
2. Carroll Wright, "Address to the Seventh Annual Convention of the Commissioners of Bureaus of Labor Statistics," *Fifth Annual Report of the Bureau of Labor Statistics, 1889* (Hartford, Conn., 1890), p. 26; idem, *Industrial Depressions: First Annual Report of the Commissioner of Labor* (Washington, D.C., 1886), pp. 5–12.
3. Carroll Wright, "The Working of the U.S. Bureau of Labor," *Bulletin of the Bureau of Labor*, no. 54 (Washington, D.C., 1904); 978.
4. *Fourth Annual Report of the Bureau of Labor for Massachusetts* (Boston, 1873), pp. 58 ff. Wright, *Industrial Depressions*, pp. 336–37.
5. *Fifth Annual Report of Bureau of Labor Statistics* (Connecticut), pp. 26–29.
6. *Fourth Annual Report of Bureau of Statistics of Labor* (Massachusetts), p. 281.
7. *Twentieth Annual Report, Bureau of Statistics of Labor for Massachusetts* (Boston, 1889), pp. 354, 363.
8. Census Office, United States Department of the Interior, *Special Census Report on the Occupations of the Population of the United States at the Eleventh Census, 1890* (Washington, D.C., 1896), pp. 5–8.
9. Ibid., p. 11. See also Carroll Wright, *First Special Report of the Commissioner of Labor: A Report on Marriage and Divorce in the United States, 1867 to 1886*, rev. ed. (Washington, D.C., 1891), pp. 144–58; idem, *Fourth Annual Report of the Commissioner of Labor, 1888: Working Women in Large Cities* (Washington, D.C., 1889), p. 76.
10. Census Office, United States Department of the Interior, *Report on the Population of the United States at the Eleventh Census, 1890*, part 1 (Washington, D.C., 1895), pp. lxv, lxvi; idem, *Report on the Social Statistics of Cities in the United States at the Eleventh Census, 1890* (Washington, D.C., 1895), pp. 8–9 ff.
11. Census Office, *Report on the Population*, pp. lxxix, clv; idem, *Special Report on Occupations*, p. 19.

CHAPTER 1

1. John L. Thomas, "Romantic Reform in America, 1815–1865," *American Quarterly* 17 (Winter 1965): 671–74. John Cawelti describes three versions of this ethic; his divisions are useful, but they are three versions of the same model. (Cawelti, *Apostles of the Self-Made Man* [Chicago: University of Chicago Press, 1965], p. 4.)
2. Ralph Waldo Emerson, *Self-Reliance* (East Aurora, N.Y., 1908), pp. 11–19.

3. Louisa May Alcott, *Little Women* (New York: Collier, 1962), p. 137.

4. Adriano Tilgher, *Work: What It Has Meant to Men through the Ages* (New York: Harcourt, Brace & Co., 1930), pp. 57–60; Lewis Mumford, *The Condition of Man* (New York: Harcourt Brace Jovanovich, 1973), p. 302; See also Charles Horton Cooley, *Personal Competition* (New York, 1899); Charles E. Rosenberg, "Sexuality, Class, and Role in Nineteenth-Century America," *American Quarterly* 25 (May 1973): 137.

5. Randolph Bourne, "In the Mind of the Worker," *Atlantic Monthly* 113 (March 1914): 375–82.

6. Cooley, *Personal Competition*, p. 162.

7. Charles E. Rosenberg, *The Trial of the Assassin Guiteau: Psychiatry and Law in the Gilded Age* (Chicago: University of Chicago Press, 1968), pp. 102–24, 244. John Higham quite rightly points out that this sense of crisis was not as deep as that felt by many Europeans. (John Higham, "The Reorientation of American Culture in the 1890's," *Writing American History: Essays on Modern Scholarship* [Bloomington: Indiana University Press, 1970], p. 100.)

8. Census Bureau, "Plan of Inquiry Respecting Misfortune and Crime in the United States: Confidential: Not Intended for Publication," *Tenth Census of the United States* (Washington, D.C., 1880), p. 6.

9. National Divorce Reform League, *Reports, 1885–1910*, vol. 1 (Boston, 1896), p. 19. According to his biographer, James Leiby, Carroll Wright was not a pessimist. (Leiby, *Carroll Wright and Labor Reform: The Origin of Labor Statistics* [Cambridge, Mass.: Harvard University Press, 1960], pp. 74–75.)

10. Frederick L. Hoffman, "Suicides and Modern Civilization," *Arena* 7 (May 1893): 682–88, 694. See also Davis R. Dewey, "Statistics of Suicides in New England," *Quarterly Publications of the American Statistical Association* 3 (June, September 1892): 158; Norman Dain, *Concepts of Insanity in the United States, 1789–1865* (New Brunswick, N.J.: Rutgers University Press, 1964), p. 90.

11. Gustavo Tosti, "Suicide in the Light of Recent Studies," *American Journal of Sociology* 3 (January 1898): 469–77. "Can Suicide Be Justified?" *Open Court* 5 (13 August 1891): 2911–13.

12. Frederick H. Wines, "Report on Crime, Pauperism, and Benevolence in the United States at the 11th Census: 1890," *Department of the Interior Census Office*, House of Representatives, 52nd Congress, 1st Session, Document 340 (Washington, D.C.; 1896), p. 11. Henry Martyn Boies, *Prisoners and Paupers; A Study of the Abnormal Increase of Criminals and Public Burden of Pauperism in the United States: The Causes and Remedies* (1893; Freeport, N.Y.: Books for Libraries Press, 1972), pp. 136, 264.

13. Roland P. Falkner, "Is Crime Increasing?" *Forum* 29 (July 1900): 596–607.

14. E. David Friedman, "Nervous Strain and Mental Hygiene," in *America and the New Era*, ed. Elisha M. Friedman (New York: E. P. Dutton and Co., 1920), p. 475. Thomas Burke, "Physical Deterioration in England," *Forum* 36 (January–March 1905): 449–51. Gustavus Meyers, "Colonizing the Tramp," *Review of Reviews* 39 (March 1909): 311. George E. McNeill, ed., *The Labor Movement: The Problem of Today* (1887; New York: Augustus M. Kelley, 1971), p. 461.

15. William Isaac Thomas, *Source Book for Social Origins*, 6th ed. (Boston, 1909), p. 173. For use of drugs in this period, see David F. Musto, *The American Disease: Origins of Narcotic Control* (New Haven, Conn: Yale University Press, 1973). See also Milton Gold, "The Early Psychiatrists on Degeneracy and Genius," *Psychoanalysis and the Psychoanalytic Review* 47 (Winter 1960): 37–55.

16. Charles W. Eliot, "The American Social Hygiene Association," *Social Hygiene* 1 (December 1914): 2–3.

17. *American Journal of Sociology* 3 (March 1898).

18. Annie Payson Call, *Power through Repose* (Boston, 1898), pp. 11–12.

19. Edward Alsworth Ross, *Social Control* (1901; Cleveland: Case Western Reserve University Press, 1969), p. vi. See also *Senate Document 705: Report*

of the *Country Life Commission*, 60th Congress, 2nd session (Washington D.C.; 1909), p. 5. Philip Rieff gives an interesting discussion of the decline of "culture" and the rise of the therapeutic in his *The Triumph of the Therapeutic: Uses of Faith after Freud* (London: Chatto and Windus, 1966).

CHAPTER 2

1. Osias L. Schwarz, *General Types of Superior Men* (Boston, 1916), p. 5. William Hirsch, *Genius and Degeneration*, 2nd ed. (New York, 1896), pp. 320–25. Lewis Terman, "The Relation of the Manual Arts to Health," *Popular Science Monthly* 78 (June 1911): 603.

2. Frederick Adams Woods, "A New Name for a New Science," *Science* 30, New Series (19 November 1909): 703–4. See also James Mark Baldwin, *Social and Ethical Interpretations in Mental Development* (1899; New York: Arno Press, 1973), pp. 154–55.

3. Eduard Toulouse, *Enquête Medico-Psychologique sur les Rapports de la Superiorité Intellectuelle avec la Neuropathie* (Paris, 1896). Arthur MacDonald, "Emile Zola," *Open Court* 12 (August 1898): pp. 457 ff.

4. Charles H. Cooley, "Genius, Fame, and the Comparison of Races," *Annals* 9 (May 1897): 317–18.

5. Francis Galton, *Hereditary Genius: An Inquiry into its Laws and Consequences* (London, 1869), p. 1.

6. Havelock Ellis, *A Study of British Genius* (New York: Houghton Mifflin Co., 1926), p. 80.

7. Cesare Lombroso, "Genius: A Degenerative Epileptoid Psychosis," *Alienist and Neurologist* 12 (July 1891): 356. See also Charles W. Pilgrim, "Genius and Suicide," *Popular Science Monthly* 42 (January 1893): 368.

8. Max Nordau, *Degeneration*, 2nd ed. (New York, 1895), pp. 171, 34. Nordau's book was practically a best seller in the United States in 1895, and went through several printings. See Howard Mumford Jones, *The Age of Energy* (New York: The Viking Press, 1970–1971), p. 342.

9. MacDonald, "Genius and Insanity," (Lewes, Del: South Counties Press, 1892), p. 12. Many American neurologists disagreed with this argument. See Nathan G. Hale, Jr., *Freud and the Americans: The Beginning of Psychoanalysis in the United States, 1876–1917*, (New York: Oxford University Press, 1971), pp. 76–81.

10. Cooley, "Genius," pp. 323–58. See, for example, James G. Kiernan, "Are Americans Degenerates?" *Alienist and Neurologist* 17 (October 1896): 447; idem, "Art in the Insane," *Alienist and Neurologist* 13 (October 1892): 247.

11. Grant Allen, "The Genesis of Genius," *Atlantic Monthly* 47 (March 1881): 380.

12. William James, "Great Men, Great Thoughts, and the Environment," *Atlantic Monthly* 46 (October 1880): 445 ff.

13. John Fiske, "Sociology and Hero Worship," *Atlantic Monthly* 47 (January 1881): 81–82.

14. William James, "The Importance of Individuals," *Open Court* 4 (7 August 1890): 2438. See also idem, "Degeneration and Genius," *Collected Essays and Reviews* (New York: Longmans, Green and Co., 1920), pp. 401–4.

15. Boris Sidis, *Philistine and Genius* (Boston, 1917), p. 51.

CHAPTER 3

1. James Mark Baldwin, *Social and Ethical Interpretations in Mental Development* (1899; New York: Arno Press, 1973).

2. "Report on the Best Methods of Dealing with Tramps and Wayfarers" *Massachusetts Association of Relief Officers Report*, 1900 (Boston, 1901), p. 33. In Europe, the great era of modern tramping was, apparently, 1870 to 1914; see

Alexandre Vexliard, *Introduction à la Sociologie du Vagabondage* (Paris: Librarie M. Riviere, 1956), p. 213.

3. Charles Ely Adams, "The Real Hobo: What He Is and How He Lives," *Forum* 33 (June 1902): 448.

4. Henry Edward Rood, "The Tramp Problem: A Solution," *Forum* 25 (March 1898): 91. E. Lamar Bailey, "Tramps and Hoboes," *Forum* 26 (October 1898): 220. Evidence of the seriousness of this problem is indicated by a study undertaken for the State Department. See "Vagrancy and Public Charities in Foreign Countries," *Special Consular Reports,* United States Department of State (Washington, D.C., 1893).

5. Charles Richmond Henderson, *Introduction to the Study of the Dependent, Defective, and Delinquent Classes,* 2nd ed. (Boston, 1901), pp. 10, 308. See also John S. Haller, Jr., *Outcasts from Evolution: Scientific Attitudes of Racial Inferiority, 1859–1900* (Urbana; University of Illinois Press, 1971).

6. J. Harold Williams, "Hereditary Nomadism and Delinquency," *Journal of Delinquency* 1 (September 1916): 209–11, 230. See also Charles Davenport, "Nomadism, or the Wandering Impulse, with Special Reference to Heredity," Carnegie Institution Pamphlet (Washington, D.C., 1915). Fernand Levillain discusses the Austrian M. Benedikt's theory that vagabonds were neurasthenics in his book *La Neurasthenie: Maladie de Beard* (Paris, 1891), pp. 310–12.

7. Jack London, *The Road* (Santa Barbara, Calif.: Peregrine Publishers, Inc., 1970), pp. ii, 180 ff; idem, *The People of the Abyss* (New York: Archer House, 1963), p. 137.

8. Josiah Flynt Willard, "The Tramp and the Railroads," *Century* 58 (June 1899): 260–63. Benjamin C. Marsh, "Causes of Vagrancy and Methods of Eradication," *Annals* 23 (May 1904): 38. Edward T. Devine, "The Shiftless and Floating City Population," *Annals* 10 (September 1897): 161–62.

9. Alice Willard Solenberger, *One Thousand Homeless Men* (New York 1911), pp. 2, 136 ff. Adams, "The Real Hobo," p. 448.

10. Josiah Flynt Willard, *Tramping with Tramps* (1889; Montclair, N.J.: Paterson Smith, 1972), pp. 2–6.

11. James B. Gilbert, *Writers and Partisans* (New York: John Wiley, 1968).

12. Devine, "Shiftless Population," p. 163. Robert Hunter, *Poverty* (New York, 1904), pp. 124–34.

13. H. A. Millis, "The Relief and Care of Dependents," *American Journal of Sociology* 3 (March 1898): 631–48. Marsh, "Causes of Vagrancy," p. 452.

CHAPTER 4

1. Charles K. Mills, "Mental Over-Work and Premature Disease among Public and Professional Men," *Smithsonian Miscellaneous Collections* 34 (May 1891): 1. Mills discusses Herbert Spencer. See also Stephen Nissenbaum, "Careful Love," (Ph.D. diss., University of Wisconsin, 1968).

2. George M. Beard, *Sexual Neurasthenia: Its Hygiene, Causes, Symptoms and Treatment,* 5th ed. (New York, 1898), p. 25, and idem, *American Nervousness, Its Causes and Consequences* (New York, 1881). Charles E. Rosenberg, "The Place of George M. Beard in Nineteenth Century Psychiatry," *Bulletin of the History of Medicine* 36 (May-June 1962): 245–50.

3. Beard, *American Nervousness,* pp. vi, 102, 185. See also Michel Foucault, *Madness and Civilization: A History of Insanity in the Age of Reason* (New York: Random House, 1965).

4. Beard, *American Nervousness,* p. 313. William James was interested in Beard's theories; see Nathan G. Hale, Jr., *Freud and the Americans: The Beginning of Psychoanalysis in the United States, 1876–1917* (New York: Oxford University Press, 1971), p. 66.

5. S. Weir Mitchell, *Wear and Tear* (Philadelphia, 1899), pp. 10, 63. This work was first published as a series of articles for *Lippincott's Magazine.*

6. See, for example, "Current Medical Literature," *American Medical Association Journal* 35 (29 September 1900): *passim*, and James Hendric Lloyd, "Medicolegal Relations of Traumatic Nervous Affections," *American Medical Association Journal* 35 (22 September 1900): 733–35. Edward Cowles, *Neurasthenia and Its Mental Symptoms* (Boston, 1891), pp. 11, 35, 62 ff.

7. H. C. Sawyer, *Nerve Waste: Practical Information Concerning Nervous Impairment in Modern Life*, 2nd ed. (San Francisco, 1889), pp. 7, 49.

8. Thomas D. Savill, *Clinical Lectures on Neurasthenia*, 3rd ed. (New York, 1907), passim.

9. "The Autobiography of a Neurasthenic," *American Magazine* 71 (December 1910): 231.

10. S. Weir Mitchell, *Fat and Blood: An Essay on the Treatment of Certain Forms of Neurasthenia and Hysteria*, 8th ed. (Philadelphia, 1902), pp. 59 ff, 212–13. Beard also advised the use of electricity.

11. Morton Prince, "The Educational Treatment of Neurasthenia and Certain Hysterical States," *Boston Medical and Surgical Journal* 139 (6 October 1898): 332–37. See also Henri F. Ellenberger, *The Discovery of the Unconscious: The History and Evolution of Dynamic Psychiatry* (New York: Basic Books, Inc., 1970).

12. W. F. Robinson, *Electro-Therapeutics of Neurasthenia* (Detroit, 1893), pp. 9–23.

13. Arthur Carey, *Nervous Prostration and Its Spiritual Cause* (Waltham, Mass., 1904), p. 21. Carey belonged to the "New Church" movement. See also Richard Clarke Cabot, *What Men Live By* (Boston, 1914), pp. xix, 13–45.

14. Boris Sidis, *Nervous Ills: Their Cause and Cure* (Boston: Richard G. Badger, 1922), pp. 334, 369.

15. Theodule Armaud Ribot, *Diseases of the Will*, trans. J. Fitzgerald (New York, 1884), pp. 45, 28–39. Horatio C. Wood, *Brain-Work and Overwork* (Philadelphia, 1880), p. 60. In his "simple life movement," French writer Charles Wagner appealed to many Americans who agreed that the rigors of industrialism were dangerous to the human personality. Among such Americans were reformers Albert Shaw and Lyman Abbott. (Charles Wagner, *My Appeal to Americans*, Intro. by Lyman Abbott [New York, 1905].)

16. John Cawelti, *Apostles of the Self-Made Man* (Chicago: University of Chicago Press, 1965), pp. 4, 168 ff. See also Jean Alter, "The Revolt from Success in the Novel of the Twenties," (Ph.D. diss., University of Chicago, 1958), pp. 4–11, and Dixon Wecter, *The Hero in America: A Chronicle of Hero-Worship* (New York: Charles Scribner's Sons, 1972), p. 485.

17. Ruth M. Elson, *Guardians of Tradition: American Textbooks of the Nineteenth Century* (Lincoln: University of Nebraska Press, 1964), pp. 43 ff. See also Richard D. Mosier, *Making the American Mind: Social and Moral Ideas in the McGuffey Reader* (New York: King's Crown Press, 1947), pp. 1 ff, 89, 110, 123. Richard M. Huber, *The American Idea of Success* (New York: McGraw-Hill Co., 1971), pp. 51–55.

18. George B. Putnam, "Clerkology," *Retail Clerks International Advocate* 15 (June 1908): 19. This same sort of ambiguity about success can also be seen in the *Book-Keeper* and *Business Magazine*. In the latter publication success is pictured more subtly and honestly, as being the result of small steps.

19. Ernest C. Johnson, *Working and Winning* (New Haven, Conn., 1914), p. 14. R. H. Thurston, "The College-Man as Leader in the World's Work," *Appleton's Popular Science Monthly* 60 (February 1902): 356–59. Gail Thain Parker, *Mind Cure in New England: From the Civil War to World War I* (Hanover, N.H.: University Press of New England, 1973), pp. 16, 167. Donald Meyer, *The Positive Thinkers: A Study of the American Quest for Health, Wealth, and Personal Power from Mary Baker Eddy to Norman Vincent Peale* (New York: Doubleday, 1965), p. 134.

20. Ernest Poole, "From Sweatshop to Factory," *Retail Clerks International Advocate* 11 (April 1904): 9.

21. Kenneth S. Lynn, *The Dream of Success: A Study of the Modern American Imagination* (Boston: Little, Brown and Co., 1955), pp. 25–47. See also Hale, *Freud and the Americans*, pp. 228–40.

22. Elwood Worcester et al., *The Moral Control of Nervous Disorders* (New York, 1908), p. 133.

23. Annie Payson Call, *Power through Repose* (Boston, 1898). For the ambiguity of churches toward modern economic conditions, see, for example, William T. Doherty, "The Impact of Business on Protestantism, 1900–1929," *Business History Review* 28 (June 1954): 141–53.

CHAPTER 5

1. Oswald Spengler, *The Decline of the West* (New York: Alfred Knopf, 1934), pp. 503–4.

2. Thorstein Veblen, *The Instinct of Workmanship; and the State of the Industrial Arts* (New York: Augustus M. Kelley, 1964), pp. 312, 319. Nels Anderson, *Dimensions of Work: The Sociology of a Work Culture* (New York: David McKay Co., 1964), p. 163.

3. Waldo Pondray Warren, *Thoughts on Business* (Chicago, 1907), p. 23. William Armstrong Fairburn, *Work, Talent, and Genius* (New York, 1916), p. 66.

4. Adriano Tilgher, *Homo Faber: Work: What It Has Meant to Men through the Ages* (New York: Harcourt, Brace & Co., 1930), p. 574. Jean Fourastie argues that the positive definition of work is relatively new in Human history. (Jean Fourastie, *Idées Majeures: Pour un Humanisme de la Société Scientifique* [Paris: Gonthier, 1936], pp. 21–31.)

5. Quoted in Raymond Williams, *Culture and Society, 1780–1950* (Garden City, N.Y.: Anchor Books, 1960), p. 152. See also Georges Friedmann, *La Crise du Progres*, 2nd ed. (Paris: Gallimard, 1936).

6. Peter F. Drucker, *The New Society* (London: William Heinemann Ltd., 1951), p. xvii. See also Robert S. Lynd and Helen Merrell Lynd, *Middletown* (New York: Harcourt, Brace & Co., 1929), p. 76.

7. Charles Fourier, *The Utopian Vision of Charles Fourier: Selected Texts on Work, Love, and Passionate Attraction*, trans. and ed. Jonathan Beecher and Richard Bienvenu (Boston: Beacon Press, 1971), p. 327. C. Wright Mills distinguishes between an older, Christian and the Renaissance view of labor; the former marked by religious sanction and satisfaction, and the latter viewing labor as valuable in its own right. I prefer to see these as emphases, not separate categories. It is hard, if not impossible, to distinguish between sectarian and religious ideas in America thought in the nineteenth and early twentieth centuries. C. Wright Mills, *White-collar: The American Middle Classes* (New York: Oxford University Press, 1953), pp. 217 ff. See also Frank Manuel, *The Prophets of Paris* (Cambridge, Mass.: Harvard University Press, 1962) and Constance M. Hall, *The Sociology of Pierre Joseph Proudhon, 1809–1865* (New York: Philosophical Library, 1971).

8. Pierre Joccard, *Histoire Sociale du Travail de l'Antiquité à nos Jours* (Paris: Payot, 1960), pp. 315–16. Pierre Joseph Proudhon, *Selected Writings*, trans. Elizabeth Fraser, ed. Steward Edwards (London: MacMillan and Co., Ltd., 1969), pp. 20, 25, 132. Tilgher, *Work*, p. 128. Leo Tolstoy, *The Slavery of Our Times* (New York, 1900), p. 39.

9. Eric Fromm, *Marx's Concept of Man: The Economic and Philosophical Manuscripts*, trans. T. B. Bottomore (New York: Frederick Ungar Publishing Co., 1961), p. 29. See also Henri Arvon, *La Philosophie du Travail* (Paris: Presses Universitaires de France, 1961), pp. 21 ff.

10. Emile Durkheim, *The Division of Labor in Society*, trans. George Simpson (New York: Free Press of Glencoe, 1933), pp. 372, 400, 409.

11. Max Weber, *Economy and Society: An Outline of Interpretive Sociology*,

eds. Gunther Roth and Claus Wittich (New York: Beminster Press, 1968), p. 223. Herbert Marcuse, *Negations*, trans. Jeremy J. Shapiro (Boston: Beacon Press, 1968), pp. 206–16.

12. Charles W. Eliot, "Content in Work," *World's Work* 8 (1904): 4959.

13. William D. P. Bliss, *The Encyclopedia of Social Reform* (1897; Westport, Conn.: Greenwood Press, 1970), pp. 502–4.

14. Reverend R. Herber Newton, "Industrial Education," in *The Labor Movement: The Problem of Today*, ed. George E. McNeill (New York: Augustus M. Kelley, 1971), p. 536.

15. Henry George, quoted in McNeill, *Labor Movement*, pp. 563 ff.

16. Frank W. Taussig, *Inventors and Money-Makers* (New York: MacMillan Co., 1915), pp. 11 ff, 66 ff.

17. Thorstein Veblen, "The Instinct of Workmanship and the Irksomeness of Labor," *American Journal of Sociology* 4 (September 1898): 187. For quote on James, see Veblen, *Instinct of Workmanship*, p. 344. See also Thorstein Veblen, *The Theory of the Leisure Class* (New York: New America Library, 1953).

18. George D. Herron, "The Social System and the Christian Conscience," *The Industrialist* 24 (July 1898): 491.

19. Francis Greenwood Peabody, *Jesus Christ and the Social Question* (New York, 1900), pp. 279, 282 ff.

20. Jane Addams, *Democracy and Social Ethics* (1902; Cambridge, Mass.: Belknap Press, 1964), p. 4.

21. Charles Roads, *Christ Enthroned in the Industrial World* (New York, 1892), p. 116.

22. Albert Shaw, *The Outlook for the Average Man* (New York, 1907), p. 141.

23. Thomas Davidson, *The Education of the Wage-Earners* (New York, 1904), p. 94.

24. William Armstrong Fairburn, *Work, Talent, and Genius*, p. 11.

25. Louis Brandeis, *Business—A Profession* (Boston, 1914), p. 34. See also Howard M. Vollmer and Donald L. Mills, *Professionalization* (Englewood Cliffs, N.J.: Prentice-Hall, Inc., 1966).

26. George Barton Cutten, *The Threat of Leisure* (New Haven, Conn.: Yale University Press, 1926), p. 12. Algie M. Simon, "The Evolution of Leisure for the Many," *Craftsman* 8 (September 1905): 777–80.

27. Georges Friedmann, *Problèmes Humains du Mechanisme Industriel* (Paris: Gallimard, 1946), p. 25.

28. Carroll D. Wright, "Hand and Machine Labor," *Thirteenth Annual Report of the Commissioner of Labor*, 1898, 2 vols. (Washington, D.C., 1899), 1:6. Carroll D. Wright, "The Apprenticeship System in its Relation to Industrial Education," *Bulletin of the United States Bureau of Education*, 1908 (Washington, D.C., 1908), pp. 65 ff. Paul Douglas, *American Apprenticeship and Industrial Education: Studies in History, Economics and Public Law* (New York: Columbia University Press, 1921), p. 54.

29. Quoted in Chessman A. Herrick, *Commercial Education: Training of Business Men as a Branch of Technical Instruction, Supplement, 5th Yearbook*, National Herbart Society, 1899 (Chicago, 1900), p. 155.

30. Carroll D. Wright, *The Industrial Evolution of the United States* (New York, 1895), pp. 346–47. See also Walter Lippmann, *A Preface to Politics* (Ann Arbor, Mich.: Ann Arbor Paperbacks, 1962), p. 54.

31. H. J. Hapgood, "The Endless Search for a Man," *Retail Clerks International Advocate* 12 (February 1905): 11.

32. Quoted in Leverett S. Lyon, *Education for Business* (Chicago: University of Chicago Press, 1922), pp. 82–83.

33. Douglas, *American Apprenticeship*, p. 107. Stuart Chase, *Men and Machines* (New York: MacMillan Co., 1929, 1935), pp. 263–64. Helen Marot, *Creative Impulse in Industry* (New York, 1918), p. 12.

34. Edwin Bjorkman, "What Industrial Civilization May Do to Men," *Worlds Work* 17 (April 1909): 11483.

35. "The Typewriter or the Muse," *Nation* 96 (6 March 1913): 226. Morris Llewellyn Cooke, *Academic and Industrial Efficiency, Bulletin of the Carnegie Foundation for the Advancement of Teaching* (New York, 1910), pp. iv, 57.

36. David Graham Phillips, "The Business Organization of a Church," *Harpers* 107 (July 1903): 210.

37. Edwin G. Knepper, *History of Business Education in the United States* (Bowling Green, Ohio, 1941), pp. 136–40. Louis T. Harnus, "The Introduction of Office Machines and Employment of Office Workers in the United States, 1900–1950" (Ph.D. diss., University of Pennsylvania, 1955), pp. 123, 357. Gilman M. Ostrander, *American Civilization in the First Machine Age; 1890–1940* (New York: Harper & Row, 1970), p. 212.

38. William H. Leffingwell, *Making the Office Pay* (Chicago, 1918), pp. 26–27.

39. Walter Rauschenbusch, "A Prayer for All Working Women," *American Magazine* (May 1910).

40. Martha B. Bruere and Robert W. Bruere, *Increasing Home Efficiency* (New York, 1912), p. 290. Abraham Myerson, *The Nervous Housewife* (1920; New York: Arno Press, 1972), pp. 26, 166.

41. Charlotte Perkins Gilman, *Women and Economics* (1898; New York: Harper & Row, 1966), pp. 67–68, 95.

42. Hamilton Wright Mabie, *Essays on Work and Culture* (New York, 1898), pp. 59, 75. Charlotte Perkins Gilman, *Human Work* (New York, 1904), p. 182.

43. Gerald Stanley Lee, *The Voice of the Machines* (Northampton, Mass., 1906), pp. 12, 19.

44. Frederick Kenyon Brown, *Man or Machine—Which?* (Boston, 1912), pp. 77, 79, 108. Henry Gantt, *Organizing for Work* (New York, 1919), p. 108.

CHAPTER 6

1. Paul de Roussiers, *La Vie Américaine* (Paris, 1892), p. 515. Jane Addams, *Twenty Years at Hull House* (1910; New York: New American Library, 1961), p. 164.

2. John Higham, "The Reorientation of American Culture in the 1890's," *Writing American History: Essays on Modern Scholarship* (Bloomington: Indiana University Press, 1970), p. 78. Henry Nash Smith, *Virgin Land: The American West as Symbol and Myth* (Cambridge, Mass.: Harvard University Press, 1950). See also Richard Slotkin, *Regeneration Through Violence: The Mythology of the American Frontier, 1600–1860* (Middletown, Conn. Wesleyan University Press, 1973).

3. Charlotte Perkins Gilman, *Human Work* (New York, 1904), pp. 102–103.

4. Henry S. Curtis, "Recreation and Play," in *America and the New Era*, by Elisha M. Friedman (New York: E. P. Dutton and Co., 1920), p. 451–52.

5. Philippe Ariès, *Centuries of Childhood: A Social History of Family Life*, trans. Robert Baldick (New York: Vintage Books, 1962), pp. 413–14. See also Foster Rhea Dulles, *A History of Recreation: America Learns to Play*, 2nd ed. (New York: Appleton-Century-Crofts, 1965), pp. 182–83, 243. See also the controversy over football in the pages of *Nation* during the 1890s.

6. William I. Thomas, "The Gaming Instinct," *American Journal of Sociology* 6 (May 1901): 750–51, 757.

7. James R. McGovern, "David Graham Phillips and the Virility Impulse of Progressives," *New England Quarterly* 39 (September 1966): 352.

8. Thorstein Veblen, *The Theory of the Leisure Class; An Economic Study of Institutions* (1899; New York: New American Library, 1953), pp. 256, 166.

9. Josiah Royce, *Race Questions, Provincialism, and Other American Problems* (1908; Freeport, N.Y.: Books for Libraries Press, 1967), pp. 241, 286.

10. Calvin M. Woodward, "Domestic and Intercollegiate Athletics," *Popular*

Science Monthly 61 (October 1902): 553. Edwin G. Dexter, "Newspaper Football," *Popular Science Monthly* 68 (March 1906): 265.

11. Theodore Roosevelt, " 'Professionalism' in Sports," *North American Review* 151 (August 1890): 187–91. See also John Betts, *America's Sporting Heritage, 1850–1950* (Reading, Mass.: Addison-Wesley, 1974), p. 126.

12. Albert Shaw, "College Reform—and Football," *Review of Reviews* 15 (December 1909): 724–29.

13. David Starr Jordan, "The American Game of Football as Related to Physical Education," *National Education Association, Journal of Proceedings and Addresses* (Winona, Minn., 1910); Charles Eliot Norton, "Some Aspects of Civilization in America," *Forum* (February 1896): 664, 650.

14. Theodore Roosevelt, *Value of an Athletic Training* (New York, 1929). Frank Ripley McDonald Young, "Football in the Gilded Age: The Origin and Social Meaning of American Football," (Ph.D. diss., University of Maryland, 1971).

15. Edward Mussey Hartwell, "On Physical Training," *Report of the United States Bureau of Education, 1897–1898* (Washington, D.C., 1899), pp. 490–555.

16. A. T. Dudley, "The Mental Qualities of an Athlete," *Harvard Monthly* 6 (April 1888): 50. See also Charles De Freminville, "How Taylor Introduced the Scientific Method into the Management of the Shop," *Bulletin of the Taylor Society* 10 (February 1925): 30–40.

17. Georges Sorel, *Reflections on Violence*, trans. T. E. Hulme, revised ed. (London, 1915), pp. 295, 133. For a comparison of Sorel and James, see Irving Horowitz, *Radicalism and the Revolt Against Reason* (London: Routledge and Kegan Paul, 1961).

18. Ralph Barton Perry, *The Thought and Character of William James as Revealed in Unpublished Correspondence and Notes, Together with his Published Writings*, 2 vols. (Boston: Little, Brown & Co., 1935), II:246–47.

19. Homer Lea, *The Valor of Ignorance* (New York, 1909), p. 41.

20. William James, "The Moral Equivalent of War," *International Conciliation Pamphlet* no. 27 (February 1910); p. 8.

21. William James, *Talks to Teachers on Psychology: And to Students on Some of Life's Ideals* (New York, 1914), p. 214.

CHAPTER 7

1. Edward Pearson Pressey and Carl Purington Rollins, *The Arts and Crafts and the Individual* (Montague, Mass., 1904), p. 22; the authors quote Mrs. Dennett. Ellen Gates Starr, "Art and Labor," in *Hull-House Maps and Papers*, by Residents of Hull House (New York, 1895), pp. 167–69.

2. Charles F. Binns, "The Arts and Crafts Movement in America" *Craftsman* 14 (June 1908): 275–76.

3. Society of Arts and Crafts, *Sixteenth Annual Report* (Boston, 1913). Society of Arts and Crafts, *Annual Report of 1903* (Boston, 1904).

4. Sara Norton and M. A. Dewolfe Howe, eds., *Letters of Charles Eliot Norton*, 2 vols. (Boston, 1913) II:430. See also Roger B. Stein, *John Ruskin and Aesthetic Thought in America, 1840–1900* (Cambridge, Mass.: Harvard University Press, 1967), p. 258.

5. Theodore D. Weld, *First Annual Report of the Society for Promoting Manual Labor in Literary Institutions* (New York: S. W. Benedict and Co., 1833), pp. 13, 23.

6. Pressey and Rollins, *Arts and Crafts*, p. 5.

7. Oscar Lovell Triggs, *Chapters in the History of the Arts and Crafts Movement* (1902; New York: Benjamin Blom, Inc., 1971), pp. 3 ff. See also W. D. P. Bliss, *The Communism of John Ruskin* (New York, 1891), p. xi.

8. John Ruskin, *The Crown of Wild Olives* (New York, 189?), pp. 10, 42. "The Gothic Revival," *Craftsman* 1 (March 1902): 2, 31. Alice Chandler, *The Dream of Order: The Medieval Ideal in Nineteenth-Century English Literature* (Lincoln; University of Nebraska Press, 1970), pp. 198, 234.

9. Claude F. Bragdon, "L'Art Nouveau and American Architecture," *Articraft* 1 (December 1903): 30. Frank Parsons founded the Ruskin College of Social Science in 1899 in the United States. Arthur Mann, *Yankee Reformers in the Urban Age* (Cambridge, Mass.: Harvard University Press, 1954), p. 130.

10. Triggs, *Chapters*, p. 150. Bragdon, "L'Art Nouveau," p. 39. For commentary on the ties between Sullivan and Morris, see A. D. F. Hamlin, "L'Art Nouveau, its Origin and Development," *Craftsman* 3 (December 1902): 129-43.

11. L. Turner, "The Little Shop: its Wares and Influence," *Articraft* 1 (March 1904): 145.

12. Gustave Stickley, "The National Spirit of Speculation: Are Not our Financial and Corporate Morals Merely the Outgrowth of the Moral Sense of the American People?" *Craftsman* 13 (December 1907): 316. Frank Lloyd Wright, "The Art and Craft of the Machine," *Articraft* 1 (May 1904): 165-67.

13. Oscar Lovell Triggs, "The Play Principle," *Craftsman* 6 (June 1904): 290.

14. Gustav Stickley, "Thoughts Occasioned by an Anniversary: A Plea for a Democratic Art," *Craftsman* 7 (October 1904): 53. See also John Crosby Freeman, *The Forgotten Rebel: Gustav Stickley and His Craftsman Mission Furniture* (Watkins Glen, N.Y. Century House, 1966), pp. 40-45.

15. Stickley, "Democratic Art," pp. 42-43, 56.

16. Stickley, "Spirit of Speculation," p. 312.

17. *Handicraft* 1-4 (1902-1912, intermittant publication). Significantly, in 1914, the magazine changed its name to *Industrial Arts Magazine*.

18. Arthur Carey, "The Past Year and its Lessons," *Handicraft* 1 (April 1902): 7-22. Mrs. Hartley Dennett, "Aesthetics and Ethics," *Handicraft* 1 (May 1902): 32-33, 46.

19. Sylvester Baxter, "The Movement for Village Industries," *Handicraft* 1 (October 1902): 145. Mary Dennett, "The Arts and Crafts," *Handicraft* 3 (April 1903): 22.

20. Walter Crane, "Modern Life and the Artistic Sense," *Cosmopolitan* 13 (June 1892): 156.

21. H. Landford Warren, "Our Work and Prospects," *Handicraft* 2 (December 1903): 185, 189. See also Parris Thaxter Farwell, *Village Improvement* (New York, 1918), pp. 13-38. George E. Waring, Jr., *Village Improvements and Farm Villages* (Boston, 1877). See also Donald K. Pickens, *Eugenics and the Progressives* (Nashville: Vanderbilt University Press, 1968), pp. 193 ff.

22. Frederic Allen Whiting, "What the Arts and Crafts Movement has Accomplished," *Handicraft* 3 (June 1910): 95.

23. Elizabeth B. Stone, "Observations of an Onlooker," *Handicraft* 3 (June 1910): 39.

CHAPTER 8

1. C. Valentine Kirby, "Craftsmanship as a Preventive of Crime," *Craftsman* 8 (May 1905): 171-77. Arthur Payne, "The Influence of the Arts and Crafts Movement upon Manual Training," *Handicraft* 4 (October 1911): 245.

2. G. Stanley Hall, *Adolescence*, 2 vols. (New York, 1905), I: 171-80.

3. Isaac Edwards Clarke, "The Democracy of Art, with Suggestions Concerning the Relations of Art to Education, Industry, and National Prosperity," *Preliminary Papers to Report on Industrial and High Art Education in the United States*, United States Commissioner of Education (Washington, D.C., 1886), p. 137.

4. William D. P. Bliss, *The Encyclopedia of Social Reform* (1897; Westport, Conn.: Greenwood Press, 1970), p. 728.

5. Daniel Coit Gilman, "A Plea for the Training of the Hand," *Monographs of the Industrial Education Association* 1 (January 1888); 4-11.

6. Bliss, *Encyclopedia of Social Reform*, p. 730. Marvin Lazerson, *Origins of the Urban School: Public Education in Massachusetts, 1870-1915* (Cambridge, Mass.: Harvard University Press, 1971), pp. 93-94.

7. Quoted by Frank A. Hill, "The Manual Training Idea—Reminiscences of Personal Growth into its Spirit," *Manual Training Magazine* 1 (October 1899): 15. See also "Editorials," *Manual Training Magazine* 1 (October 1899): 53–57.

8. *Official Catalogue of Exhibitors, Universal Exposition,* St. Louis, Department of Anthropology (St. Louis, 1904), pp. 9, 17.

9. See John Spargo for the effect of manual training on immigrants; "The Regeneration of Ikey—The Story of a School Where Dull or Vicious Little Brains are Awakened by Training the Hands to do Useful Work," *Craftsman* 7 (September 1907): 642–46. See also Charles F. Pidgen, "The Apprenticeship System," *Annual Report of the Massachusetts Bureau of Statistics of Labor,* part 1 (Boston, 1906), p. 58.

10. Isaac Clarke, "Democracy of Art," in *Preliminary Papers to Report on Industrial and High Art Education,* pp. cxxi, cxvi, 139.

11. Leslie W. Miller, "The Possible Relations of a State School of Art to the Industries of the Commonwealth," *Massachusetts Board of Education Bulletin* (Boston, 1913), p. 33.

12. Lois Coffey, "The Mission of Industrial Arts," *Arts and Industry in Education* (New York, 1912), p. 37.

13. Herman Schneider, *Education for Industrial Workers, School Efficiency Series,* ed. Paul H. Hanus (Yonkers-on-Hudson, New York, 1915), pp. 55 ff.

14. Henry Demarest Lloyd, *Man, the Social Creator,* ed. Jane Addams and Anne Withington (New York, 1906), pp. 203, 273, 173.

15. Reverend Francis E. Clark, "The Next Step Forward," *Proceedings of the First Annual Convention of the Religious Education Association* (Chicago, 1903), pp. 3–14.

16. Charles Henderson, "The Manual-Training School as a Factor in Social Progress," *Manual Training Magazine* 2 (October 1900): 8.

17. "Manual Training and Citizenship," *Craftsman* 5 (January 1904): 407–10.

18. Foster H. Irons, "A Study: Manual Training for City Children," *Manual Training Magazine* 1 (July 1900): 196.

19. Schneider, *Education for Industrial Workers,* p. 17.

20. Lazerson, *Origins of the Urban School,* p. 178.

21. Colin A. Scott, *Social Education* (Boston, 1908), pp. 237–55.

22. John Dewey, "The Place of Manual Training in the Elementary Course of Study," *Manual Training Magazine* 2 (July 1901): 197. John Dewey, "Ethical Principles Underlying Education," *Third Yearbook of the National Herbart Society* (Chicago, 1897), pp. 8, 13–17.

CHAPTER 9

1. See for example, Joel H. Spring, *Education and the Rise of the Corporate State* (Boston: Beacon Press, 1972). Colin Greer, *The Great School Legend: A Revisionist Interpretation of American Public Education* (New York: Basic Books, Inc., 1972). Michael B. Katz, *The Irony of Early School Reform; Educational Innovation in Mid-Nineteenth Century Massachusetts* (Cambridge, Mass.: Harvard University Press, 1968), pp. 36, 43–53.

2. Horace Mann, "The Powers of Common Schools to Redeem the State from Social Vices and Crimes," and "Education and Crime," in *Report of the Commissioner of Education for the Year, 1898–99,* 2 vols. (Washington, D.C., 1900), II: 1254–55, 1282.

3. William T. Harris, "Compulsory Education in Relation to Crime and Social Morals," *Report of the Commissioner of Education for the Year 1898–99,* 2 vols. (Washington, D.C., 1900) II:1317. See also Zachariah Montgomery, *The School Question From a Parental and Non-Sectarian Standpoint* (1889; New York: Arno Press, 1972), pp. 3–10, and J. McKeen Cattell, "The School and the Family," *Popular Science Monthly* 74 (January 1909): 84–95.

4. William T. Harris, "Moral Education in the Common Schools," Address to the

Sixth meeting of the Illinois Social Science Association, Chicago, 16 October 1883, William Torrey Harris Manuscripts, Library of Congress, Washington, D.C.

5. Henry Suzzallo, "Introduction" to George Herbert Palmer's "Ethical and Moral Instruction in Schools," *Riverside Educational Monographs*, ed. Henry Suzzallo (Boston, 1909), p. v. See also Gustav Spiller, *Report on Moral Instruction and on Moral Training* (London, 1909), pp. 284 ff, and William T. Harris, "Herbert Spencer," *Proceedings of the Department of Superintendence*, National Educational Association, 1904 (Chicago, 1904), p. 54.

6. Palmer, "Moral Instruction," pp. 17–31. For the importance of this movement see Edward H. Griggs, *Moral Education* (New York, 1904), p. 279.

7. Felix Adler, *Moral Instruction of Children* (New York, 1892), p. 269.

8. F. A. Cavenagh, ed., *Herbert Spencer on Education* (Cambridge: At the University Press, 1932), pp. 56–57.

9. Janine Assa et al., *Traité des Sciences Pédagogique, Histoire de Pédagogie* 2 vols. (Paris: Presses Univérsitaires de France, 1971), II:366. Walter B. Kolesnik, *Mental Discipline in Modern Education* (Madison: University of Wisconsin Press, 1958).

10. John Dewey, "Ethical Principles Underlying Education," *Third Yearbook of the National Herbart Society* (Chicago, 1897), pp. 12–14.

11. John Dewey, "Interpretation of the Savage Mind," *Psychological Review* 9 (May 1902): 219–20, 229.

12. John Dewey, *The School and Society*, revised ed. (Chicago, 1915), pp. 134–35.

13. John Dewey, *Schools of Tomorrow* (1915, New York: E. P. Dutton, 1962), pp. 121, 173.

14. Dewey, *School and Society*, p. 136.

15. Dewey, *Schools of Tomorrow*, p. 181.

16. Dewey, *School and Society*, p. 18.

17. John Dewey, *Democracy and Education, an Introduction to the Philosophy of Education* (New York, 1916), p. 356.

18. Dewey is quoted by Helen Wooley in "Charting Childhood," in *Readings in Vocational Guidance*, ed. Meyer Bloomfield (Boston, 1915), p. 237.

CHAPTER 10

1. Charles Horton Cooley, *Personal Competition* (New York, 1899), pp. 78, 106–7.

2. Hugo Munsterberg, *Vocation and Learning* (St. Louis, 1912), pp. 11, 24.

3. Charles W. Eliot, "The Value During Education of the Life-Career Motive," *Journal of Proceedings and Addresses*, National Education Association (Winona, Minnesota, 1910), pp. 134, 140. Meyer Bloomfield was one of the leading advocates of vocational guidance; he credited this speech with setting the direction of vocational guidance. Meyer Bloomfield, *The Vocational Guidance of Youth* (1911; New York: Arno Press, 1969), p. 25.

4. Frank Parsons, *Choosing a Vocation* (Boston, 1909), pp. 20–21, 114. See also William B. Whiteside, *The Boston Y.M.C.A. and Community Need* (New York: Association Press, 1951), pp. 125–152. John Brewer, historian of vocational guidance, agrees on the central role of Parsons. (John Marks Brewer, *History of Vocational Guidance; Origins and Early Development* [New York: Harper and Brothers, 1942], p. 49.)

5. Roy Willmarth Kelly, *Training Industrial Workers* (New York: Ronald Press Co., 1920), p. 348.

6. C. A. Prosser, "Practical Arts and Vocational Guidance," in Meyer Bloomfield, *Readings in Vocational Guidance* (Boston, 1915), p. 352.

7. Herman Schneider, "Effect of Noise, Fatigue, and Environment on Workers," in Bloomfield, *Readings in Vocational Guidance*, pp. 379–85.

8. Louis R. Harlan, *Booker T. Washington, The Making of a Black Leader, 1856–1901* (New York: Oxford University Press, 1972), pp. 63–64.

9. Oscar Lovell Triggs, "A School of Industrial Art," *Craftsman* 3 (January 1903): 216.

10. "Toward a Profession," *American Teacher* 2 (January 1913): 9; Henrietta Rodman, "Vocational Guidance and Training," *American Teacher* 1 (February 1912): 10–13. See also Marvin Lazerson, *Origins of the Urban School: Public Education in Massachusetts, 1870–1915* (Cambridge, Mass.: Harvard University Press, 1971), pp. 200, 255–57.

11. See Brewer, *History of Vocational Guidance*, pp. 5, 259 ff.; Whiteside, *Boston Y.M.C.A.*, pp. 108–53, and Sol Cohen, "The Industrial Education Movement, 1906–1907," *American Quarterly* 20 (Spring 1968): 96. Entries concerning the Boston Vocation Bureau are frequent in the *Readers' Guide to Periodical Literature* after 1910.

12. Bloomfield, *Vocational Guidance of Youth*, pp. x, 31–32 (his italics).

13. Vocation Bureau of Boston, *Vocation Guidance and the Work of the Vocation Bureau of Boston* (Boston, 1915), pp. 5, 8. In 1915 the Vocation Bureau of Boston listed as sponsors and officers: A. Lincoln Filene of Filene's Store, E. J. Bliss, president of the Boston Chamber of Commerce, several other important businessmen, and one labor leader. See also Edmund C. Lynch, *Meyer Bloomfield and Employment Management; Studies in Personnel and Management*, no. 22 (Austin, Tex.: Bureau of Business Research, 1970), pp. 4, 36.

14. Rodman, "Vocational Guidance," p. 11. See also Edward L. Thorndike, "The University and Vocational Guidance," in Bloomfield, *Readings in Vocational Guidance*.

CHAPTER 11

1. New York State Board of Charities, *Field Work Manual*, Eugenics and Social Welfare Bulletin no. 10 (Albany, New York, 1917), p. 12.

2. Massachusetts Association of Relief Officers, *Report on the Best Methods of Dealing with Tramps* (Boston, 1901), p. 4.

3. Arthur MacDonald, "Moral Education," *American Monthly Magazine* 32 (June 1908): 1. See also Peter A. Speek, "The Psychology of Floating Workers, *Annals* 69 (January 1917): 72–78, and Henry M. Boies, *The Science of Penology: The Defence of Society Against Crime* (New York, 1901), p. 43.

4. Arthur MacDonald, *Statistics of Crime, Suicide, Insanity and Other Forms of Abnormality . . . in Connection with a Bill to Establish a Laboratory for the Study of Criminal, Pauper, and Defective Classes*, United States Congress, Senate Document 12, 58th Cong., 1st Sess. (Washington, D.C., 1903). See also Hugo Münsterberg, *On the Witness Stand, Essays on Psychology and Crime* (New York, 1909).

5. See David Rothman, *The Discovery of the Asylum; Social Order and Disorder in the New Republic* (Boston: Little, Brown and Co., 1971), p. 237, and Norman Dain, *Concepts of Insanity in the United States, 1789–1865* (New Brunswick, N.J.: Rutgers University Press, 1964), pp. xiii, 161.

6. Orlando F. Lewis, *The Development of American Prisons and Prison Customs, 1776–1845* (1922; Montclair, N.J.: Patterson Smith, 1967), p. 130. See also Blake McKelvey, *American Prisons: A Study in American Social History Prior to 1915* (Montclair, N.J.: Patterson Smith, 1968), pp. 21, 39.

7. Francis Paul Prucha, "Indian Reform Policy and American Protestantism," in *People of the Plains and Mountains*, ed. Ray Allen Billington (Westport, Conn.: Greenwood Press, 1973), pp. 120–45.

8. Jack M. Holl, *Juvenile Reform in the Progressive Era: William R. George and the Junior Republic Movement* (Ithaca, N.Y.: Cornell University Press, 1971), pp. 231, 240, 185.

9. Florence Finch Kelly, "An Undertow to the Land: Successful Efforts to Make Possible a Flow of the City Population Countryward," *Craftsman* 11 (December 1906): 294–308.

10. New York State Board of Charities, *State Industrial Farm Colony, Annual Report of 1912* (Albany, New York, 1913), p. 27. See also "Tramp Colony Assured," *Survey* 26 (5 August 1911): 633 and "The Farm Colony for Tramps," *Independent* 71 (27 July 1911): 269–70.

11. Orlando F. Lewis, *Vagrancy in the United States,* A paper presented to the thirty-fourth annual session of the National Conference of Charities and Corrections, 14 June 1907 (New York, 1907), pp. 3–56.

12. Zebulon R. Brockway, *Fifty Years of Prison Service* (1912; Montclair, N.J.: Patterson Smith, 1969), pp. 318, 345. See also S. J. Barrows, *The Reformatory System in the United States, Reports Prepared for the International Prison Commission,* United States Congress, H. Document 459, 56th Cong., 1st Sess. (Washington, D.C., 1900).

13. William D. P. Bliss, *Encyclopedia of Social Reform* (1897; Westport, Conn.: Greenwood Press, 1970), p. 553.

14. R. C. Bates, "Character Building at Elmira," *American Journal of Sociology* 3 (March 1898): 578–80.

15. Enoch Cobb Wines, *The State of Prisons and of Child-Saving Institutions in the Civilized World* (1880; Montclair, N.J.: Patterson Smith, 1968), p. 699.

16. Hamilton D. Wey, *Physical and Industrial Training of Criminals: Monographs of the Industrial Education Association* 1 (New York, May 1888): 4–6.

17. Stanley E. Grupp, "Criminal Anthropological Overtones: New York State Reformatory at Elmira, 1876–1907," *Correction* 24 (May-June 1959): 11–15.

18. Henry H. Goddard and Helen F. Hill, "The Wayward Girl and the Binet Test," *The Review* 1 (December 1911): 11–12. Goddard worked at Vineland, New Jersey, Training School. *The Review* had, for consultants, financier Jacob Schiff and educator Felix Adler.

19. Arthur MacDonald, *Statement to Support Bill no. S. 3066, To Establish a Laboratory for the Study of the Criminal, Pauper, and Defective Classes,* United States Congress, Senate, Committee on Education and Labor, *Hearings,* 60th Cong., 1st Session (Washington, D.C., 1908), pp. 7, 39.

20. Charles H. North, "The Mind of the Criminal," *The Delinquent* 6 (December 1916): 9–11.

21. Roscoe Pound, "Introduction" to Raymond Saleilles, *The Individualization of Punishment,* trans. Rachel Szold Jastrow (Boston, 1911), xvii. Jerome Hall discusses two dominant schools of criminology, a positivist, biological, and statistical one, and a more classical and moral one. See Hall, "Criminology," *Twentieth-Century Sociology,* ed. George Gurvitch (New York: Philosophical Library, 1945), pp. 345–46.

CHAPTER 12

1. Emile Durkheim, *Le Suicide,* 2nd ed. (Paris: Presses Univérsitaires de France, 1967), p. 418 (my translation).

2. Arthur MacDonald, "Scientific Study of Baseball," in "Studies of Modern Man," I (Collection of Pamphlets and Articles, Library of Congress, Washington, D.C.), p. 22; also printed in the *American Physical Education Review* (March 1914), p. 22.

3. Lewis M. Terman, *The Intelligence of School Children* (Boston, 1919), p. 224.

4. Hugo Münsterberg, *On the Witness Stand; Essays on Psychology and Crime* (New York, 1909), p. 257.

5. Hugo Münsterberg, *American Problems, from the Point of View of a Psychologist* (1910; Freeport, N.Y.: Books for Libraries Press, 1969), p. 35.

6. Francis Galton, *Hereditary Genius: An Inquiry into its Laws and Consequences* (London, 1869), p. 1. See also Francis Galton, "The Possible Improvement of the Human Breed Under the Existing Conditions of Law and Sentiment," *Popular Science Monthly* 60 (January 1902): 218–33.

7. Havelock Ellis, *A Study of British Genius* (New York: Houghton Mifflin Co., 1926), p. 80. Published in 1900 in *Popular Science Monthly.*

8. Francis Galton, *Finger Prints* (1892; New York: De Capo Press, 1965), pp. 2–17. For an attack upon Galton's theories, see Charles H. Cooley, "Genius, Fame, and the Comparison of Races," *Annals* 9 (May 1897): 317–58.

9. Cesare Lombroso, "Genius: A Degenerative Epileptoid Psychosis," *Alienist and Neurologist* 12 (July 1891): 356. See also Cesare Lombroso, "A Paradoxical Anarchist," *Popular Science Monthly* 56 (January 1900): 312–15. Samuel Smith comments on the popularity of Lombroso in the United States; see Samuel G. Smith, "Typical Criminals," *Popular Science Monthly* 56 (March 1900): 539.

10. "Arthur MacDonald," (Obituary), *Rochester Democrat and Chronicle,* Rochester, New York (2 April 1920).

11. Arthur MacDonald, *Statement to support Bill no. S. 3066, to Establish a Laboratory for the Study of the Criminal, Pauper, and Defective Classes,* United States Congress, Senate, Committee on Education and Labor, *Hearings,* 60th Cong., 1st Sess. (Washington, D.C., 1908), p. 102.

12. Arthur MacDonald, "Study of Man," in "Studies of Modern Man," p. 1.

13. Arthur MacDonald, *Statistics of Crime, Suicide, Insanity and Other Forms of Abnormality . . . in Connection with a Bill to Establish a Laboratory for the Study of Criminal, Pauper, and Defective Classes,* United States Congress, Senate Document 12, 58th Cong., 1st Sess. (Washington, D.C., 1903), p. 77.

14. Arthur MacDonald, "Statement," *Hearings on the Bill to Establish a Laboratory for the Study of the Criminal, Pauper, and Defective Classes,* United States Congress, House Committee on the Judiciary, 57th Cong., 1st Sess. (Washington, D.C., 1902), p. 15. See also Charles A. Drew, "Signs of Degeneracy and Types of the Criminal Insane," *American Journal of Insanity* 57 (April 1901): 697.

15. Charles Kassel, "Physiognomy and Genius," *Popular Science Monthly* 78 (February 1911): 159–63 and Charles Kassel, "Genius and Stature," *Popular Science Monthly* 67 (December 1910): 579–81.

16. J. Abbott Cantrell, *Pleasure and Work* (New York, 1913), p. 122. Language usage was also thought to be an indication of character. See Frederick Howard Wines, *Punishment and Reformation: An Historical Sketch of the Rise of the Penitentiary System* (1895; New York: Benjamin Blom, Inc., 1971), and Henry Dwight Sedgwick, *The New American Type and Other Essays* (Boston, 1908).

17. Katherine M. H. Blackford and Arthur Newcomb, *Analyzing Character; the New Science of Judging Men,* 8th ed. (New York: Henry Alden, 1920), p. 10.

18. John S. Haller, Jr., *Outcasts from Evolution: Scientific Attitudes of Racial Inferiority, 1859–1900* (Urbana: University of Illinois Press, 1971), pp. 17–32.

19. Donald Pickens, *Eugenics and Progressives* (Nashville, Tenn.: Vanderbilt University Press, 1968), p. 166. See also Hamilton Cravens, "American Scientists and the Heredity-Environment Controversy" (Ph.D. diss., University of Iowa, 1969), pp. 10–14, 86–105.

20. William Healy, *An Individual Delinquent* (New York, 1915).

21. Münsterberg, *On the Witness Stand,* p. 234.

CHAPTER 13

1. Clark Wissler, *The Correlation of Mental and Physical Tests* (New York, 1901), pp. 1–59.

2. "Psychological Examining in the United States Army," in *National Academy of Sciences Official Report,* ed. Robert Yerkes, submitted to the Surgeon General of the Army by the Division of Psychology of the Office of the Surgeon General, 15 vols. (Washington, D.C., 1920), 15:19.

3. Luther Lee Bernard, *The Transition to an Objective Standard of Social Control* (Chicago, 1911), pp. 91, 96.

4. Frederic Harrison, *On Society* (London, 1918), p. 193.

5. C. E. Seashore, "The Consulting Psychologist," *Popular Science Monthly* 78 (March 1911): 285, 290.

6. Charles H. Carpenter, *History of American Schoolbooks* (Philadelphia: University of Pennsylvania Press, 1963), pp. 243–44.

7. E. Digby Baltzell, *The Protestant Establishment* (New York: Random House, 1964), p. 170.

8. Thorstein Veblen, *The Higher Learning in America: A Memorandum on the Conduct of Universities by Business Men* (1918; New York: Augustus M. Kelly, 1965), p. 6. For a discussion of older forms of "mental science," see John D. Davies, *Phrenology: Fad and Science, A Nineteenth Century American Crusade* (New Haven, Conn.: Yale University Press, 1955).

9. Edwin G. Boring, *A History of Experimental Psychology* (New York: Century Co., 1929), pp. 545–48. See also Philip Hunter DuBois, *A History of Psychological Testing* (Boston: Allyn and Bacon, Inc., 1970), pp. 12–14, and Kimball Young, "The History of Mental Testing," *Pedagogical Seminary* 31 (March 1924): 6.

10. Joseph Peterson, *Early Conceptions and Tests of Intelligence Measurement and Adjustment Series* (Yonkers-on-Hudson, New York: World Book Co., 1925), pp. 73–74, 78–93.

11. Young, "Mental Testing," p. 15.

12. Geraldine M. Joncich, *The Sane Positivist: A Biography of Edward L. Thorndike* (Middletown, Conn.: Wesleyan University Press, 1968), pp. 99 ff.

13. Edward L. Thorndike, "The Intelligence of Monkeys," *Popular Science Monthly* 59 (July 1901): 273–79.

14. Edward L. Thorndike, "The Evolution of Human Intelligence," *Popular Science Monthly* 60 (November 1901): 65.

15. Ibid., p. 60.

16. Edward L. Thorndike, *The Psychology of Learning*, vol. 2 of *Educational Psychology* (New York, 1913), p. 185.

17. Edward L. Thorndike, "The Permanence of Interests and Their Relation to Abilities," *Popular Science Monthly* 81 (November 1912): 456. See also DuBois, *Psychological Testing*, pp. 71, 77, and E. David Friedman, "Nervous Strain and Mental Hygiene" in Elisha M. Friedman, *America and the New Era* (New York: E. P. Dutton and Co., 1920), pp. 487–88.

18. Tsura Arai, "Mental Fatigue," *Columbia University Contributions to Education*, no. 54 (New York, 1912), pp. 11–15. For a discussion of Thorndike and others, see Max Offner, *Mental Fatigue*, trans. Guy Montrose (Baltimore, 1911); Walter Kolsenik, *Mental Discipline in Modern Education* (Madison; University of Wisconsin Press, 1958), 26 ff; and Thomas Russell Garth, "Mental Fatigue during the Continuous Exercise of a Single Function," *Archives of Psychology* 26 (August 1918): preface.

19. W. Townsend Porter, "On the Application to Individual School Children of the Mean Values Derived from Anthropological Measurements by the Generalizing Method," *Quarterly Publications of the American Statistical Association* 3 (December 1893): 586; see also Young, "Mental Testing," p. 36.

20. Lewis M. Terman, "Genius and Stupidity: A Study of Some of the Intellectual Processes of Seven 'Bright' and Seven 'Stupid' Boys," *Pedagogical Seminary* 13 (September 1903): 307–73.

21. Lewis M. Terman, "A Preliminary Study in the Psychology and Pedagogy of Leadership," *Pedagogical Seminary* 11 (December 1904): 432.

22. Lewis M. Terman, *Intelligence of School Children* (Boston, 1919), p. 309. See also Lewis Terman and Melita H. Oden, *The Gifted Group at Mid-Life, Thirty-Five Years' Follow-up of the Superior Child* (Stanford, Calif.: Stanford University Press, 1959), p. viii.

23. "Psychological Examining," in *National Academy of Sciences Official Report*, ed. Yerkes, 15:779–815. See also Robert M. Yerkes, "Forward" to *A Study of American Intelligence*, by Carl C. Brigham (Princeton, N.J.: Princeton University Press, 1923), p. vii; and Josiah Morse, "A Comparison of White and Colored Children Measured by the Binet Scale of Intelligence," *Popular Science Monthly* 84 (January 1914): 75.

24. Boring, *Experimental Psychology*, pp. 580–88.

25. Erich Kahler, *The Tower and the Abyss: An Inquiry into the Transformation of Man* (New York: Viking Press, 1957), pp. 6, 14. Robert A. Nye, "Two Paths to a Psychology of Social Action: Gustave LeBon and Georges Sorel," *Journal of Modern History* 45 (September 1972): 411–38.

26. Gustave LeBon, *The Crowd; A Study of the Popular Mind*, 2nd ed. (Dunwoody, Georgia: Norman S. Berg, 1968), p. 153.

27. Ibid., p. v. For Joshia Royce's reaction to LeBon, see Royce, *Race Questions, Provincialism, and Other American Problems* (1908; Freeport, N.Y.: Books for Libraries Press, 1967), pp. 80–95.

CHAPTER 14

1. Ralph Barton Perry, *The Thought and Character of William James As Revealed in Unpublished Correspondence and Notes, Together with His Published Writings,* 2 vols. (Boston: Little, Brown and Co., 1935), 2:329.

2. Gay Wilson Allen, *William James: A Biography* (London: Rupert Hart-Davis, 1967), pp. 6–10. Two other sons, Garth Wilkinson and Robertson, will not be considered here. See also Alice James, *The Diary of Alice James* (New York: Dodd, Mead and Co., 1964).

3. Henry James, *Notes of a Son and Brother* (New York, 1914), p. 180. See also Henry James, *A Small Boy and Others* (New York, 1913). Two interesting works on James are: Craig R. Eisendrath, *The Unifying Moment: The Psychological Philosophy of William James and Alfred North Whitehead* (Cambridge, Mass.: Harvard University Press, 1971), and Erik H. Erikson, *Identity: Youth and Crisis* (New York: W. W. Norton and Co., 1968).

4. Henry James, *Notes of a Son*, p. 180. See also Henry James, Sr., "On Creation, between a Father and Son," Henry James, Sr., Manuscripts, Houghton Library, Harvard University, Cambridge, Massachusetts (Hereafter cited as Henry James, Sr., MSS. By permission of the Houghton Library.)

5. Sig Synnestvedt, *The Essential Swedenborg* (Twayne Publishers, 1970), p. 49. See also Allen, *William James*, pp. 18–20.

6. Henry James, Sr., "The European and American Order of Manhood," Henry James, Sr., MSS, p. 9.

7. Herbert Schneider, *A History of American Philosophy*, 2nd ed. (New York: Columbia University Press, 1963), pp. 263–74. See also Francis O. Matthiessen, *The James Family: Including Selections* (New York: Albert Knopf, 1947), p. v.

8. William James to F. W. H. Myers, Cambridge, Mass., 17 December 1893, in Perry, *Thought and Character*, 2:159. See also Myers's response, F. W. H. Myers to William James, 16 November 1893, William James Papers, Houghton Library, Harvard University, Cambridge, Massachusetts (Hereafter cited as William James MSS. By permission of the Houghton Library.)

9. William James's diary for 1869–1870, William James MSS.

10. Henry James, *Notes of a Son*, p. 179. Henry James to William James, quoted in Perry, *Thought and Character*, 1: 428.

11. William James to Carl Stumph, Bad-Nauheim, 10 July 1901, Perry, *Thought and Character*, 2:199.

12. William James to Theodore Flournoy, 1892, Perry, *Thought and Character,* 1:442. Henry James, Jr., reports that the father was hostile to formal schooling; see Henry James, *Notes of a Son*, p. 112.

13. William James, *Talks to Teachers on Psychology: And to Students on Some of Life's Ideals* (New York, 1914), p. 57.

14. William James to Theodore Flournoy, 27 January 1903, *Letters of William James and Theodore Flournoy,* ed. Robert LeClaire (Madison; University of Wisconsin Press, 1966), p. 138.

15. William James to F. C. S. Schiller, Cambridge, Mass., 18 May 1907, in Perry, *Thought and Character*, 2:506.

16. William James, *Some Problems of Philosophy: a Beginning of an Introduction to Philosophy* (New York: Longmans, Green, and Co., 1924), pp. 6–7. For earlier essay, see "The Teaching of Philosophy in Our Colleges," Letter to the *Nation* in Perry, *Thought and Character*, 1:373.

17. Charles W. Eliot, *Education for Efficiency and the New Definition of the Cultivated Man* (Boston, 1909), pp. 34–45. See also Charles W. Eliot, "Service of Universities to a Democracy," in *Training for an Efficient Life* (1915; Freeport, New York: Books for Libraries Press, 1970), p. 82.

18. William James, "The Ph.D. Octopus," *Memories and Studies* (1911; New York: Greenwood, 1968), p. 334.

19. William James to L. T. Hobhouse, Chocorua, N. H., 12 August 1904, in Perry, *Thought and Character*, 2: 246.

20. James, *Talks to Teachers and Students,* p. 214.

21. William James, "Vacations," *Nation* 17 (7 August 1873): 91.

22. William James, "Power through Repose," *Nation* 52 (19 March 1891): 246.

23. William James, "Great Men, Great Thoughts, and the Environment," *Atlantic Monthly* 46 (October 1880): 445–48.

24. Henry James, Jr., ed., *The Letters of William James,* 2 vols. (Boston: Atlantic Monthly Press, 1920), 1:100–101.

25. William James, "On the Social Value of the College-Bred," *Memories and Studies,* p. 319.

26. William James, *Pragmatism: A New Name for Some Old Ways of Thinking* (New York, 1907), p. 100.

27. William James, "Moral Equivalent of War," *International Conciliation Pamphlet,* no. 27 (February 1910), p. 8.

28. William James, *Talks to Teachers and Students,* p. 273.

29. James, *Memories and Studies,* p. 102.

30. William James, *The Will to Believe,* new ed. (London: Longmans, Green and Co., 1937), p. 131. See also William James, *The Principles of Psychology,* 2 vols. (New York, 1890), and Herbert Schneider, *History of American Philosophy,* pp. 495–503. In this latter work Schneider discusses James's "two psychologies."

31. William James, "Brute and Human Intellect," *Journal of Speculative Philosophy* 12 (July 1878): 246.

32. William James to H. G. Wells, Chocorua, N.H., 11 September 1906, in Henry James, Jr., *Letters of William James,* 1:259–60.

33. William James, "Opening Remarks," Lowell Lectures, 1878, William James MSS.

34. William James, *The Meaning of Truth* (1909, New York: Greenwood Press, 1968), p. 58.

35. William James, quoted in Matthiesson, *James Family,* p. 673.

CHAPTER 15

1. William James to J. H. Hyslop, 95 Irving St., Cambridge, Mass., 25 October 1903, William James MSS. James later withdrew from the organization.

2. William James to G. C. Robertson, 13 August 1885, Chocorua, N.H., William James MMS.

3. Gardner Murphy and Robert Ballou, eds., *William James on Psychical Research* (New York: Viking Press, 1960), p. 41. See also Alta L. Piper, *The Life and Work of Mrs. Piper* (London: Kegan Paul, Trench, Trubner, and Co., 1929), pp. 21–23, and Gay Wilson Allen, *William James: A Biography* (London: Rupert Hart-Davis, 1967), pp. 282–85.

4. William James, "Presidential Address," *Presidential Addresses to the Society for Psychical Research, 1882–1911* (London, 1912), p. 83.

5. Quoted in Murphy and Ballou, eds., *James on Psychical Research,* p. 45. See also Henri Ellenberger, *Discovery of the Unconscious; the History of Dynamic Psychiatry* (New York: Basic Books, Inc., 1970).

6. William James, "The Hidden Self," *Scribner's Magazine* 7 (March 1890): 361–73. See also William James, "Notes on Automatic Writing," in *Proceedings of the American Society for Psychical Research* (March 1889), 1:548–64.

7. William James, *A Pluralistic Universe and Essays in Radical Empiricism* (1909, 1912; Gloucester, Mass.: Peter Smith, 1967), p. 298. For a discussion of James's work, see Boris Sidis and Simon P. Goodhart, *Multiple Personality; An Experimental Investigation into the Nature of Human Individuality* (New York, 1905).

8. Quoted in Ralph Barton Perry, *The Thought and Character of William James As Revealed in Unpublished Correspondence and Notes, Together with His Published Writings*, 2 vols. (Boston: Little, Brown and Co., 1935), 2:122–23.

9. Henry James, Jr., ed., *The Letters of William James*, 2 vols. (Boston: Atlantic Monthly Press, 1920), 2:71.

10. Murphy and Ballou, eds., *James on Psychical Research*, p. 27.

11. William James, "Psychical Phenomena at a Private Circle," *Journal of the American Society for Psychical Research* 3 (February 1909): 109.

12. William James, "Statement *re* American Psychopathological Society," pp. 4–5, William James MSS.

13. Murphy and Ballou, eds., *James on Psychical Research*, p. 45.

14. William James, "Demonical Possession," Notes to Lowell Lectures, 1893, William James MSS.

15. Allen, *William James*, pp. 166–67.

16. William James to Boris Sidis, 11 September 1902, Chocorua, N.H., William James MSS.

17. William James, *The Varieties of Religious Experience: A Study in Human Nature* (1902; New York: Colliers Books, 1961), p. 273.

18. William James, *Pragmatism: A New Name for Some Old Ways of Thinking* (New York, 1907), pp. 29–30. See Morrison I. Swift, *Human Submission*, 2nd part (Philadelphia, 1905).

19. William James, *Talks to Teachers on Psychology: And to Students on Some of Life's Ideals* (New York, 1914), pp. 247, 257, 275.

20. William James, "The True Harvard," *Memories and Studies* (1911; New York: Greenwood Publishers, 1968), pp. 351, 353.

21. William James, "Thomas Davidson," *Memories and Studies*, pp. 102–3. For an interesting essay on William James see Paul K. Conkin, *Puritans and Pragmatists; Eight Eminent American Thinkers* (New York: Dood, Mead and Co., 1968), (esp.) p. 336.

22. William James, *Some Problems of Philosophy: A Beginning of an Introduction to Philosophy* (New York: Longmans, Green, and Co., 1924), p. 51. For the definition of philosophy, see the review of James by W. R. Sorley, "A Pluralistic Universe," *Hibbert Journal* 8 (October 1909): 20.

23. William James, *Some Problems of Philosophy*, p. 230.

24. William James, *Pragmatism*, pp. 27, 301.

25. William James, *The Will to Believe*, new ed. (London: Longmans, Green and Co., 1937), p. 302.

26. William James, *Psychology: Briefer Course* (1892; New York: Collier Books, 1962), p. 158.

27. William James, *Pragmatism*, p. 58. See also William James, *Talks to Teachers and Students*, p. 29.

28. William James, *Memories and Studies*, p. 374.

29. William James, *Collected Essays and Reviews* (1920; New York: Russell and Russell, 1969), p. 71 (my translation).

30. William James, *Varieties of Religious Experience*, p. 392.

31. Perry, *Thought and Character*, 2:442. See also Bernard P. Brennan, *William James* (New York: Twayne Publishers, 1967), p. 131.

32. William James, "Presidential Address," p. 83.

33. William James, *The Meaning of Truth,* A Sequel to "Pragmatism" (1909; New York: Greenwood Press, 1968), p. 36 (his italics).

34. Perry, *Thought and Character,* 2:383.

35. Owen Wister to William James, 10 January 1908, Philadelphia, Pa., William James MSS.

CONCLUSION

1. Paul Goodman, *Growing up Absurd* (New York: Vintage, 1960), pp. xiv, 142.

Library of Congress Cataloging in Publication Data

Index